JUST GIVE
MONEY TO
THE POOR

JUST GIVE
MONEY TO
THE POOR

The Development Revolution from the Global South

Joseph Hanlon, Armando Barrientos and David Hulme

MANCHESTER
1824

The University of Manchester
Brooks World Poverty Institute

Chronic Poverty
Research Centre

UK**aid**

from the Department for
International Development

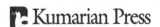

Kumarian Press

A Division of Lynne Rienner Publishers, Inc. • Boulder & London

Published in the United States of America in 2013 by
Kumarian Press
A division of Lynne Rienner Publishers, Inc.
1800 30th Street, Boulder, Colorado 80301
www.kpbooks.com
www.rienner.com

and in the United Kingdom by
Kumarian Press
A division of Lynne Rienner Publishers, Inc.
Gray's Inn House, 127 Clerkenwell Road, London EC1 5DB

Library of Congress Cataloging-in-Publication Data
Hanlon, Joseph.
Just give money to the poor : the development revolution from the global
  south / by Joseph Hanlon, Armando Barrientos, and David Hulme.
    p. cm.
  Includes bibliographical references and index.
  ISBN 978-1-56549-334-6 (cloth : alk. paper)
  ISBN 978-1-56549-333-9 (pbk. : alk. paper)
1. Transfer payments—Developing countries. 2. Economic assistance—
Developing countries. 3. Poverty—Developing countries. I. Barrientos,
Armando. II. Hulme, David. III. Title.
  HC59.72.P63H36 2010
  339.5'22—dc22

                                                        2009048967

British Cataloguing in Publication Data
A Cataloguing in Publication record for this book
is available from the British Library.

Printed and bound in the United States of America

10   9   8   7   6

CONTENTS

ILLUSTRATIONS

TABLES

FIGURES

FOREWORD

THREE NEW AND COMPELLING IDEAS ABOUT REDUCING POVERTY IN DEVEL-
oping countries have emerged over the last decade.

The first is that the poor need access to savings and asset accumulation
services just as much as—and possibly more than—they need access to
credit. CGAP, a World Bank affiliate, puts it this way: "When savings
accounts in financial institutions serving the poor outnumber micro-loan
accounts seven to one, one thing is certain: microfinance clients want
savings services." And at the same time, advocates of asset development for
the poor (also a novel idea) have asked, "Savings for what?" spawning new
programs and policies worldwide to enable the poor to leverage their
savings for land, livestock, homes, businesses, and the like.

The second is conditional cash transfers, or CCTs, which reward the
poor with cash payments if and only if they do the kinds of things that
governments, NGOs, and other non-poor donors want them to do: keep
their kids in school, take them to the doctor, eat the right foods, and so
on. CCTs made their debut in Mexico in 1997 and have since spread
throughout Latin America and to Africa, Asia, Central Europe, and the
United States. Research results have demonstrated that many positive
economic, social, and health outcomes are associated with CCTs, so they
are likely to spread even further.

The third new idea—the subject of *Just Give Money to the Poor: The
Development Revolution from the Global South*—may be the most simple,
and radical, of all. In their inspiring, well-researched new book, Joseph

Hanlon, Armando Barrientos, and David Hulme argue that simply giving money to the poor—no strings, no conditions, no kidding—may be the most promising approach not just for avoiding hardship and reducing poverty, but for long-term development as well.

The authors present data from direct cash transfer programs around the world and conclude that (1) such transfers are affordable for governments and other donors; (2) recipients use the money efficiently; (3) cash transfers reduce immediate hardship and poverty effectively; and (4) they have the potential to reduce longer-term poverty by facilitating both economic and social development.

However, not all cash transfer programs are created or implemented equally. Experience has shown that these four outcomes are most likely to be achieved when the programs are "fair and assured"—that is, when there is agreement among citizens and policymakers about who is eligible to receive the cash, and when those recipients can be assured of receiving regular, monthly payments. In fact, this book offers five principles to guide those aiming to adopt cash transfer programs worldwide: Such programs should be *fair; assured; practical* (Are the civil service and banking infrastructures sufficient to administer the program?); *not pennies* (Are the cash payments large enough to make a difference?); and *popular* (Are the programs politically acceptable?).

The authors don't deny the importance of a good education, health services, and access to financial services and productive assets, but they wisely observe that "the biggest lesson has been that people must have at least enough money to take advantage of the schools, health facilities, and land that are available. And if they do have that money, they can take the lead in their own development."

The authors are refreshingly honest about the limitations of cash transfer programs and about two related areas of intense debate: targeting and conditions. Although it is clear that such programs must be well targeted in order to be politically acceptable, achieving this in practice is challenging. Moreover, as much as the authors passionately argue for unconditional cash transfers—admirably trusting the poor to make the best decisions about how to use the money—they acknowledge the powerful donor and policymaker preference (especially outside the Global South) for reciprocity. "Not only must you be among the 'deserving' poor; you're also going to use our funds in ways that we see fit for your well-being" is the common command; hence the popularity of conditional cash transfers.

Thankfully, the authors don't shortchange these important questions and debates but, rather, offer good examples and data to make their case for targeted but unconditional transfers.

Hanlon, Barrientos, and Hulme also buck another powerful trend in academic and policymaker circles worldwide: the tendency toward "soft paternalism" and the larger "behavioral economics" framework behind it. The premise of this anti-neoclassical theory of economics is that human beings are anything but rational when it comes to decisions about their health, wealth, and happiness. Indeed, the theory goes, we often make decisions *against* our self-interest and cannot, therefore, be trusted. Because of our general inability to look out for ourselves, policymakers and others need to make decisions for us, "nudge" us to do the right things, construct a "choice architecture," and establish "default" settings to help ensure that we make the "best" choice. The Obama administration is smitten by this approach, and new academic centers have sprung up at Harvard and elsewhere to apply this thinking to poverty, pensions, and potbellies around the world.

It's hard to imagine a premise more offensive to the authors of *Just Give Money to the Poor*. Instead, they trust the ability of the poor to make decisions that promote their own well-being, and they are convinced that donors (whose strategies over the last generation are reviewed in the book) will continue making poor decisions on behalf of the poor.

Now, I happen to believe that the behavioralist approach holds real promise, because many of the results of its application thus far are encouraging. However, concerns are surfacing about the loss of freedom this approach implies; perhaps paternalism has gone too far. *Just Give Money to the Poor* makes it clear that there is a real debate about this issue. Do poor people simply lack the money to improve their own lives and thus, over time, the economic status of their community and country? And if unencumbered by conditions, will they largely make the right choices about how to use cash transfers? Or do they also need paternalistic nudges to push them toward being healthier and happier human beings? I don't think we know the answer yet, nor have we debated the question enough.

Wherever we fall on the freedom/paternalism, or the trust/non-trust, or the conditional/unconditional assistance, or the credit/savings spectrum, we owe a great debt to Joseph Hanlon, Armando Barrientos, and David Hulme for writing *Just Give Money to the Poor*. They have enriched an important and timely debate with their brave, powerful, well-documented, and often counterintuitive arguments for direct cash transfers to the poor—a debate on which the lives and livelihoods of hundreds of millions of people depend.

—Ray Boshara
Vice President, New America Foundation
Washington, DC

JUST GIVE
MONEY TO
THE POOR

1

Introduction

"I BAKE 100 ROLLS PER DAY AND SELL EACH FOR ONE NAMIBIAN DOLLAR [12¢]. I make a profit of about N$400 per month [$50]" said Frieda Nembaya.[1] She began baking rolls in 2008 when she started to receive a grant of N$100 [$12] per month and thus, for the first time, had the money to buy flour and firewood.[2] In neighboring South Africa, younger adults living in pensioner households are significantly more likely to go out and look for work, because the older person can afford to provide child care and small amounts of money for food and bus fare for the job seeker.

In Mexico, families receiving a child benefit (averaging $40 per family per month) eat better—spending more on protein and fruit and vegetables—which improves the health of the entire family, cutting days off work due to illness by one-fifth. Mexican children who do not go to school hungry do better in class and are much less likely to fail at the end of the year.[3] "Before, we ate tortillas with chili and salt, and that was it. Now we live better. Sometimes we can even buy meat," said Elvira Francisco Casimira, from Ixtlahuancillo, Veracruz, Mexico.[4] In South Africa, social pensions have a direct effect on children. Children living in pensioner households are better nourished[5] and more likely to go to school.

These stories point to a wave of new thinking on development that is sweeping across the Global South. Instead of maintaining a huge aid industry to find ways to "help the poor," it is better to give money to poor people directly so that they can find effective ways to escape from poverty.

These stories come from studies of programs in Mexico, South Africa, and Namibia that give cash to people on a long-term basis. And they point to a little-understood reality of the developing world: The biggest problem for those below the poverty line is a basic lack of cash. Many people have so little money that they cannot afford small expenditures on better food, sending children to school, or searching for work. It is not a lack of motivation; people with little money spend their days actively trying to find a way out of poverty. It is not a lack of knowledge; they know what they need and manage their money extremely well. Mexico, South Africa, and Namibia are not alone. Brazil, Indonesia, India, and many other countries have introduced programs to give regular cash payments to large numbers of people on a longer-term basis, and there are countless stories of small amounts of money making a huge difference.

In Brazil, 18 million households (74 million people, or 39% of the population) benefit from cash transfers—a family grant (Bolsa Família) or pension. South Africa's child benefit reaches 8 million children (55% of all children), and a social pension reaches 2 million older or disabled people (85% of all older people). In Mexico a family grant (Oportunidades) goes to over 5 million households (24 million people, or 22% of the population; in the three poorest states, it reaches more than half of all families). In Indonesia a grant went to 19 million poor families (40% of the population). In India, over 43 million households benefit from an employment guarantee scheme.

Taking into account the outcomes of these programs, an African Union conference in 2006 issued the "Livingstone Call for Action," which maintained that every African country should have social transfer programs "including the social pension and social transfers to vulnerable children, older persons and people with disabilities."[6]

This book draws on this rapidly growing pool of research to highlight the potential and limitations of cash transfers for transforming the lives of people in poverty in developing countries. There is quite a broad consensus that many cash transfers have proved remarkably successful, and this has led at least 30 other developing countries to experiment with giving money to people directly, through "cash transfer" programs.

Four conclusions emerge repeatedly: These programs are affordable, recipients use the money well and do not waste it, cash grants are an efficient way to directly reduce current poverty, and they have the potential to prevent future poverty by facilitating economic growth and promoting human development. But two areas remain the subject of intense debate: targeting and conditions. Should smaller grants be given to many people or larger grants to a few? Should recipients be asked to satisfy conditions, such as sending their children to school or doing voluntary labor? Important challenges surround the financing and delivery of these programs, especially in low-income countries. And transfer programs remain controversial; some people are still skeptical about their ability to reduce long-term poverty. These issues, too, are discussed in this book.

Changed Thinking

In industrialized countries, there was a major change in thinking in the 20th century, and cash transfers are now considered an effective and normal means of addressing poverty. There are child benefits (for example, £18.80 a week for the first child and £12.55 a week for each additional child in Britain, and €166 per month for the first two children and €203 for subsequent children in Ireland) paid without regard to income. Britain gives winter fuel payments of £200 a year to everyone over 60.[7]

Other cash transfers are income-related. In Britain, a housing benefit and income support are available for those of working age, and the government guarantees that no one over 60 receives less than £124 per week. In Canada, the child benefit is reduced for higher-income families. Some benefits are made conditional on actions by the recipient; an example is the job seekers allowance in Britain. Thus in industrialized countries we have become accustomed to giving cash. Indeed, Article 25 of the Universal Declaration of Human Rights, adopted by the United Nations in 1948, states that everyone has the right to an "adequate" standard of living.

But this right had been questioned in two ways with respect to less developed countries. First, it had been assumed that social grants were a luxury for the relatively rich. Poorer countries could not "afford" to give money to their own poorest, because so many of their citizens have low incomes, so these countries would have to wait until economic growth made them more "modern" before they could extend this right to their poorest citizens. Second, the right does not distinguish between the deserving and the undeserving poor. The rich and powerful always argue that the poor are at least partly responsible for their own poverty and therefore unworthy of support; poor people must be guided or even compelled to act in the best interests of their children.

Over the past decade, countries in the developing world have challenged both of these beliefs. They argue that they cannot afford *not* to give money to their poorest citizens. And not only is it affordable to do so, it is often much more efficient than systems promoted by conventional international aid and financial agencies. They argue that people living in poverty use the money well. And responsibility for eradicating poverty, as the Human Rights declaration implies, is shared by all.

Cash transfers represent a paradigmatic shift in poverty reduction. These grants are not short-term, emergency "safety nets" or charitable donations; they do not assume poor people are poor because of stupidity and cupidity. Instead they are often broadly based, covering a significant part of the population in poverty; they are seen as partly satisfying the right to an adequate standard of living. Although the cash clearly reduces immediate poverty, these grants are seen not just as palliatives for current poverty but also as building productive capacity among those in poverty and promoting development programs. This is the southern challenge to an aid and development industry built up over half a century in the belief that development and the eradication of poverty depended solely on what international agencies and consultants could do for the poor, while discounting what the citizens of developing countries, and the poor among them, could do for themselves. The response has been an exceptional amount of research on southern cash transfer programs. And researchers have been surprised to find that, by and large, families with little money have honed their survival skills over generations and that they use a little extra money wisely and creatively—without armies of aid workers telling "the poor" how to improve themselves.

A quiet revolution is taking place based on the realization that you cannot pull yourself up by your bootstraps if you have no boots. And giving "boots" to people with little money does not make them lazy or reluctant to work; rather, just the opposite happens. A small guaranteed income provides a foundation that enables people to transform their own lives. In development jargon, this is the "poverty trap" model—many people are trapped in poverty because they have so little money that they cannot buy things they know they need, such as medicines or schoolbooks or food or fertilizer. They are in a hole with no way to climb out; cash transfers provide a ladder.

In industrialized countries, cash transfers are seen in part as a form of redistribution; that is, money paid in taxes by the better off goes to those less well off. In Europe, government grants have largely replaced charity and discretional payments. The more developed countries in the South are using cash transfers as a means to redistribute much-needed support to the worst off. At a global level, there is now a growing recognition of the need for redistribution, between developed and underdeveloped countries and between the better off in the North and the less well off in the South. So far, we have a system that describes itself as "aid" coming from "donors"—the classic charity language. The change in thinking coming from the South is to apply globally the positive lessons of industrialized countries and build institutions that can redistribute at a national level, helped by global redistribution.

ANTI-POVERTY AND DEVELOPMENT

"The N$100 [$12] we receive seems small but it is a blessed money. Many things have changed in our lives. We have bought blankets, clothes, school clothes, paid school fees and a strong plastic to put on the roof of our house. We do not any more suffer from the severe hunger we were in before," explained grant recipients Johannes and Adolfine Goagoses in Otjivero, Namibia. And the grant has changed the community. "We don't any more hear of people complaining of hunger or asking food around. The theft cases have also reduced tremendously. Many people bought corrugated zincs and repaired their houses."[8]

Each country has done its cash transfers differently; some use pensions and child benefits, and others use family grants aimed at the poorest. But there is substantial research to show that most cash transfers reach those with the least money and reduce poverty levels in both developed and less developed countries. Money is spent on immediate needs such as food and medicine, and then on children—particularly for clothes, shoes, and school supplies. Quite small amounts of money reduce the intense pressure on cash-poor families, and this has longer-term implications. Children can go to school instead of walking the streets selling sweets or single cigarettes. None of this is because an NGO worker came to the village and told people how to eat better or that they should go to a clinic when they were ill; people in the community already knew that, but they never had enough money to buy adequate food or pay the clinic fee.

The major cash transfer programs all report substantial contributions to poverty reduction. In Brazil, the percentage of people in poverty remained stubbornly at 28% for nearly a decade. Then in 2001 the government introduced Bolsa Escola, and in 2003 this school grant was integrated with several other programs into a family grant (Bolsa Família); most commentators credit these programs, along with the increase in the minimum wage, with poverty levels' dropping dramatically to 19% in 2006 and continuing to fall to 17% in 2008. Extreme poverty fell from 7% in 2003 to below 5% in 2006.[9] In northeast Brazil, the country's poorest region, Bolsa Família brought a 45% reduction in chronic child malnutrition (stunting, measured by height for age).[10] Brazil is still one of the most economically inequitable countries in the world, but innovative social policies have brought about a substantial decrease in poverty and inequality.[11]

Halfway across the world in Mongolia, one of the poorest countries in Asia, a new child benefit has reduced the percentage of children in poverty from 42% to 27%.[12] India's rural employment guarantee scheme is reported to have "had a significant impact on rural poverty," leading not only to an important increase in food consumption but also to a 40% increase in the purchase of clothing.[13]

Children are the main beneficiaries of all cash transfers, not just of child benefits. Cash transfers in whatever form, including pensions, improve child health and reduce malnutrition, increase school attendance, and reduce child labor. For example, a non-contributory rural pension in Brazil not only increases the income of the elderly but also significantly increases school registration and attendance by children in the household.[14] Millennium Development Goal 4, to reduce under-five mortality by two-thirds, is unlikely to be met. The United Nations warns that "between 1990 and 2006, about 27 countries—the large majority in Sub-Saharan Africa—made no progress in reducing childhood deaths. In Eastern Asia and Latin America and the Caribbean, child mortality rates are approximately four times higher than in developed regions."[15] The respected British medical journal *The Lancet* cites "regular cash transfers, such as child benefits or pensions, as one crucial intervention to get Millennium Development Goal 4 back on track."[16]

Moving families out of malnutrition and improving their health and housing could be considered justification enough for cash transfers. But the real impact is felt in the longer term. The poverty trap stretches over generations, because children who are malnourished and badly educated are likely to remain in poverty as adults. *The Lancet* adds, "Even more compelling is the argument that the effect of lifting households with young children out of poverty will last for many generations to come." South Africa shows the impact: a child benefit in the first two years of life improves nutrition so much that the average child will be 3.5 cm taller as an adult.[17] Because of their impact on children, cash transfers break the intergenerational poverty cycle and help to prevent future poverty.

Virtuous Spiral

Transfers can create a virtuous development cycle at the household and community level—and nationally. Families with an assured, though small, income begin to take small risks by investing in their future: buying better seeds to try to increase farm production, purchasing goods that can be resold locally, or even spending more time looking for better jobs. In impoverished communities, it is hardly worth starting a business because no one has money to buy. When they have a bit of extra income, most families spend the money locally, buying food, clothing, and inputs. This stimulates the local economy, because local people sell more, earn more, and buy more from their neighbors, creating the rising spiral.

This basic insight challenges two aspects of the received wisdom that governed global development policy in the 20th century. The first is the extreme free market, or "neo-liberal," view espoused by the International Monetary Fund and World Bank, promoted by the US Treasury over the past three decades, and often imposed on the least developed countries. Proponents of this view argue that removing restrictions on global trade and domestic markets will create rapid growth from which everyone will gain—a rising tide lifts all boats. But recent history has shown that growth is not enough to ensure that those in extreme poverty can escape from their predicament. Many are left behind, vulnerable to the instability in the global economy that caused the Asian financial crisis of the late 1990s and the global financial crisis of 2008. And a rising tide *sinks* leaky boats, especially among those so poor that they cannot participate in the new global market.

The second aspect of the received wisdom is that money spent on people in poverty is merely charity, is "unproductive," and takes resources away from real development. Mozambique has a cash grant program giving $4 to $10 per month to more than 150,000 people, mainly elderly women, but the country's minister of women's affairs and social welfare, Virgilia Matable, wants to reduce this. "Whether we want to admit it or not, these are alms," she said, and the government should not give alms.[18] But the new revolution in thinking is that money spent on those with little cash can be productive and developmental if it is guaranteed and provided in the longer term. If they can depend on receiving a grant sufficient to ensure subsistence, even people with little money can afford to send their children to school or experiment with new crops or new businesses. Thus regular and reliable transfers to families in poverty can be an investment in growth and in the future.

Indeed, research on cash transfers shows two important differences between the relatively poor and the relatively rich. Poorer people spend more on food and locally produced goods, whereas those who are better off buy more imports, so any transfer from rich to poor stimulates the domestic and local economy. Second, poorer people are much more likely to use small amounts of money to try to leverage increases in income—by investing in their farm, by trading, or by looking for work. Thus grants can be explicitly developmental.

A final change in thinking that has come from the South is the realization that social protection in the industrialized world has been primarily job related; that is, deductions from salary (matched by government) provide unemployment insurance and pensions. But these benefits are not available to many women and casual workers, and in the developing world they exclude the vast majority who are small farmers or work in the informal sector. In developing countries, where informality is rife, cash transfers are the alternative to job-related protection.

FAILING TO MAKE POVERTY HISTORY

The number of people living in chronic poverty is actually increasing.[19] Those who campaigned in 2005 to "Make Poverty History" increasingly ask what went wrong. Two best-selling books, Dambisa Moyo's *Dead Aid: Why Aid Is Not Working and How There Is a Better Way for Africa* and Paul Collier's *The Bottom Billion,* claim that aid has failed and largely blame poor countries for misusing the money. Moyo, who worked for Goldman Sachs and the World Bank, says that aid prevents development and forces countries to borrow and be disciplined by the banks.[20] Oxford professor and former World Bank research director Paul Collier calls on donors to impose yet more "good governance" conditions on aid.[21] The theme of less aid and more conditions feeds nicely into the agendas of governments trying to cut spending after the 2008 economic crisis, while still maintaining a large industry to "help" the poor.

The South desperately needs the money. When you remove China's phenomenal poverty reduction from the 1990–2010 global figures, it becomes clear that life has improved relatively little in the rest of the world. The poverty in Africa, South Asia, and other parts of the world remains dire. And the North often forgets that these countries still bear the marks of distorted economic, social, and governance systems caused by the slave trade, colonialism, unfair trade, overthrow of governments, and the "hot wars" that were fought in the South during the Cold War era. There is a debt to be paid.

Aid has not failed; what has failed is an aid and anti-poverty industry that thrives on complexity and mystification, with highly paid consultants designing ever more complicated projects for "the poor" and continuing to impose policy conditions on poor countries. This book offers the southern alternative: Give the money directly to those who have the least of it, but who know how to make the best use of it. Cash transfers are not charity or philanthropy but, rather, investments that enable poor people to take control of their own development and end their own poverty. Thus, this book is a direct challenge to Moyo, Collier, and much of the current popular writing on aid.

Moyo herself estimates that 500,000 people are employed by the aid industry and have strong incentives to maintain the status quo.[22] Indeed, in 2000, when Joseph Stiglitz, then senior vice president and chief economist of the World Bank, pointed out that growth was most rapid in China, which did not follow IMF and World Bank policies, he was pushed out and the Fund and Bank did not change their policies.

Both Moyo and Collier acknowledge the past failures of these policies. Moyo cites banks' bad lending to developing countries for more than two centuries and the very recent disruption of poor country development by banks "jumping in and out to garner short-term gains," and Collier acknowledges failures of conditionality since the 1980s. Yet both have a breathtaking belief that *this time*, when the rich North tells the poor South what to do, the North will finally be getting it right.

The history of northern prescriptions has not been good. International banks in the 1970s promoted excessive borrowing by corrupt dictators in countries from Zaire to the Philippines, leading to the 1980s debt crisis. Banks even paid kickbacks to Philippine dictator Ferdinand Marcos to encourage him to borrow $2.3bn for the Bataan nuclear power station, which was knowingly built on an earthquake fault at the foot of a volcano. (Thankfully, though completed in 1984, the power station was never used.)[23] Moyo was writing her book in praise of the reformed bankers just as the economic crisis was taking hold—a crisis attributable to "subprime lending" in the United States identical to the uncontrolled lending to poor countries in the 1970s. As for good governance, one of us (JH) has written extensively on Mozambique,[24] where the government has always wanted universal primary education. Imposed "good governance" conditions meant in 1995 that it had to accept (and say, publicly and loudly, that it accepted) that it was too poor to afford universal primary education. Then in 2000, with the Millennium Development Goals, "good governance" meant Mozambique had to aim for universal primary education, but without more teachers and thus with classes sometimes including more than 100 pupils. Then, suddenly, in 2005 the donor community decided that "good governance" meant Mozambique had to hire 10,000 more teachers whom it had not been allowed to train the year before. People in Mozambique, the Philippines, and the now Democratic Republic of Congo are not impressed by the "good governance" discipline imposed by donors, banks, and the World Bank, which has been based on rapidly changing fads and has led to great waste of aid and to policies that kept the majority in poverty.

An alternative to Moyo and Collier is offered by Roger Riddell in his 2007 book *Does Foreign Aid Really Work?*[25] which is a much more nuanced look at aid. Riddell is a member of the British government's Independent Advisory Committee for Development Impact, and his book concludes, "Aid works, but not nearly as well as it could." Riddell studied aid in detail and concludes that there must be fundamental change, not just the "marginal change" (into which Collier and Moyo put their trust) that does "not even begin to address some of the most fundamental problems which continue to impede the greater impact of aid." The core problem, says Riddell, is that hundreds of donors remain in almost total control of their aid and that, because of political, strategic, and commercial interests, they are not prepared to give up that control. Thus "the aid which is provided is not allocated in any systematic, rational or efficient way to those who need it most."

"Just give cash to those who need the aid," concludes Riddell. The refusal of donors to give money to poor people is "linked to the paternalistic and condescending view that poor people do not know how best to use it. These beliefs sit uncomfortably alongside the increasingly mainstream view that beneficiary choice and participation are fundamental to the aid relationship." Cash transfers have proved effective, and "the case for significantly enhancing the impact of aid by giving it directly to poor people would seem to be compelling."

Just Give Money to the Poor?

The southern response is a quiet revolution that has created a new development paradigm. It says that, rather than international sources giving aid to government bureaucrats and consultants, North and South, it should be given directly to poor people so they can pull themselves out of the poverty trap. Cash transfers are a direct challenge to the traditional belief, explicit or at least subconscious, that impoverished people are at least partly responsible for their plight. The new paradigm dovetails in many ways with contemporary thinking on the politics of development. The fall of the Berlin wall marked the end of an era of state-dominated economic development. But the successor vision of global development led by international corporations and banks lasted only 15 years before it, too, was shown to be a failure.

Individuals were supposed to be at the heart of both visions: a socialist vision in which each individual would be provided for, and a capitalist vision in which individuals would realize their potential as free agents in the market. But what actually characterized both failed visions was a belief that very large institutions could somehow micro-manage global development, and the individuals became marginalized.

The new development paradigm draws from both failed visions. Cash transfers recognize the right of each individual to an adequate standard of living. But cash transfers also provide the resources for people, individually and collectively, to participate in the economy and develop themselves and their countries.

Of course, no one argues that all social spending or aid money should suddenly be given to poor people. Spending on health, education, infrastructure, and government itself remains essential. But without cash, poor people cannot make adequate use of these facilities. Thus giving money directly to poor people is just as important as spending on health and education.

FAIR AND ASSURED

Cash transfers in developing countries are mainly a phenomenon of the last decade and so are still being developed. There seems broad agreement on one overriding principle, however: *Cash transfers work when they are fair and assured.* They must be seen to be fair in that most citizens agree on the choice of who receives money and who does not, and to be assured in the sense that every month the money really arrives and families can depend on it.

There will always be too many demands and too little money, so resource allocation is always fraught. Furthermore, taxpayers and finance ministers instinctively resist simply handing out money. And it is obvious that a cash transfer program cannot be run by driving through the countryside throwing $10 bills or 10 peso notes out of a car window.

So far, each country has handled cash grants in a different way, the main differences being in aspects of allocation and control. There is a natural desire to give money to the poorest, but very strict targeting is expensive—in general the smaller the percentage of people to receive grants, the higher the administrative costs—and strict targeting can be inaccurate and socially divisive. Therefore, different countries have selected recipients in a wide range of ways. Some governments give money to everyone; Alaska, in the United States, distributes oil revenues to all residents of the state ($2,069 per person in 2008). Others give to categories of people, such as children or the elderly; Lesotho gives an old-age grant to all citizens aged 70 or over. And some countries identify only the most impoverished, as in Zambia, where a donor program seeks to give money only to the 10% of the population who are "ultra-poor" and cannot work. There is a similar wide range of views on whether conditions should be imposed on recipients.

This book looks at the extensive experiences of cash transfer programs in the past decade. These programs are only a decade old, and cash transfers are on the cutting edge of development policy. They have been extensively researched, and the results have been used to improve existing programs. In such a rapidly evolving area, only a small part of the research is published in peer-reviewed academic journals. Research institutes, often within the country, have carried out many evaluations. Donor agencies and the World Bank have done other studies. Inevitably, some of the studies are contradictory or disputed, and in the footnotes we supply detailed references and websites so that readers can refer to the original reports.

In this book, we describe the extensive experience of cash transfer programs, examine their successes and limitations, review intense debate over issues of design and implementation, and explore the still unresolved debates on the extent of targeting and the effectiveness of conditionality. We identify and discuss the main challenges ahead, especially in the context of low-income countries. It is possible to give money directly to the poor, but each country must design its own program. And cash transfers do not work alone; rather, they are the essential additional factor that makes health services, education, and road building much more effective in reducing poverty and promoting development.

Cash transfer programs are already being introduced across the South, as an explicit alternative to the development model promoted by the rich countries and their institutions. These programs work, and many southern governments see cash transfers as the front line in their battle against poverty and their efforts to promote development.

NOTES

1. Nearly all names of grant recipients in the book are pseudonyms, but all quotations are taken from actual interviews conducted by some of the many research projects that have done family histories.

2. Claudia Haarmann et al., *Towards a Basic Income Grant for All,* Basic Income Grant Pilot Project First Assessment Report (Windhoek, Namibia: Basic Income Grant Coalition, 2008), available at www.bignam.org.

3. Santiago Levy, *Progress Against Poverty* (Washington DC: Brookings Institution, 2006), pp. 44–45.

4. Mauricio Carrera, *Oportunidades: Historias de Éxito* (Mexico: Secretaría de Desarrollo Social, Coordinación Nacional del Programa de Desarrollo Humano Oportunidades, 2008), p. 123.

5. Esther Duflo, "Child Health and Household Resources in South Africa: Evidence from the Old Age Pension Program," *American Economic Review,* 90, no. 2 (2000): 393.

6. "The Livingstone Call for Action," adopted at the African Union Intergovernmental Regional Conference "A Transformative Agenda for the 21st Century: Examining the Case for Basic Social Protection in Africa," Livingstone, Zambia (March 20–23, 2006).

7. As of August 2009: UK child benefit $31 and $21 per week, Ireland child benefit $232 and $284 per month, UK winter fuel $330 per year, UK over-60 income guarantee $205 per week.

8. Claudia Haarmann et al., *Making the Difference! The BIG in Namibia,* Basic Income Grant Pilot Project Assessment Report, April 2009 (Windhoek, Namibia: Namibian BIG Coalition, 2009), available at www.bignam.org.

9. Marcelo Côrtes Neri, "Poverty, Inequality and Income Policies" (Rio de Janeiro: O Centro de Políticas Sociais [CPS], Fundação Getulio Vargas, 2007), available at http://www3.fgv.br/ibrecps/RET3/engl/index.htm; poverty defined as below R$125 per month per capita in 2006 and extreme poverty as US$1 per day per capita. Updated to 2008 on "Evolução da Miséria" (Rio de Janeiro: O Centro de Políticas Sociais [CPS], Fundação Getulio Vargas), available at http://www.fgv.br/cps/pesquisas/miseria_queda_grafico_clicavel/. In addition to Bolsa Família, other factors that contributed to the drop in poverty were job-creating economic growth and a real increase in the minimum wage. See also "FGV: Bolsa Família Contribui para Diminuição da Pobreza" (Brasilia: Fome Zero, Presidência da República, 2006), available at http://www.fomezero.gov.br/noticias/fgv-bolsa-familia-contribui-para-diminuicao-da-pobreza.

10. Diana Oya Sawyer, *Sumário Executivo—Avaliação de Impacto do Programa Bolsa Família* (Brasilia: Ministro do Desenvolvimento Social e Combate à Fome, 2007).

11. Degol Hailu and Sergei Soares, "What Explains the Decline in Brazil's Inequality?" One Pager 89 (Brasilia: International Policy Centre for Inclusive Growth [formerly International Poverty Centre], 2009). Sergei Soares, "Distribuição de Renda no Brasil de 1976 a 2004 com Ênfase no Período entre 2001 e 2004" (Brasilia: Instituto de Pesquisa Económica Aplicada, 2006), Texto para Discussão 1166.

12. Anthony Hodges et al., "Child Benefits and Poverty Reduction: Evidence from Mongolia's Child Money Programme," Working Paper MGSoc/2007/WP002 (Maastricht: School of Governance, Maastricht University, 2007).

13. Shamika Ravi and Monika Engler, "Workfare in Low Income Countries: An Effective Way to Fight Poverty? The Case of NREGS in India," Indian School

of Business Working Paper (Hyderabad: Indian School of Business, 2009), available at http://www.isb.edu/WorkingPapers/Workfare_LowIncomeCountries.pdf.

14. Marcelo Medeiros et al., "Targeted Cash Transfer Programmes in Brazil: BPC and the Bolsa Família," Working Paper 46 (Brasilia: International Poverty Centre, 2008).

15. United Nations, *The Millennium Development Goals Report 2008* (New York: United Nations Department of Economic and Social Affairs, 2008), p. 21, available at http://mdgs.un.org/unsd/mdg/Resources/Static/Products/Progress2008/MDG_Report_2008_En.pdf.

16. *The Lancet* Editorial, "Cash Transfers for Children—Investing into the Future," *The Lancet,* 373, no. 9682 (2009), citing Jennifer Yablonski with Michael O'Donnell, *Lasting Benefits: The Role of Cash Transfers in Tackling Child Mortality* (London: Save the Children, 2009), available at http://www.savethechildren.org.uk/en/docs/Lasting_Benefits.pdf.

17. Jorge M. Agüero et al., "The Impact of Unconditional Cash Transfers on Nutrition: The South African Child Support Grant," Working Paper 39 (Brasilia: UNDP International Poverty Centre, 2007).

18. Speaking at the ministry's coordinating council, May 10, 2007. Quoted by AIM, Mozambique News Agency, May 10, 2007.

19. Chronic Poverty Research Centre, *The Chronic Poverty Report 2008–09* (Manchester, UK: Chronic Poverty Research Centre, 2008).

20. Dambisa Moyo, *Dead Aid: Why Aid Is Not Working and How There Is a Better Way for Africa* (New York: Farrar, Straus and Giroux, 2009).

21. Paul Collier, *The Bottom Billion* (Oxford: Oxford University Press, 2008), especially p. 108 ff.

22. Moyo, *Dead Aid,* p. 54.

23. Joseph Hanlon, "Defining 'Illegitimate Debt': When Creditors Should Be Liable for Improper Loans," In *Sovereign Debt at the Crossroads,* edited by Chris Jochnick and Fraser A. Preston (Oxford: Oxford University Press, 2006), pp. 109–31.

24. Joseph Hanlon and Teresa Smart, *Do Bicycles Equal Development in Mozambique?* (Woodbridge, Suffolk, UK: James Currey, 2008).

25. Roger C. Riddell, *Does Foreign Aid Really Work?* (Oxford: Oxford University Press, 2007), pp. 380 ff, 406.

2

From Alms to Rights and North to South

HELPING POOR PEOPLE IS ONE OF THE FUNDAMENTAL DUTIES PRESCRIBED in all of the world's major religions. In a phrase probably written in the 7th century BCE, the Jewish Torah and Christian Bible (Deuteronomy 15:11) say that "The poor will never cease to be in the land; therefore I command you, saying, 'You shall freely open your hand to your brother, to your needy and poor in your land.'"

As the phrase "your land" in Deuteronomy shows, in peasant societies it was largely the family and clan that provided those support systems. Over the centuries, production systems and our attitudes have slowly changed. Our "land" has become the entire world, and we no longer accept that the poor will always be with us. Ending poverty has become a global goal.

Over recent centuries, there have been four paradigm shifts in thinking about the poor and about the well-being of the vulnerable—those who could become poor if they lost their jobs or had a health problem. Each new paradigm builds on its predecessors:

- In 16th-century England, a government for the first time accepted the collective responsibility for ensuring subsistence for all.
- In late-19th-century Europe, government social spending increased, and pensions and sickness and old-age insurance were introduced.
- In the mid-20th century, an adequate standard of living became a human right and a government responsibility, and the rich North accepted a responsibility toward the poorer South.

15

- At the beginning of the 21st century, countries of the Global South took the lead in construing cash transfers as a right and in using them as a way to end poverty and promote development—the subject of this book.

A brief review of some of the milestones that occurred in each phase will put these paradigms in context.

SHIFTS IN THINKING ABOUT THE POOR

Poor Laws to Increase Labor Mobility

More intensive agriculture, landlessness, and population growth led to changes in thinking about poverty. Traditionally, the poor depended on charity from churches and the wealthy. But in England during the reign of Elizabeth I (1558–1603), a series of "poor laws" were introduced. These were some of the first in the world, and they created the first social security system in which the government accepted the collective responsibility for ensuring subsistence for all. In 1572, for the first time, government and taxpayers took responsibility for the poorest citizens. The parish (a town or neighborhood with its own church, then the smallest administrative unit) was given responsibility for its own poor citizens, and a compulsory poor tax was introduced. A 1662 law made parishes responsible for people born in the parish, no matter where they lived. This created a social security system that covered the entire county, and for the first time ever, people could expect to be provided for, wherever they were in the country.

Simon Szreter, Cambridge University reader in history and public policy, points out that this encouraged labor mobility; farmers and landowners could more easily hire and lay off short-term labor.[1] Social security for workers, combined with provision for the aged, meant that peasants were less dependent on the land and family for social security and could take the risk of moving to towns in search of work. This, in turn, spurred economic growth. Szreter argues that England "moved from a position as a small, average economy on the European periphery to that of world leader, primarily because of the increased efficiency of its agrarian economy." Around the middle of the 17th century, England became the first country to escape national famine-related deaths.

Szreter argues that English history has direct implications for developing countries today. He says that "the self-righteous (and hypocritical) western rhetoric denouncing 'corruption' in government and throughout society in the world's poorest countries is in part a deep mis-reading and misunderstanding." Without a social security system, it is highly rational to try to accumulate wealth and to cultivate patrons who will protect you. It is often claimed that less developed countries cannot afford social security, but Szreter argues that the lesson of history is that poorer countries cannot afford *not* to develop social security systems, which are an essential precursor to economic growth and which encourage market growth and the mobility of labor and capital.

Principles Behind the "Poor Laws"

The Elizabethan poor laws established a pattern of thinking about poverty that in many ways has persisted until today. In 1563, three groups were defined:

- **Those who would have worked but could not:** the able-bodied or deserving poor for whom jobs or wages should be created to support them until they were needed again on farms or in workshops.
- **Those who could have worked but would not:** the feckless or idle poor who were responsible for their own poverty and should be punished. William Hogarth's 1750 print "Gin Lane," which shows at its center a drunken mother letting her baby fall from her arms, has become the iconic image of the undeserving poor.
- **The old and ill:** those who had little money and could not work through no fault of their own, who were to be looked after in almshouses or hospitals. This category also included **orphans and children of poor people,** who deserved help so that they could and would work when they grew up.

Progress and Obstacles

Over the next 250 years, there was slow growth in support for people living in poverty in England, first in response to the need to feed landless agricultural workers during the winter when there was no farm work, and later in response to economic crises, famines, and food riots. Social spending also began to grow in other parts of Europe, but it remained limited; by the end of the 18th century, only England, Belgium, and the Netherlands were spending 1% of national income on poor people. In England spending reached 2%.[2]

The mid-19th century saw a total reversal. The rich and powerful argued that the system was too generous, and for nearly 50 years the poor were blamed for their poverty and were often incarcerated in workhouses or forced-work colonies. After passage of the New Poor Law of 1834, English spending was slashed from 2% to 1% of national income, and recipients were stigmatized. Slowly a movement grew in reaction to this. The title character in Charles Dickens's 1839 novel *Oliver Twist* became a powerful symbol of this reaction against neglect and exploitation of the poor. (As part of a group of workhouse boys desperately hungry for more gruel, Oliver steps forward, bowl in hand, and makes his famous request: "Please, sir, I want some more.") A similar debate was occurring elsewhere in Europe; Victor Hugo's novel *Les Misérables* was published in 1862.

Late-19th-Century Social Spending

The mid-19th century did, however, see the rise of public primary schooling. In 1840, only in Prussia, Norway, and the United States were more than half of all children enrolled in state primary schools. But by the end of the century, tax-funded primary schooling was common across much of Europe and in other countries ranging from Japan to Jamaica.

Around 1880 there was a radical change in attitudes. For the next 50 years, social spending increased and covered more areas. This probably reflects the expansion of democracy and literacy. Five countries took the lead: Denmark enacted the first public pension law in 1891; Germany made employer-funded accident, sickness, and old-age insurance mandatory in the 1880s; and Sweden, Norway, and Britain were all spending more than 2% of GDP on social transfers by 1930.

These social changes had dramatic economic effects. In 1913 Sweden guaranteed a state pension to all men and women over the age of 67 and, beginning in 1917, developed a universal health-care system that indirectly brought about a rapid decline in infant mortality. Historically, having children was the only viable old-age insurance system, and birth rates fall when people trust that they will be protected in old age. With fewer workers, Sweden moved to a highly skilled, high-wage, more productive economy. Thus a cash transfer (the non-contributory pension) and universal health care were essential precursors to the economic development of Sweden.[3] Notre Dame University Professor J. Samuel Valenzuela has compared Chile to Sweden. At the start of the 20th century, these countries were very similar in development, population, and natural resources, with high levels of poverty and child mortality. Up to the 1920s they were identical in gross domestic product (GDP) per capita.[4] But Chile did not develop pensions and universal health care, so fertility levels remained high, and growth in GDP per capita in Chile fell far behind that in Sweden. Health care and the pension made the difference, argues Valenzuela.

Mid-20th-Century Rights

The Great Depression of the 1930s made more people realize that it was not just the undeserving who could become impoverished, and economic growth after World War II made larger social transfers possible. But the most dramatic change in thinking was to challenge the assumption that the poor will always be with us and to replace that assumption with the belief that people have a right not to be poor. The Universal Declaration of Human Rights was adopted by the United Nations General Assembly on December 10, 1948. Article 25 says, "Everyone has the right to a standard of living adequate for the health and well-being of himself and of his family, including food, clothing, housing and medical care and necessary social services, and the right to security in the event of unemployment, sickness, disability, widowhood, old age or other lack of livelihood in circumstances beyond his control." Everyone also has the right to "social security" (Article 22), the right to work and to protection against unemployment (Article 23), and the right to free primary education (Article 26).

Two major political changes occurred, as governments attempted to put the principles behind these rights into practice. Three different groups of countries created their own development policies based on equity: the socialist and communist countries, the Scandinavian social democracies, and the "Asian Tigers" such as South Korea. The second political change was a slow globalization of these new rights. Industrialized countries accepted a responsibility to their former colonies and other less developed countries, and there was a new focus on what was then called the Third World and is now called the Global South. Industrialized countries made a serious attempt, through aid and development programs, to help not only poor people but poor countries as well. Just as in the past, these social programs also had economic content, and "aid" was linked to the need to acquire raw materials and to gain new markets. These processes continued through the 1970s.

A 21st-Century Revolution from the South

And just as had happened a century before, there was another paradigm shift in thinking about poverty. But while the North dithered, this radical change in thinking was for the first time led by the Global South. Beginning in the late 1990s, better understandings of neoliberalism, social protection, and aid came together to shape a totally new way of thinking. Most important was a growing realization that blaming poor people for poverty had failed as a development strategy for countries of the Global South, while the unfettered globalization of financial flows caused first the 1997–1998 Asian financial crisis and then the 2008–2009 world depression. In three southern countries that took the lead on cash transfers (South Africa, Mexico, and Brazil), the overwhelming majority of people attribute poverty to an unfair society, not to any failings of the poor themselves. This insight enabled those countries to make this crucial paradigm shift.

Internationally, there are substantial national differences in attitudes toward the causes of poverty, and this drives very different responses to poverty. In opinion surveys in a wide range of countries (before the recent global economic crisis), respondents were asked why they thought some people in their own country lived in need. Table 2.1 sets out the responses. And the differences are dramatic. In the US and Japan, 61% and 57%, respectively, blame the poor for their poverty. But in Europe, 65% to 87% blame an unfair society.

Equally important in the paradigm shift have been changes in the nature of work, the family, and the role of women. In the industrialized world, social protection had been provided largely through insurance for a century. Workers and their employers paid into social funds (run or regulated by government) that provided pensions, insurance against impoverishment via accident or unemployment, and in some countries health insurance as well. This approach is based on a model of (mainly) male workers spending most of their lives working for the same company, or at least in the same industry, and being the chief breadwinners for their families. By the late 20th century, however, women made up nearly half the workforce, and people changed jobs more often. At the same time, the neoliberal economic model reduced workers' rights and relaxed regulations on social funds, making them less effective. It has proved difficult for the North to change its traditional social protection systems. Meanwhile, in the Global South, development was no longer based on formal-sector jobs with registered employers who could pay into social funds, but instead was based on what was called "informal" employment: self-employment or working in tiny, unregulated businesses that had no links to social funds. Indeed, most people could not be included in job-based insurance programs. This meant that the paradigm shift took place first in the Global South, because the problem was greater there.

The new southern cash transfer paradigm rests on four principles: It is rights-based; it is non-contributory, with money coming from government;

Table 2.1 Why Are People in Need?

	Percent of respondents answering that poor people are poor because of laziness and lack of will power	Percent of respondents answering that poor people are poor because of an unfair society
United States	61%	39%
China	58	42
Japan	57	43
Australia	50	51
Korea	49	51
India	42	58
Chile	40	60
Norway	35	65
South Africa	34	66
Argentina	26	74
Mexico	25	75
Sweden	22	78
Armenia	22	78
Brazil	21	78
Pakistan	20	80
Spain	19	81
Germany	13	87

Notes: In a range of surveys between 1995 and 2000, people were asked: "Why, in your opinion, are there people in this country who live in need?"

The survey was not carried out in the United Kingdom.

Source: World Values Survey, http://www.worldvaluessurvey.org/.

transfers (or at least guarantees) are usually longer-term, eligible recipients can be confident of receiving them, and the transfers cover a significant part of the population; and cash transfers are seen as a central part of a broader development strategy. The six countries that initially developed big cash transfers—South Africa, Mexico, Brazil, India, Indonesia, and China—are newly industrialized countries that can afford to pay for the grants from taxes. And they have the domestic political support for the programs. Later in this book, we will argue that even the poorest countries can afford to pay for cash transfers from the government budget.

OECD COUNTRIES

Cash transfers are normal in all industrialized countries. But as we have already noted, industrialized countries developed insurance schemes that were initially based on male, formal-sector workers. The fourth paradigm shift now taking place in the South is toward direct government-funded transfers and away from insurance schemes. In the Organisation for Economic

Co-operation and Development (OECD) countries, cash transfers are nearly 16% of GDP (13.2% is from social insurance schemes and 2.5% is from the kind of social, government-funded cash transfers discussed in this book, according to World Bank estimates).[5]

In 2008 OECD published a major study provocatively titled *Growing Unequal?*[6] which concluded that "there has been an increase in income inequality that has gone on since at least the mid-1980s and probably since the mid-1970s." The numbers of those living in poverty have also risen over the past two decades. But the study added that "governments have been taxing more and spending more to offset the trend towards more inequality—they now spend more on social policies than at any time in history." The study explicitly cautions that "work is not sufficient to avoid poverty. More than half of all poor people belong to households with some earnings, due to a combination of low hours worked during the year and/ or low wages. Reducing in-work poverty often requires in-work benefits that supplement earnings."

The OECD study then looks in much more detail at the combination of public cash transfers to households and the taxes and social security contributions paid by households. Across the OECD countries, tax systems are progressive and reduce inequality, but the public cash transfers have a much greater impact on reducing inequality and poverty.[7] And the study shows that cash transfers and a progressive tax system can dramatically reduce poverty in individual countries.[8] Using slightly different definitions that do not distinguish between social and insurance transfers, the OECD itself estimates cash transfers as 12% of GDP on average, half or more of which is typically accounted for by pensions and the next large chunk by family grants, including child benefits, as Table 2.2 shows. The table also shows the huge variation in poverty reduction. For this estimate, the income poverty line is set at 50% of median income, which means that before tax and benefit, between half and one-third of people are in poverty. But Sweden uses the tax system and cash transfers to pull 80% of those people out of poverty. And the average among the OECD countries is that more than half of households are taken out of poverty. The United States is the main exception; there, two-thirds of the income-poor remain in poverty. The table also shows that, in general, larger cash transfers are linked to greater poverty reduction.

But just as a century before, there was a backlash, particularly in the 1980s and 1990s, that affected both the industrialized countries themselves and their "aid" programs. Memories of the 1930s depression and of

Table 2.2 Poverty Reduction and Cash Transfers in Selected OECD Countries

Country	Poverty rate (%) before taxes and transfers	Poverty rate (%) after taxes and transfers	Poverty reduction (%)	Cash transfers, as % of GDP, 2005		
	Mid-2000s			Old age	Family	Total
Sweden	27%	5%	80%	7%	1.5%	14%
France	31	7	77	11	1.4	17
Hungary	30	7	76	8	1.9	14
Austria	23	7	71	12	2.4	18
United Kingdom	26	8	68	5	2.2	10
Germany	34	11	67	11	1.4	16
Italy	34	11	66	12	0.6	17
OECD average	26	11	60	6	1.2	12
Australia	29	12	57	3	2.2	8
Canada	23	12	48	4	0.9	7
Japan	27	15	45	7	0.3	10
United States	26	17	35	5	0.1	8

Note: Poverty threshold = 50% of median income
Source: Data extracted on October 2, 2009, from OECD.Stat.

colonialism faded, and poor countries and poor people were blamed for their plight. Wealth was glorified, and the United States and many other industrial economies adopted what came to be called neoliberal economic policies, which entailed a smaller role for government and less redistribution. Welfare and social spending was cut, and the gap between rich and poor widened dramatically. Indeed, for some neoliberal radicals, increased inequality was seen as a good thing, in the sense that it would lead to increased competition and more growth. Both *Oliver Twist* and *Les Misérables* were reincarnated as successful stage musicals 120 years after the novels' publication, just as the anti-poor backlash was intensifying. And, reminiscent of the response of Dickens and Hugo a century before, there was increased writing and discussion of the harm that neoliberal policies were doing to the weakest. Progressive thinkers also warned that helping the rich and penalizing the poor was failing to bring growth and development to poor countries.

There have been shifts in thinking in the industrialized North, both with respect to its own social protection policies and in attitudes toward the Global South. But these changes have been slow and inconsistent, and the psychological and political impact of the 2008 financial crisis remains unclear.

Meanwhile, "aid" to poor countries in the late 20th century went though much the same changes of thinking that affected help to poor people in the 19th century. Aid peaked in 1992 and then fell by one-quarter in the next five years, returning to 1992 levels only in 2002.[10] Initially construed as a form of charity, aid increasingly became a way of changing the behavior of those living in poverty, who were again seen as responsible for their plight. But just as 19th-century workhouses and harsh treatment of the poor failed to end poverty and bring economic growth, the neoliberal policies and social spending cuts that were imposed failed to bring development to poor countries. And, just as in the late 19th century, there was a growing realization that industrial growth depended on cheap labor and that keeping labor cheap required housing and other support. Thus, in the late 20th century there was an understanding that globalization depended on poor countries providing cheap commodities. The fair trade movement grew, and aid was increasingly understood as compensation for ever lower commodity prices.

With aid falling, the 1990s saw cuts in social spending in poor countries and the creation of "safety net" programs to provide temporary relief to those in poor countries who were harmed by imposed neoliberal policies of structural adjustment. The Millennium Development Goals called for a reversal of cuts in health and education spending, and aid increased. But poor people were still seen as responsible for their own long-term poverty, particularly by not sending their children to school and to health services.

Divisions have grown within the aid community, many of them characterized by growing gaps between the attitudes in Europe and in the Washington-based institutions (World Bank, IMF, USAID) and even within these institutions.[11] Just as a century earlier democratization meant that those with little money had rights and could vote, so the 1990s saw the growth of a "rights-based" approach to aid, which began to take seriously the 1948 Universal Declaration of Human Rights. Aid was seen less as alms for the poor and more as a transfer of resources to help to satisfy their right to a decent standard of living. The rights-based approach reflects awareness that donors can no longer impose harsh conditions on what they see as the undeserving poor. But as recent books on the failure of aid, cited in Chapter 1, make clear, this new thinking remains seriously contested.

THE SOUTHERN REVOLUTION
BUILDS ON NORTHERN HISTORY

In the North, thinking about the poor and vulnerable went through three phases: First, government accepted collective responsibility for ensuring subsistence for all (England in the 16th century); next, old-age insurance and sickness benefits were introduced (Europe in the late 19th century); and finally, an adequate standard of living became a human right (United Nations, the mid-20th century). These changes created a firmer underpinning for development in the industrialized countries by giving people more security and promoting labor mobility. There were backlashes in the mid-19th century and the late 20th century, as the rich accused the poor of being responsible for their poverty and thus being "undeserving" of assistance. Surveys show that these attitudes persist primarily in the United States.

At the very end of the 20th century, a group of six large southern countries led a fourth paradigm shift, creating a new model. They were responding to two problems. First, the neoliberal economic model promoted by the rich North had failed to spur development in the South, and poverty was increasing, while the global economic model triggered the Asian financial crisis of the later 1990s. Meanwhile, the northern model of social protection was based on insurance programs that assumed male workers in relatively steady employment, whereas in the South many people work in the informal sector without security or are peasant farmers. The southern response was cash transfers from the state that were neither contributory nor insurance-based but, instead, were funded by tax revenue. The cash transfer paradigm challenged the neoliberal model by assigning a greater role to the state and by giving money to large numbers of poor people. Cash transfers are seen as a central part of a broader development strategy. They are granted on a long-term basis, eligible recipients can be confident of their continued availability, and they cover a significant part of the population.

NOTES

1. Simon Szreter, "A Right to Registration: Development, Identity Registration, and Social Security—A Historical Perspective," *World Development*, 35, no. 1 (2007): 67–86.

2. Peter H. Lindert, *Growing Public: Social Spending and Economic Growth Since the Eighteenth Century* (Cambridge: Cambridge University Press, 2004).

3. J. Samuel Valenzuela, "The Missing Links: Families, Welfare Institutions and Economic Development in Latin America," paper presented at the Annual Meetings of the Society for the Advancement of Socio-Economics, Copenhagen, July 2007; and Timothy Scully, J. Samuel Valenzuela, and Eugenio Tironi, eds., *El Eslabón Perdido: Familia, Modernización y Bienestar en Chile* (Santiago, Chile: Taurus, 2006).

4. Angus Maddison, "Statistics on World Population, GDP and Per Capita GDP, 1–2006 AD," datafile, part of *Historical Statistics of the World Economy: 1–2006 AD* (2009), available at http://www.ggdc.net/maddison/. Note also that these statistics show that claims that the neoliberal economic policies of Augusto Pinochet created strong economic growth are in fact a myth. GDP per capita in Chile was lower in 1985 than when Pinochet took over in a coup in 1973.

5. Christine Weigand and Margaret Grosh, "Spending on Social Safety Nets: Comparative Data Compiled from World Bank Analytic Work," Spreadsheet dated June 30, 2008 (Washington, DC: World Bank), http://siteresources.worldbank.org/SAFETYNETSANDTRANSFERS/Resources/SN_Expenditures_6-30-08.xls.

6. OECD, *Growing Unequal? Income Distribution and Poverty in OECD Countries* (Paris: Organisation for Economic Co-operation and Development [OECD], 2008), 15–19.

7. Peter Whiteford, "How Much Redistribution Do Governments Achieve? The Role of Cash Transfers and Household Taxes," Chapter 4 of OECD, *Growing Unequal?* particularly p. 112.

8. Michael Förster and Marco Mira d'Ercole, "Poverty in OECD Counties: An Assessment Based on Static Income," Chaper 5 of OECD, *Growing Unequal?* particularly p. 141.

9. Data from OECD.Stat.

10. ODA (Official Development Assistance) at constant prices, from OECD DAC, downloaded from stats, www.oecd.org. At constant 2007 prices, aid was as follows: 1992, $83bn; 1997, $65bn; 2003, $85bn; 2005, $117bn; 2008, $114bn.

11. See, for example, Joseph Stiglitz, *Globalization and Its Discontents* (New York: Penguin, 2002).

3

Cash Transfers Today

ECONOMIC AND FINANCIAL CRISES OF THE LATE 1990S LED SIX OF THE MOST important newly industrializing countries (Mexico, Brazil, South Africa, India, China, and Indonesia) to formulate a southern response to widespread poverty and vulnerability. Recognizing that poverty is often multidimensional and persistent, they opted for new strategies giving money to the poor directly, as an entitlement, not charity, and guaranteed for a period of time. Encountering incredulity on the part of the North and their own conservatives, who were sure the feckless poor would simply waste the money, the first three in the group set up ongoing evaluations of their cash transfers. Each of the six countries has handled the transfer differently, but the studies offer strong evidence that cash transfers work both to reduce immediate poverty and to promote longer-term human development.

This, in turn, has triggered an avalanche of other cash transfer programs in the South, ranging from small pilot projects to nationwide schemes. Each is different, responding to different levels of social development, institutional structure, perceived needs and priorities, and political conditions. A program in Zambia gave ZMK 30,000 ($6) per family per month to "reduce extreme poverty, hunger and starvation in the 10% most destitute and incapacitated (non-viable) households."[1] By contrast, Indonesia gave an unconditional grant of Rp100,000 ($8) per month to 19 million families—more than 40% of the population—to ease the impact of rising prices.[2]

Most programs have multiple goals. Non-contributory pensions and child benefits are now provided by a growing number of countries, reflecting the recognition that children and older people are more likely to live in poorer households and that society has a responsibility to the young and old. Grants are often implicitly or explicitly intended to build human development, and it is usually expected that the money will be spent locally and will promote economic growth. A core issue of development is that the children of poorer people tend to be poor themselves, so many grants have a goal of reducing intergenerational poverty. If the poor cannot afford to invest in their children, can money be directed to promote better nutrition, regular school attendance, and less child labor? Many programs have a particular focus on the extreme poor, who might be stuck in "poverty traps." Brazil's family grant reaches 12 million families (25% of the population) and has the dual goals of reducing deprivation in poor households and breaking the cycle of the intergenerational transmission of poverty. Nicaragua's Red de Protección Social (Social Protection Network) gave C$12 (US$19) per month to selected poor families, with some of the most precise goals: increasing food expenditure by the poorest, increasing attendance and reducing dropout rates during the first four years of primary school, and increasing health center visits by children under age 3.[3]

Mexico's Progresa-Oportunidades is intended explicitly to "redistribute income to families in extreme poverty," and its two other goals are to encourage completion of primary and secondary education and to improve the health and nutritional status of poor households, in particular so that children's school performance is not affected by ill health or malnourishment.[4]

BALANCING GOALS

The design of a cash transfer program depends on the goals and priorities set by policy makers: Who is it supposed to benefit and what are the objectives? Every cash transfer program is different because each country has made different choices. In this section, we divide the goals and objectives of cash transfers into four broad groups. Every program chooses from this list; none can meet all of the goals, and some possible goals can be contradictory, so it is important to be clear about objectives.

Social Protection and Security

In developing countries, cash transfers have as their core purpose raising the income of the poor and poorest. There are three general types of objectives related to protection and security.

- **Young, old, and disabled.** Societies have always acknowledged their responsibility to those who cannot be productive. We were all young once, and most of us will have children and will one day be old; thus the broader community and state increasingly share the responsibility to provide the support required by these groups. In developed countries, social insurance schemes assist the young, pregnant mothers, and the old through funds that pool contributions from workers and distribute them to those in need. In developing countries, where social insurance schemes cover at best a small fraction of the labor force, non-contributory pensions, family allowances, and child grants have become the southern preference. Figure 3.1 shows how severe child poverty is in Africa, and Figure 3.2 shows that a child benefit can take many children out of poverty.
- **Raising incomes of the working poor.** Most of the chronically poor are actually working,[5] but either they do not earn a living wage or the incomes from their tiny fields are too small to support their

Figure 3.1 Poverty in Some African Countries

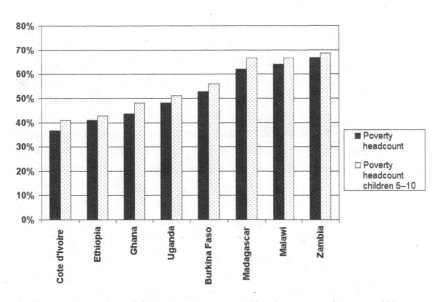

Note: Percentage of population and percentage of children between 5 and 10 years old living in poverty. Data from 1997–2001.

Source: Nanak Kakwani, Fabio Soares, and Hyun Son, "Conditional Cash Transfers in African Countries," Working Paper 9 (Brasilia: International Poverty Centre, 2005).

Figure 3.2 How Much Would a Child Benefit Reduce Poverty?

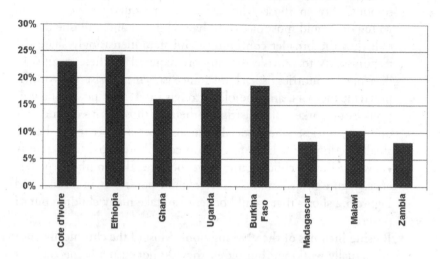

Note: Simulated impact of a child benefit. For the countries in Table 3.1, this is the percentage of children now in poverty who would be taken out of poverty by a child benefit which transferred 30% of the poverty line to all children under 16.

Source: Nanak Kakwani, Fabio Soares, and Hyun Son, "Conditional Cash Transfers in African Countries," Working Paper 9 (Brasilia: International Poverty Centre, 2005).

families. Cash transfers have an immediate effect in bringing those earnings nearer to the poverty line.

- **Safety nets.** The old attitudes of help for the "deserving poor" (those who would work but cannot) remain strong. Thus there is broad acceptance of help for those who cannot work because they are ill or injured, or who cannot find jobs during economic downturns, or whose crops fail because of bad weather. In developed countries, insurance and employee social funds play a key role. But even in advanced countries such as the United States, there are state benefits, including food and food vouchers, as well as job creation schemes such as labor-intensive road building and tree planting. And there is a long history of simply giving people cash, either through unemployment insurance programs in industrialized countries or through government cash payments. Short-term emergency measures for the victims of floods and other disasters are common; the United States gives $500 to any family displaced by a major disaster.[6] Cash has also been used to compensate people for temporarily higher living costs. In 2008 every adult and child who lived in Alaska—more than 600,000 people—received $1,200 from the state, to offset higher fuel costs.[7]

Development and Economic Growth

More than simply preventing immediate hunger and suffering, cash transfers should be a springboard for the economic growth of poor countries. Poor people (and poor communities) are caught in what is called the poverty trap. That is, their poverty and marginalization make it more difficult and more expensive for the poor to do things than for the better off. Borrowing, starting a business, sending their children to school, and even just obtaining documents are all more difficult for poorer people. Without any kind of insurance, it is much more dangerous for poor people to risk growing new crops or going further afield to search for work. It has been argued that governments cannot afford to provide cash transfers and social protection until after development and economic growth have occurred, but the opposite is actually true: Cash transfers are essential to promote growth and development.

Increased understanding of the "poverty trap"—appreciation of the fact that you cannot pull yourself up by your bootstraps if you have no boots—has led to the use of cash transfers as a way of enabling people to participate actively in the economy. Cash transfers compensate them for the higher opportunity costs and higher risks experienced by those with the least money. Cash transfers work to stimulate economic growth at three levels: Individuals can invest and earn more, the local economy is stimulated by increased spending, and this positive spiral of local economic growth helps to promote economic growth on the national level. Thus cash transfers are important in the following three ways:

- **Stimulating demand.** Cash grants are a direct way of stimulating demand, because poor people spend the extra money locally. The total amount of money spent on grants may be small, typically 1% of GDP. But it can increase the spending power of poor families by 20%, and this can give a huge boost to a local community. UNCTAD, the United National Conference on Trade and Development, in its *Least Developed Countries Report 2006*, stressed that "domestic demand makes the largest contribution to economic growth."[8] UNCTAD goes on to point to the "massive informalization of non-agricultural employment" and to emphasize that "the critical factor which enables increased informal sector earnings is the stimulus of demand." Even developed countries use cash transfers to stimulate demand. In early 2009 the Australian government gave 1% of GDP as a one-off grant of A$950 (then US$700, £440) to 14 million low- and middle-income Australians (more than half the population of the country) to support jobs.[9]

- **Security to promote investment.** UNCTAD also argues that "all-pervasive economic insecurity at the household level associated with generalized poverty adversely affects entrepreneurship as it leads to short-termism and limits risk-taking."[10] An assured cash transfer provides a form of insurance; families know that a certain amount of money will be available each month, which reduces insecurity and decreases the need to save for emergencies such as sickness or crop failure, releasing money for investment. This, in turn, makes smaller levels of saving tolerable and thus allows more investment (such as buying stock for trading, inputs for manufacturing, or fertilizer and improved seeds for farming) and more risk taking (such as experimenting with new, higher-yielding crops, making a different product to see whether there is a market, or going further afield to look for work).
- **Start-up capital.** Rich people tend to assume that cash transfers will be used only for immediate consumption, but in fact they are used partly for productive investment. The World Bank, in its *World Development Report 2006: Equity and Development,* argues that "markets in developing countries are highly imperfect, and those who do not have enough wealth or social status tend to underinvest." The report cites various studies showing that the poor and those with lower social status have less access to credit and are charged higher interest rates, yet their investments tend to be more productive and have higher rates of return. This means that redistribution can actually be an efficient way to promote investment and economic growth.[11] Cash transfers often provide the initial capital that enables the poor and socially marginalized to invest.

Human Capital and Breaking the Intergenerational Poverty Cycle

Cash transfers directly improve the well-being of people on low incomes:

- **Nutrition** is improved because grants provide money to buy food.
- **Health** standards are raised by better nutrition, by increased ability to attend clinics, and by having more money for medicines and treatment.
- **Education** standards are raised because children are better fed and can go to school instead of working; indeed, reducing child labor is

an explicit goal in many programs. Cash grants can increase the school attendance of girls.

Although improved health and education can be seen as valuable gains in themselves, they also improve the productive capacity of poor households. The main assets that poor people have are themselves and their labor power, and cash transfers can boost their productive capacities—increasing what economists call their human capital.

In its *World Development Report 2006: Equity and Development*, the World Bank declares that the

> adverse effects of unequal opportunities and political power on development are all the more damaging because economic, political, and social inequalities tend to reproduce themselves over time and across generations. We call such phenomena "inequality traps." Disadvantaged children from families at the bottom of the wealth distribution do not have the same opportunities as children from wealthier families to receive quality education. So these disadvantaged children can expect to earn less as adults. Because the poor have less voice in the political process, they— like their parents—will be less able to influence spending decisions to improve public schools for their children. And the cycle of underachievement continues.

The Bank also notes that "intergenerational immobility is also observed in rich countries: new evidence from the United States (where the myth of equal opportunity is strong) finds high levels of persistence of socioeconomic status across generations: recent estimates suggest that it would take five generations for a family that earned half the national average income to reach the average."[12]

- **Breaking the intergenerational poverty link** has become a major explicit goal of cash transfers, because they are a key way to redress inequalities by helping to ensure that children in poor families are better fed, are healthier, and have more education than their parents.

"My life would have been different if there had been something like Oportunidades [the Mexican family grant] in my time. I simply wasn't able to study," notes Andrés Ponce Hernández. In the tiny village of Zongozotla in a coffee-growing area of Mexico, he lives in a makeshift house of bricks and cardboard that leaks when it rains. But his children "are not going to live like us. They will have a better life. They don't know so much

poverty anymore, or at least not as we have known poverty." The key thing
has been that he was able to send his daughters to secondary school. "If I
didn't have the help of Oportunidades, I would have had to tell my daughters that they could not study anymore and should just join with some fellow to support them."[13]

Because of the importance placed on breaking the intergenerational
poverty chain, cash transfers are often combined with access to public services, and many are conditional (for example, they may require attendance
at school, clinics, or parenting classes). Whether conditions are necessary
is intensely debated and is discussed in Chapter 8.

Rights, Equity and Fairness

Many proponents of cash transfers see them as having important ethical or
moral components and as encouraging fairness, equity, and empowerment.

- **The right to an adequate standard of living** is guaranteed to everyone, deserving and undeserving, by the Universal Declaration of Human Rights,
  and this right can be accorded to recipients through cash transfers.
- **Redistribution** of money from the richer to the poorer, along with the
  attendant reduction in inequality, is often an implicit goal, because in
  more unequal societies redistribution is the only way to reduce poverty.
  The growth of European social democracy was built on a belief that societies should be more equal and that there should be some redistribution of wealth from the rich to at least the "deserving poor," with cash
  transfers running in parallel with a progressive tax system and state-
  funded services, particularly for education and health. Table 3.1 gives two
  measures of income inequality for a range of countries. In Sweden, which
  is quite equal, the richest ten percent earns 6 times the income of the poorest fifth; Britain and the United States are less equal, with ratios of 14:1
  and 16:1; whereas Brazil and South Africa are among the most unequal
  countries in the world, with ratios of 41:1 and 35:1. The other measure
  of income inequality is the Gini index, which measures the extent to
  which the distribution of income is unequal: 0 reflects total equality and
  100 indicates complete inequality (one person has all the income). Cash
  transfers and other policies have made Sweden more equal. Figures 3.3
  and 3.4 give the proportion of national income that goes to five groups
  of people. As Figure 3.4 shows, in Sweden the poorest fifth of the population has 9% of national income, compared to 5% in the United States
  and only 3% in Brazil. A number of studies[14] show that more equal societies are happier, are healthier, and experience more rapid economic

Table 3.1 Measures of Inequality

Country	Ratio of income of richest 10% to that of poorest 10%	Gini Index
Sweden	6	25
Bangladesh	6	31
Mongolia	9	33
United Kingdom	14	36
Indonesia	11	39
United States	16	41
Ghana	16	43
Mexico	21	48
Brazil	41	55
South Africa	35	58

Source: World Bank World Development Indicators online database. Data from: Sweden 2000, Bangladesh 2005, Mongolia 2005, United Kingdom 1999, Indonesia 2005, United States 2000, Ghana 2006, Mexico 2006, Brazil 2007, and South Africa 2000.

development. Cash transfers can be part of a program to redistribute money and reduce inequality.

- **Empowerment and choice** can be explicit or implicit goals of cash transfers. Raising income above the poverty line means that people need no longer be chained to the demands of immediate survival. Rather, they have more time and resources to make choices about their own lives and to be politically active, which promotes democracy. Cash transfers sometimes replace food aid or subsidies on particular goods such as maize; giving people money instead of goods enables them to choose how the money is spent. This, in turn, can increase competition between providers and may improve quality and efficiency via supply-side impacts.
- **Improve status of women.** Child and family benefits are normally given to women, which is a direct gain for women struggling to feed a family. Having an additional income can also raise the status of women within the household. Young women in many countries face sexual demands from teachers and employers, and a regular income makes it possible for some young women to resist these sexual pressures. Social (non-contributory) pensions also benefit women more than men, partly because women live longer and tend to be poorer, but also because men are more likely to have had a job that included them in a formal pension system.
- **Distribute mineral revenues.** The "resource curse," in which corrupt elites of Nigeria or Guinea divert revenues from oil or minerals to their own use instead of national development, has become an increasingly urgent issue. Cash transfers can be used to distribute the income from natural resources more fairly, to reduce poverty and support citizenship instead of lining

Figure 3.3 Income Inequality

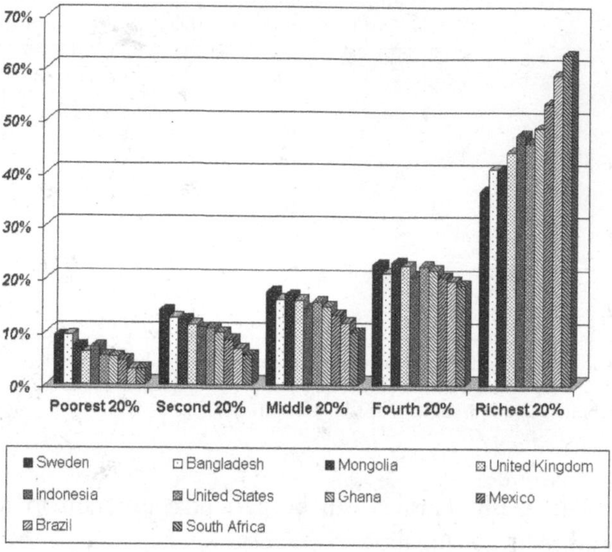

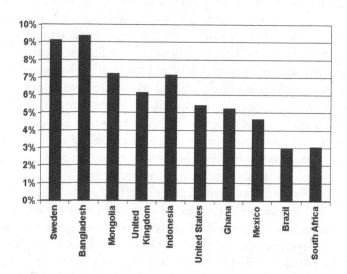

Note: Share of income of population divided into fifths (quintiles).

Source: World Bank World Development Indicators online database. Data from: Sweden 2000, Bangladesh 2005, Mongolia 2005, United Kingdom 1999, Indonesia 2005, United States 2000, Ghana 2006, Mexico 2006, Brazil 2007, and South Africa 2000.

Figure 3.4 Share of Income of the Poorest 20%

Source: World Bank World Development Indicators online database. Data from: Sweden 2000, Bangladesh 2005, Mongolia 2005, United Kingdom 1999, Indonesia 2005, United States 2000, Ghana 2006, Mexico 2006, Brazil 2007, and South Africa 2000.

ministers' pockets. Mongolia, Bolivia, and the US state of Alaska distribute part of the income derived from oil, gas, and metals as cash transfers.

Brazilian researchers Degol Hailu of the International Policy Centre for Inclusive Growth and Sergei Suarez Dillon Soares of the Institute for Applied Economic Research (IPEA) note that "the economics profession has long debated whether there is a tradeoff between growth and equity. Countries that pursued inequality-reducing strategies have been warned that growth will be affected, and hence that poverty increases. The harbingers of doom advocated a growth-focused strategy. Their assumption was that the income of the poor rises in direct proportion to economic growth. The truth is more like this: economies with more equal income distribution are likely to achieve higher rates of poverty reduction than very unequal countries."[15]

Cash transfers do not automatically reduce inequality. Many pension systems actually benefit the better off.[16] Other transfers do reduce extreme poverty, but often by redistributing cash from the middle classes to the poor, so they do little to change overall inequality. Furthermore, the amount transferred, typically 1% of GDP, will not on its own have a major impact on inequality. Nevertheless, as part of a broader program, cash transfers can play a part in reducing inequality. Not all countries will see this as a priority, and differing attitudes toward wealth and poverty will lead countries to have varying attitudes toward redistribution. Thus clear goals will be important in the design of a cash transfer program.

Mixing Goals

All cash transfers are designed in an effort to satisfy several of these aims. A child benefit provided as part of society's recognition of the need to give extra money to families with children may also be conditional on sending those children to school as part of ending intergenerational poverty. Similarly, increasing evidence that less developed countries grow more rapidly if they are more equal means that redistribution can have direct developmental impacts.

The African Union 2006 Livingstone Call for Action underlines the multiple goals.[17] It cites five different purposes for social transfers: directly reducing poverty and inequality; addressing generalized insecurity; providing cash directly to poor people to enhance economic growth; increasing human capital by helping people to stay healthy, by assisting them in educating their children, and supporting families affected by HIV/AIDS; and stimulating local markets to benefit whole communities.

It is difficult to fulfill all purposes at once. Thus there are huge differences between programs in different countries because of different starting points, priorities, social attitudes, and spending levels. In this book we will look at the differences and consider the range of choices and outcomes. This approach underlines our view that there are no universal models that can be directly applied. We believe that cash transfers are proving effective and should be more widely used, but each country must shape its own program.

CASH TRANSFERS TODAY—THE LEADING SIX

The combination of a global economic crisis, the increasingly obvious failure of the neoliberal development model, and domestic political considerations demanding an engagement with poverty led Brazil, India, Mexico, South Africa, and China all to begin cash transfer programs in the late 1990s; Indonesia joined them soon afterwards. More than 90 million families receive cash transfers in these six countries. These programs have been heavily evaluated, and there have been many changes, but they remain the largest programs and continue to provide data and experiences from which other countries can learn. These grants are not simple and are characterized by changing eligibilities and varying grant levels.

SOUTH AFRICA ended white minority rule (apartheid) and Nelson Mandela was elected president in 1994, but this did not bring job creation or dispel poverty for the majority. Under apartheid, there had been some racially determined social protection, and the initial demand was to extend these programs to all citizens.

In 1928 the South African state introduced non-contributory old-age pensions for poor white and "colored" people, and in 1944 this was extended to "African" people, although at a much lower rate, with black pensioners receiving $\frac{1}{12}$ of what was given to whites.[18] By the 1950s, black South Africans were a majority of the recipients of non-contributory pensions, and by the end of the apartheid era, pensions had become one of the most important sources of income for rural black South Africans.[19] Only in 1993, in the dying days of apartheid, did the white government agree that all non-contributory pensions would be at the same level.[20] By 2009 there were 2.3 million people receiving a social pension (85% of the population 63 and older) and another 1.3 million receiving a similar disability grant. Whereas the majority of white older people live alone or with other older people, three-generation households are the rule among black South African families with pensioners. This means that social pensions directly improve the lives of millions of non-pensioners. There are six people in the average South African pensioner household; households with a pension are larger and have more children than households without a pension. One-third of black children under the age of 16 live with a social pensioner.[21]

In 1998 South Africa introduced the child support grant, which in mid-2009 went to more than 8.5 million children (55% of all children). The grant is R240 ($27) per month, and it goes to families where the main caregiver has a monthly income below R800 ($89) in formal dwellings in urban areas and below R1100 ($122) in informal dwellings and rural areas.[22] The grant began in 1998 for children under 7 years old, but it has been steadily extended, and by 2009 it was available for children under 15.

South Africa's grants are not conditional, but applicants do have to satisfy a verified means test. The means test for the child support grant is quite complex; that for the pension is less so. Cash delivery is very straight-forward. One-quarter of beneficiaries receive their money electronically, and the rest collect the cash from shops, banks, and mobile cash machines.

In the 2009–2010 financial year, South Africa expects to spend R80 billion ($9bn) on grants and cash transfers; this represents 12% of the total national budget and 3.5% of GDP. "This makes South Africa one of the world's biggest spenders on social grants," says the South African Treasury.[23]

BRAZIL faced a series of economic crises in the mid-1990s and was affected by the Asian financial crisis of 1998. Fernando Henrique Cardoso, president from 1994 to 2002, introduced a series of cash transfers during 1996–1999, including money for very poor households to buy food and gas and the Child Labour Eradication Programme ($11–17 per child per month for poor households with children aged 7–14 working in hazardous or degrading conditions, a program that had 866,000 beneficiary children in 2002). The Bolsa Escolar (school grant) program started as a local program in municipalities. Initiated in Brasilia in 1995 by the newly elected Worker's Party (PT), it had reached 100 municipalities when it was made national in 2001. The grant was $5–15 per household for poor households with children aged 6–15; 8.2 million children, living in 5 million households, were covered in 2002, representing 5% of the population.

Luiz Inácio Lula da Silva of the PT was elected president in 2002 and reelected in 2006 to serve until 2010. In 2003 he consolidated the cash transfers into one family grant (Bolsa Família). In mid-2009, 11.6 million families (50 million people,[24] representing 26% of the population) were receiving grants. Eligibility is linked to the minimum wage, and families with a per capita monthly income of less than R$69 ($35, 15% of the minimum wage) receive a family grant of R$62 ($31) per month. In addition, all families with a per capita monthly income below R$137 ($69, 30% of the minimum wage) are covered, and children receive R$20 or R$30 per month per child (depending on age) up to five children. The maximum benefit is R$182 ($91).[25] People must apply for the grant, but municipalities largely accept a family's declaration of income. The grant requires clinic attendance and 85% school attendance, but these are "soft" conditions. That is, if the conditions are not met, the grant is not cut off, but social services are called in to support the family. The system is highly decentralized and is administered at the municipal level. Payments are made through agents—banks, shops, lottery sales agents—and cash machines.

There are also two social pension schemes, both of which pay a benefit equivalent to the minimum wage. A non-contributory rural pension (Previdencia Rural) was introduced in 1991 and, two years later, an urban pension (Benefício de Prestação Continuada, or BPC, which replaced the Renda Mensal Vitalicia, or RMV). In 2007 pensions were paid to 1.2 million individuals aged 65 and over living in households with per capita household income below a quarter of the minimum wage; a disability pension was paid to 1.3 million people, and a rural pension was paid to 5.4 million people who had worked in the informal sector.[26] Half of pensioner households also include children. The average pensioner household contains 3 people, and 24 million people are in families benefitting from these pensions.[27] Thus 74 million people, or 39% of the population, benefit from cash transfers.[28] The three pensions cost R$31bn in 2007, and Bolsa Família that year cost $R8bn for a total of R$39bn ($22bn at the exchange rate in 2007), or 1.5% of GDP for all the cash transfer programs.[29]

MEXICO faced a major crisis in the mid-1990s. Its joining the North American Free Trade Agreement in 1994 triggered the Zapatista rebellion in Chiapas province. Ernesto Zedillo took office as president on December 1, 1994, and immediately faced a major economic crisis. The poor were badly hit, threatening to make a sick joke of Zedillo's campaign slogan "well-being for your family" (Bienestar para tu familia). Over the next two years, the Mexican government completely rethought anti-poverty programs. Food subsidies on bread, tortillas, maize, beans, and other staples had been in place for up to 30 years, but it was argued that the subsidies largely benefitted the better off who consumed more. In 1997 Mexico launched its cash transfer program, Progresa, giving money to 300,000 families. This program was steadily expanded. Renamed Oportunidades in 2002, it reached 5 million families in all 31 states by 2004, thus serving 24 million people, or 22% of the population. In the three poorest states, it reaches more than half of all families. The cash grant averages $38 per month, which is 27% of the average household income of the rural poor and 20% of that of the urban poor. The 2008 budget for Oportunidades was 42 billion pesos, about $4bn, which is just 0.3% of GDP.

Poor households that are to receive the grants are identified by a point system (called a proxy means test) based on the age, gender, and education of each family member, on whether the house has electricity and tap water, and on whether there are assets such as a radio, television, and bicycles. The grant is quite complex, depending on age and school level. Part of the grant is paid to the mother or to whoever is responsible for the children. But children who attend school more than 85% of the time receive their own cash transfer, which increases as children become older. Finally, families receive food supplements and free medicines. For the entire family, the average cash transfer is $30 per month, and in-kind transfers are worth $6 per month. The maximum cash transfer per family is $153 per month. There are no restrictions on how the money is spent.[30]

Unlike the programs in Brazil and South African, the Mexican program imposes a set of conditions on recipients. In part this reflects the influence of attitudes of the neighboring United States on Mexican elites as well as on the Inter-American Development Bank, which played a major role in designing the program.[31] As in Brazil, mothers must attend health clinics with their children, to ensure that the children are monitored and that they receive vaccinations. But in Mexico mothers must also attend talks on health, nutrition, and reproductive health, must attend community meetings, and must take part in community labor such as cleaning schools or sweeping streets. Teenagers must attend talks related to reproductive health and drug addiction. Those who fail to comply lose their grants. Also unlike Brazil and South Africa, "Oportunidades is not a programme to reduce poverty in the short-term. It was designed to break the 'inter-generational circle of poverty' through a medium- and long-term process of human capital construction," explains Mercedes González de la Rocha of the Mexican Social Anthropology Research Institute (CIESAS).[32] The program was unusual in that there was extensive independent research and evaluation from the start, not only by Mexican researchers and academics but also by the Washington-based International Food Policy Research Institute (IFPRI).

INDIA has adopted a very different strategy with its National Rural Employment Guarantee Scheme (NREGS). This program guarantees each rural household 100 days of unskilled wage labor per year at a wage of no less than Rs 60 ($1.25) per day. It is sometimes called workfare[33] because it requires the recipient to actually work to earn the money, but it differs from traditional public works programs in that it guarantees a right to work, and thus a right to an income when the recipient needs it, which is typically when there is no agricultural work. One-quarter of Indians are poor, and three-quarters of those live in rural areas; most are small farmers or landless farm workers who cannot find work during slack farming seasons—around April in many parts of India. The program began in Maharashtra state in 1979 and was tried in other states, including Bihar; work was promised within 2 weeks of an application, and if work was not available, approved applicants would still be paid the minimum wage.

When the Congress Party of India returned to power in 2004, it took up the idea, and the national program was launched in 2006. It was rapidly expanded to all 600 rural districts by 2009 and was planned to involve 44 million households. Most of the work is on labor-intensive, small-scale construction projects for roads, water supply, irrigation, flood control, land development, and reforestation. Total expenditure is $4bn per year (0.3% of GDP); the average salary is $1.70 per day, and the average household does 40 days of work per year. Projects are intended to encourage higher agricultural productivity and improve market access, and they are partly selected by local development committees. The guarantee means that projects are demand driven and must be designed to handle large variations in labor supply.

CHINA was faced with the collapse of its old safety nets, and the Minimum Livelihood Guarantee Scheme (Di Bao) was introduced in Shanghai in 1993 and expanded to other Chinese cities in 1999. By 2005 it covered 22.3 million people in 7.4 million families. Although the numbers are large, the grant is relatively small, and the program covers only a small fraction of the population. Di Bao is restricted to "registered" urban residents, and thus it excludes many migrants from rural areas who do not have a formal right of residency and are often the poorest people in urban areas. The grant is unconditional and goes to all registered families below a poverty line set at the municipal level, which averages Yuan 230 ($28) per person per month. It now covers about 6% of urban residents and costs 0.1% of GDP. Families claim the grant by reporting an income below the poverty line, and local authorities and neighborhood committees try to ensure that recipients are genuinely eligible by looking at assets such as consumer durables and at housing conditions. The World Bank estimates that Di Bao covers only one-quarter of urban households below the poverty line. The grant is small, averaging Yuan 26 ($3) per person per month and representing only 10% of the income of recipients. It is accepted that this small transfer will be largely spent on food, so many areas have introduced separate medical assistance programs.[34] Di Bao is being expanded into rural areas, and in August 2009 China announced plans for a rural pension that would combine personal pension payments by farmers and a government subsidy, apparently guaranteeing Yuan 260 per month to everyone over 60.[35]

INDONESIA was hit hard by the 1997–1998 Asian financial crisis, and poverty increased sharply; popular uprisings forced President Suharto to resign in 1998. Various anti-poverty and safety net programs were introduced, particularly around community infrastructure development. In 2005 a fuel subsidy (which largely benefitted the better off) was replaced by a cash transfer program that gave Rp100,000 ($8) per month to 19 million poor families (40% of the population) for 12 months in 2005–2006. It was called the Program Bantuan Langsung Tunai (BLT) and cost about 0.5% of GDP. In response to the rise in fuel prices, BLT was given again for 9 months in 2008–2009. By then Indonesia was already designing a different kind of cash transfer program, one that is longer term, carries conditions, and gives more money to fewer families. Program Keluarga Harapan (PKH) by late 2009 covered 2 million households and aimed to reach 6.5 million poor families. Each family will receive money for 6 years. Transfers will depend on the size of the family, will range from Rp50,000 ($4) to Rp183,000 ($15) per month, and will average Rp116,000 ($10). BLT was unconditional, but PKH is explicitly modeled on Mexico's Oportunidades and requires school attendance and visits to clinics. Targeting is based on a proxy means test, and the household must have a child; money is given to women heads of households and is collected from the post office.[36]

The six big cash transfer programs already in operation show just how varied such programs can be. They are unconditional, soft conditional, and hard conditional; are targeted narrowly and broadly; and vary greatly in what proportion of household income they provide.

OTHER CASH TRANSFERS IN THE SOUTH[37]

Social Pensions

BOLIVIA is the only country in Latin America to have a universal non-contributory pension. Bolivia is one of South America's poorest countries; 29% of the population live on less than a dollar a day, and most people work in the informal sector with no secure income. Bolivia introduced Bonosol in 1996, using funds from the privatization of Bolivia's utility companies. In 2001 Bonosol was providing an annual pension of Bs900 ($125) to every man and woman over the age of 65; this pension was increased to Bs1800 ($250) in 2003. In 2008 it was renamed Renta Dignidad and reformulated to be financed from a tax on gas exports following renationalization. The age of eligibility was reduced to 60, and benefits were set at two levels: Bs2400 for those without any pension and Bs1800 for those with some kind of contributory pension.[38]

There are clusters of countries with social pensions in South Asia (INDIA, BANGLADESH, NEPAL), southern Africa (SOUTH AFRICA, BOTSWANA, NAMIBIA, LESOTHO, SWAZILAND, MAURITIUS), and South America (CHILE, ARGENTINA, BRAZIL, URUGUAY, ECUADOR).[39]

Families and Children

At least 26 countries have introduced child benefits or family grants. Three such programs are large and cover a significant portion of the children in the country.

MONGOLIA, one of Asia's poorest countries, introduced a targeted Child Money Program (CMP) after both main political parties promised it during 2004 elections.[40] Targeting proved ineffective, however, and in 2006 CMP was converted to a universal child benefit, over the objection of donors. The initial program provided Tog 36,000 ($31) per child per year. In 2007 this was increased to Tog 136,000 ($117) per year, which made possible a 35% increase in spending for the poorest tenth of households. This child benefit has reduced the percentage of children in poverty from 42% to 27%. The cost of CMP increased from 0.8% of GDP to 3.9% of GDP; CMP is largely funded from a new tax on mineral exports and is publicly presented as sharing the mineral wealth of the country. The program started with a range of conditions, but now it requires only school attendance.

ECUADOR has one of the biggest of the newer programs. Bono de Desarrollo Humano was launched in 2003, and by 2006 it covered 5 million people in more than 1 million households—40% of the population. Beneficiaries are selected by a proxy means test, and the program is unconditional. The cost is 0.6% of GDP.

PERU's Programa Juntos had reached 125,000 households with $33 per month by 2006. The target is to reach the 1.5 million households in extreme poverty, 28% of the population, which would cost 2% of GDP. The poorest communities are selected, and then a proxy means test is applied to select poor households; there is a community validation.

The members of another group of programs reach around 15% of the population:

COLOMBIA's Familias en Acción is a child benefit that had reached 1.7 million households, more than 15% of the population, by 2007. The grant is $8–33 per child, depending on age, and is conditional on school and clinic attendance. The cost is 0.2% of GDP.

HONDURAS gives $113 per year to 240,000 households in the 1,000 poorest communities, reaching 15% of the population. The cost is 0.3% of GDP.

ARMENIA has a family grant that in 2003 gave $15 per month to 141,000 households, about 17% of the population, at a cost of 0.9% of GDP. Eligibility is by a proxy means test, and the program has been scaled down from its peak in 1999, when it reached 212,000 families at a cost of 2% of GDP.

PANAMA's Red de Oportunidades reaches 50,000 households (15% of the population) with $35 per month, costing 0.4% of GDP. There is a geographic selection of the poorest communities, and then a proxy means test is used to select the poorest households. The grant is conditional on attendance at schools and clinics and on mothers attending human development lessons.

JAMAICA has a combined child benefit, pension, and disability benefit aimed at the poorest. By 2008 it had reached 300,000 people, or 12% of the population. Grants range from $7 to $12 per month per person. The cost is 0.2% of GDP.

GHANA's Livelihood Empowerment Against Poverty (LEAP) aims to reach the 19% of the population who are identified by the Ghana Living Standard Survey (GLSS) as falling into the category of extremely poor. Grants are $6–10 per household per month. LEAP started in 2008 with 8,000 households and had reached 35,000 by 2009. It expects to reach 165,000 households by 2012 at a cost of 1% of GDP.

Ten programs reach less than 15% of the population, sometimes with quite small amounts of money, but each gives money to more than 1 million people:

The PHILIPPINES picked the 150 poorest municipalities and cities and then used a proxy means test to select the 380,000 poorest households, which receive $11 per month plus $7 per month for each child, up to age 3. The program is conditional on attending school and health clinics. The cost is 0.1% of GDP.

CHILE has two cash transfers. Subsidio Unitario Familiar (SUF) gives $10 per month to poor households and reaches 1.2 million people (7% of the population). Chile Solidario gives extra money and explicitly tries to support families in extreme poverty and to change their behavior, setting family and government responsibilities for action on seven dimensions of poverty; it requires regular meetings with a social worker. The program targets the 5% of households estimated to be in extreme poverty. Grants start at $21 per month and decrease to the $10 per month of SUF after 18 months. The cost is 0.1% of GDP.

The KYRGYZ REPUBLIC has two main benefits that cover 500,000 poor children, about 10% of the population, at a cost of 0.6% of GDP.

BANGLADESH gives a stipend of Tk100 ($1.50) per month to 5.3 million poor primary school pupils at a cost of 0.2% of GDP. The old-age pension scheme, introduced in the face of donor resistance, now provides Tk250 ($3.75) per month to almost 1 million old people (mainly widows).

In PAKISTAN, in Punjab state, 450,000 girls at secondary school receive $3 per month. A food support program gives a quite small amount of money, a single annual payment of PRs 3000 ($36) per family to a large number of people—1.5 million households, 6% of the population. The cost is 0.04% of GDP.

Other programs include the following:

EL SALVADOR's Red Solidaria gives up to $20 per month to 100,000 extremely poor households in the 100 poorest municipalities.

CAMBODIA has a conditional program for education of poor girls and ethnic minority children, which gives $45–90 to 15,000 children in 75 secondary schools located in the poorest communes of 17 provinces.

PARAGUAY has two programs that reach 22,000 families with $18–36 per month, at a cost of 0.1% of GDP.

MALAWI had several pilot programs targeting the 10% of families that are ultra-poor and lack sufficient labor. This program started in four districts, had expanded to seven districts and 24,000 families by 2009, and plans to cover the entire country and reach 273,000 households by 2013. The grant averages $14 per month and is projected to cost 1.4% of GDP by 2013. Malawi also offers a fertilizer subsidy, costing up to 4.7% of GDP, that reaches families with land and labor.

Smaller family programs, typically pilots reaching fewer than 20,000 households, are being run in ZAMBIA, BURKINA FASO, KENYA, TANZANIA, and NIGERIA.

Workfare

ETHIOPIA is the only African country to opt for a labor-based program similar to India's. Its Productive Safety Nets Programme (PSNP) began in 2005 and was initially financed by a consortium of donors as an alternative to repeated emergency food aid programs. It is targeted at 262 chronically food-insecure *woredas* (districts) and aims to provide predictable cash transfers for 5 years. By 2008 it had reached more than 7 million people and had an annual budget of $500 million (2% of GDP, which makes this the largest program in Sub-Saharan Africa, after South Africa). The main part of PSNP is a public works program paying 8 birr ($1) per day for 5 days of work per month between January and June, when less labor is needed for farming. The second component is direct support, which gives money to vulnerable households with no able-bodied members who can be employed on public works projects. One-third of PSNP households also benefit from a package of production-increasing services such as credit and agricultural extension.[41]

GIVING MONEY TO 110 MILLION FAMILIES

At least 45 countries in the Global South now give cash transfers to more than 110 million families. This policy revolution has swept the South in the past decade and is challenging attitudes in the North. Every program is different and there are huge variations, from universal child benefits in Mongolia to pensions in Africa to family grants in Latin America. Some grants are tiny—only $3 per month—whereas others give families more than $100 per month; some cover more than one-third of the population, and others aim only for the very poorest. The size of public spending also varies enormously, from as little as 0.1% of GDP up to 4% of GDP, although most programs fall in the range of 0.4% to 1.5%. Six countries took the lead and still have the biggest programs—Brazil, Mexico, South Africa, India, Indonesia, and China—but several countries (including Mongolia, Ecuador, Peru, and Ghana) are introducing cash transfers that will reach a large portion of their population.

The huge variation in cash transfers reflects significant differences in local politics, history, resources, and goals. Each transfer program chooses from a broader menu of possible goals:

- **Social protection and security.** Alleviating immediate poverty with money for the young, old, and disabled and for the working poor, as well as creating "safety nets" for those temporarily in poverty.

- **Development and economic growth.** Giving poor people enough additional money to enable them to invest profitably in new crops, trade, or the search for a better job, while providing a small buffer that makes it easier to take risks. Initial spending is within the local community, which creates demand and promotes an upward spiral of local economic growth. Local growth in poor areas then spurs national economic development.
- **Breaking intergenerational poverty.** Children of poor parents are less likely to be poor if they are better fed, healthier, and better educated, all of which can be promoted by cash transfers.
- **Rights and equity.** Cash transfers help to satisfy the human right to a decent standard of living. They can also reduce income inequality, and less inequality tends to promote development. They can promote the status of women. And they can be important in a fair distribution of mineral revenues, preventing the "resource curse."

Cash transfers are becoming popular precisely because they are tools that can be effectively used for a range of goals, but they are always based on the understanding that it makes sense to give money directly to poor people because they will use it productively and wisely.

NOTES

1. Bernd Schubert, "The Pilot Social Cash Transfer Scheme Kalomo District—Zambia" (Lusaka: GTZ, 2004).

2. Stella A. Hutagalung, Sirojuddin Arif, and Widjajanti I. Suharyo, "Problems and Challenges for the Indonesian Conditional Cash Transfer Programme—Program Keluarga Harapan (PKH)," to be published in *Social Protection in Asia* (IDS Sussex, 2009).

3. John A. Maluccio and Rafael Flores, "Impact Evaluation of a Conditional Cash Transfer Program—The Nicaraguan Red de Protección Social," Research Report 141 (Washington, DC: International Food Policy Research Institute, 2005), p. 62.

4. Santiago Levy, *Progress Against Poverty: Sustaining Mexico's Progresa-Oportunidades Program* (Washington, DC: Brookings Institution, 2006), p. 21.

5. Tony Addison, Caroline Harper, Martin Prowse, and Andrew Shepherd, *The Chronic Poverty Report 2008–09: Escaping Poverty Traps* (Manchester, UK: Chronic Poverty Research Centre, 2008), p. vii.

6. During hurricanes Katrina and Rita in 2005, $2,000 grants known as expedited assistance were made via debit cards, followed by a $2,358 transitional

housing assistance program. More than 450,000 families received grants (http://www.ohsep.louisiana.gov/archive/2003_2007/katrina23billion.htm, accessed May 25, 2009). This policy was changed in 2008 to give $500 "displacement assistance" to anyone displaced more than 7 days (http://www.fema.gov/good_guidance/download/10320, accessed May 25, 2009).

7. This was in addition to the normal oil revenue distribution, which was $2,069 in 2008. Rachel D'Oro, "Alaskans to Receive $3,269 Each," *Anchorage Daily News*, September 5, 2008.

8. UNCTAD, *The Least Developed Countries Report 2006: Developing Productive Capacities* (Geneva and New York: UNCTAD, 2006), p. 263 ff.

9. Office of the Prime Minister of Australia, "$950 One-off Cash Bonus to Support Jobs," media release February 2009 (http://www.pm.gov.au/media/Release/2009/media_release_0778.cfm, accessed May 25, 2009).

10. UNCTAD, *The Least Developed Countries Report 2006*, p. 110.

11. World Bank, *World Development Report 2006: Equity and Development* (Washington, DC: World Bank, and New York: Oxford University Press, 2005), pp. 91, 96, 101, 102.

12. World Bank, *World Development Report 2006*, p. 6.

13. Mauricio Carrera, *Oportunidades: Historias de Éxito* (Mexico: Secretaría de Desarrollo Social, Coordinación Nacional del Programa de Desarrollo Humano Oportunidades, 2008), p. 112.

14. Richard Wilkinson and Kate Pickett, *The Spirit Level: Why More Equal Societies Almost Always Do Better* (London: Allan Lane, 2009).

15. Degol Hailu and Sergei Soares, "What Explains the Decline in Brazil's Inequality?" One Pager 89 (Brasilia: International Policy Centre for Inclusive Growth (formerly International Poverty Centre).

16. Margaret Grosh, Carlo del Ninno, Emil Tesliuc, and Azedine Ouerghi, *For Protection and Promotion* (Washington, DC: World Bank, 2008), p. 33.

17. "The Livingstone Call for Action," adopted at the African Union Intergovernmental Regional Conference "A Transformative Agenda for the 21st Century: Examining the Case for Basic Social Protection in Africa," Livingstone, Zambia, March 20–23, 2006.

18. Michael Samson et al., "Final Report: The Social and Economic Impact of South Africa's Social Security System," Report commissioned by the South Africa Department of Social Development, EPRI Research Paper 37 (Cape Town: Economic Policy Research Institute, 2004), http://www.epri.org.za/rp37.htm p. 28.

19. South Africa continues to use the racial classifications "white," "colored," "Indian/Asian," and "African" in official publications; see, for example, the publications of Statistics South Africa.

20. Jeremy Seekings, "Prospects for Basic Income in Developing Countries: A Comparative Analysis of Welfare Regimes in the South" (Cape Town: Centre for Social Science Research, 2005), http://www.cssr.uct.ac.za/index.html.

21. Armando Barrientos, "Pensions and Development in the South," *Geneva Papers on Risk and Insurance,* 28 no. 4 (2003).

22. South African Social Security Agency: http://www.sassa.gov.za/content .asp?id=1000000555, downloaded July 12, 2009; South African National Treasury, "A People's Guide to the 2009 Budget."

23. South African National Treasury, "A People's Guide to the 2009 Budget."

24. There are 4.3 people in the average Bolsa Família family. Ministério do Desenvolvimento Social e Combate à Fome, "Perfil Das Famílias Do Programa Bolsa Família No Cadastro Único," 2009, http://www.mds.gov.br/institucional/secretarias/ secretaria-de-avaliacao-e-gestao-da-informacao-sagi/arquivo-sagi/pesquisas.

25. Programa Bolsa Família, http://www.mds.gov.br/bolsafamilia/, accessed July 12, 2009.

26. Ministério da Previdência Social, http://www1.previdencia.gov.br/aeps 2007/16_01_01_03.asp and Ministério do Desenvolvimento Social e Combate à Fome, http://www.mds.gov.br/institucional/secretarias/secretaria-de-avaliacao-e- gestao-da-informacao-sagi/arquivo-sagi/pesquisas, accessed July 12, 2009.

27. Armando Barrientos, "Comparing Pension Schemes in Chile, Singapore, Brazil and South Africa," IDPM Discussion Paper 67. Manchester: University of Manchester, 2005.

28. There is not much overlap between households with Bolsa Família and a pension, because few households receive both. The pension is much larger than Bolsa Família benefits.

29. Armando Barrientos and Claudio Santibañez, "New Forms of Social Assistance and the Evolution of Social Protection in Latin America," *Journal of Latin American Studies,* 41, no. 1 (2009), 1–26.

30. Santiago Levy, *Progress Against Poverty,* ch. 2.

31. Santiago Levy, *Progress Against Poverty,* p. 114.

32. Mercedes González de la Rocha, "Households and Social Policy in Mexico," presentation made at the Bi-Regional Conference on Social Protection and Poverty Reduction, Cape Town, South Africa, June 6–9, 2007.

33. Shamika Ravi and Monika Engler, "Workfare in Low Income Countries: An Effective Way to Fight Poverty? The Case of NREGS in India," Indian School of Business Working Paper (Hyderabad: Indian School of Business, 2009), http:// www.isb.edu/WorkingPapers/Workfare_LowIncomeCountries.pdf.

34. Bjorn Gustafsson and Deng Quheng, "Social Assistance Receipt and its Importance for Combating Poverty in Urban China," Discussion Paper No. 2758 (Bonn: IZA (Institute for the Study of Labor, 2007); Shaohua Chen, Martin Ravallion, and Youjuan Wang, "Di Bao: A Guaranteed Minimum Income in China's Cities?" Policy Research Working Paper 3805 (Washington, DC: World Bank, 2006); Limin Wang, Sarah Bales, and Zhengzhong Zhang, "China's Social Protection Schemes and Access to Health Services: A Critical Review" (Washington, DC: World Bank, 2006).

35. "New Pension Plan to Benefit China's 900 [Million] Farmers," August 5, 2009, www.xinhuanet.com.

36. Stella A. Hutagalung, Sirojuddin Arif, and Widjajanti I. Suharyo, "Problems and Challenges for the Indonesian Conditional Cash Transfer Programme—Program Keluarga Harapan (PKH)," to be published in *Social Protection in Asia,* 2009.

37. Armando Barrientos, Rebecca Holmes, and James Scott, "Social Assistance in Developing Countries Database," version 4 (Manchester: Brooks World Poverty Institute and CPRC, 2008).

38. Fiona Clark, "Renta Dignidad" (New York: Global Action on Aging, 2008), http://www.globalaging.org/pension/world/2008/Renta.htm; Sebastian Martinez, "Pensions, Poverty and Household Investments in Bolivia," paper presented at Perspectives on Impact Evaluation Conference, Cairo, Egypt, April 2009 (Washington, DC: Human Development Network, World Bank, 2009).

39. Armando Barrientos, "Social Pensions in Low Income Countries." In *Closing the Coverage Gap: The Role of Social Pensions and Other Retirement Transfers,* edited by R. Holzman, D. Drobalino, and N. Takayama (Washington DC: World Bank, 2009), pp. 73–84; Armando Barrientos and Claudio Santibañez, "Social Policy for Poverty Reduction in Low Income Countries in Latin America: Lessons and Challenges," *Social Policy & Administration,* 43, no. 4 (2009): 409–24.

40. Anthony Hodges et al., "Child Benefits and Poverty Reduction: Evidence from Mongolia's Child Money Programme," Working Paper MGSoc/ 2007/WP002 (Maastrict: School of Governance, Maastrict University, 2007).

41. Daniel Gilligan, John Hoddinott, and Alemayehu Seyoum Taffesse, "The Impact of Ethiopia's Productive Safety Net Programme and Its Linkages," Discussion paper 839 (Washington, DC: International Food Policy Research Institute [IFPRI], 2008); Stephen Devereux et al., "Ethiopia's Productive Safety Net Programme" (Brighton, UK: Institute of Development Studies, and Addis Ababa: Indak International, 2008).

4

Eating More—and Better

"THE GRANT DOESN'T COVER EVERYTHING. IT'S ONLY ENOUGH TO BUY FOOD and keep my son in school," explains Lúcia, a mother in Bacabel, northeastern Brazil.[1] A study in Brazil showed that the main increases in spending were on food, children's clothing, and costs related to children's health and education,[2] and this is true of most cash transfers. In general, half the grant is spent on more, better, and more varied food—typically more meat or fish, as well as more fruit and vegetables. In Colombia the grant "greatly increased" total food consumption and particularly increased consumption of food rich in proteins: milk, meat, and eggs.[3] After food, the main increase in spending was on children's clothing and shoes. In Mchinji, Malawi, families in the cash transfer program ate meat or fish three times a week, compared to once every three weeks for families not in the program.[4] In South Africa, for those families that receive the child support grant, it accounts for 40% of household income, and half of all family expenditure is on food.[5] Indeed, without the grant, most households would not have sufficient income to cover their food needs. Of the 12 million South Africans who receive social grants, 70% are still below the poverty line, but without the grants it would be 94%.[6]

In poor households in Mexico before Oportunidades, diet was monotonous, with 75% of calories coming from grains. Oportunidades meant that people ate 8% more calories, but what was striking was the increase in vegetables, fruit, and meat and animal products, particularly in the poorest households. Most of the improvement is due simply to increased income, but part of the increase in variety of foods seems to be attributable to health talks given to mothers.[7] Children in Oportunidades who are between one and five years of age have a 12% percent lower incidence of illness than children outside the program, and adult beneficiaries have 17% fewer days incapacitated by illness and can to walk 7% farther than non-beneficiaries.[8]

Whatever their precise targets, most cash transfer programs are shared across the family, but with an emphasis on children (even in the case of pensions), and all cash grants, whether or not the grants have conditions, improve child health and school attendance. Children usually have priority in the family, so high levels of child mortality,[9] malnutrition, and illness are indicators of family poverty. Each year, more than 9 million children die before they reach the age of five—one child every 3 seconds. As Figures 6.3 and 6.4 in Chapter 6 show, in some African countries between 1 in 10 and 1 in 5 children die before their fifth birthday. In Bangladesh and Indonesia it is more than 1 in 13 for the poorest children. Undernutrition is an underlying cause in more than one-third of all deaths in children under five, according to the United Nations, and most of these deaths could have been prevented with a few dollars' worth of food.[10]

Lack of money, and thus lack of food, is one of the key causes of malnutrition, and thus the most important marker of the success of cash transfer programs should be decline in child mortality and malnutrition. In northeast Brazil, Bolsa Família brought a dramatic reduction of 45% in chronic child malnutrition (stunting, measured by height for age).[11] Studies in both Nicaragua and Mexico show significant improvements in child nutrition as a consequence of grants.[12] An elegant study in South Africa used the introduction of the child support grant to compare height for age of children born more than a year before their mothers received the grant with height for age of children born after the start of the grant. Children born before the grant were significantly shorter than average, whereas children born after mothers began receiving the grant were significantly taller than average—and were likely to be 3.5 cm taller as adults.[13] Children in pensioner households in South Africa were also taller.[14] Most cash transfers report a decrease in stunting, although the amount of the grant matters; grants that make a substantial contribution to household income are more effective.[15] Children in Oportunidades are 1 cm taller after two years, and even after six years they are 0.67 cm taller.[16]

Key mental and physical development takes place in the first two years of life, and any losses that occur then are irreversible. Malnutrition in early childhood permanently undermines physical and cognitive development, educational achievement, adult height, and even adult earning capacity.[17] The period of the transition from breastfeeding to other foods is particularly important. The importance of early childhood nutrition was underlined in a study in Mexico of Oportunidades. Teresa Cen, of Tixmehuac, Yucatán, explained that "my two sons could not pass the second grade because they did not learn how to read. One learned to read in two hours when we told him we would buy him a toy airplane, but the other has a hard head and cannot learn to read for anything." Maribel Lozano Cortés of the Universidad de Quintana Roo, who carried out the study, comments, "These deficiencies are, without a doubt, what health experts have labeled as a product of the poor nutrition that the children of South Yucatán receive. This generates low intellectual and physical productivity levels that will stay with them for the rest of their lives."[18] Oportunidades was too late for one of Teresa Cen's sons.

Children in poorer households are more likely to be in poor health and to be shorter and more poorly nourished than those in wealthier households. Their mental development is restricted, and as they grow older they have a smaller vocabulary than richer children, which affects their earning capacity as adults. A World Bank study in Ecuador confirmed this general pattern but found that cash transfers could significantly change it.[19] A relatively modest cash transfer to poor women "led to substantial improvements in child outcomes for the poorest children." The study looked at Bono Solidario,[20] which began in 1998 and provided an unconditional grant of $15 per month to poor families; this represented only 10% of family expenditure, but it was enough to make a difference. Because of the way the program was rolled out, it was possible to compare participating families with similar ones the grant had not yet reached. As expected, the children in poor families receiving the grant were healthier, but the study looked more closely at mental development and found the children to have a significantly larger vocabulary and better short- and long-term memory as well. They were also noticeably better behaved. Similar improvements in cognitive development due to a cash transfer were found in Nicaragua.[21]

More money in poor households makes possible the purchase of more soap, warm clothing, and shoes, which also has a direct impact on child health.[22] Several programs, including those in Colombia, Malawi, and Zambia, report large decreases in children's illness.[23] In South Africa, pension income is also used to upgrade household sanitation facilities.[24]

More Kids in School

All cash transfer programs produce an increase in school enrollment and attendance, regardless of conditions and of whether or not such an increase is an explicit goal of the program. This even occurs where primary school attendance is already required by law. Both South Africa and Mexico have high primary school attendance rates, and the grants in both countries increase school attendance. In South Africa primary school attendance was already 96%, but the child support grant cut non-attendance in half, with 98% of children in grant families going to school. This is a greater impact than in Mexico, where the increase on a similar base was just over 1%. This is surprising, because school attendance is a condition of the grant in Mexico, and the South African grant is unconditional.[25]

"One notices the difference with Oportunidades: the kids are better dressed," said teacher Eloisa Cobá of Tixmehuac, Yucatán, Mexico.[26] Socorro Palma Cazabal, a mother in San Felipe Teotlancingo, in the state of Puebla, confirms this: "Before Oportunidades, there weren't many children who went to school well dressed. They went with their shoes broken or with very simple clothes. Now, they go wearing new clothes, or very neat. There are more children and the school is improving."[27]

For Mexico, the major changes are beyond primary school (grades 1–6). Teenagers in Oportunidades are 33% more likely to be enrolled in middle school or junior high school (grades 7–9, called *secundaria* in Mexico). Children in Oportunidades are 23% more likely to finish grade 9 than those outside the program. In rural areas, high school (*medio superior,* grades 10–12) enrollment has doubled.[28] Before Oportunidades it was rare for poor pupils to stay on for secondary school, but now it is the norm. "Many more students are reaching high school. I am the director of a primary school, and today I find that almost all of my students go on to high school," reports Efren Hernandez of Tzucacab, Yucatán. A study showed that graduation rates of high school students in the southern Yucatán had greatly increased, in large part thanks to Oportunidades. High school principal Casimiro Dzib of Chacsinkin, Yucatán, argues that "they come to school because of the scholarships; if they were to be taken away, the students would no longer come."[29]

Some programs have shown a proportionately greater increase in attendance by girls, reducing the gender imbalance. Oportunidades has differential scholarships for girls and boys; by grade 12, girls receive $15 per month more. The schooling and attendance gender gap has disappeared in grades 7–12.[30] "I would have liked to continue studying. I took the test to enter senior high and passed, but my parents had no money. I missed out on studying," says Miguelina Ramírez Álvarez in Zacate Colorado, Veracruz, Mexico. She sighs sadly: "If Oportunidades had existed back then, I would most certainly have continued studying."[31]

And it is not just Mexico. In Brazil the unconditional rural pension increased the school registration of children in the household, especially girls between 12 and 14 years old.[32] The northeast is Brazil's poorest region, which is home to 30% of the national population, but to 49% of those who are poor and 63% of those considered indigent.[33] Not surprisingly, half of Bolsa Família recipients are in the northeast. Because of the way Bolsa Família has been rolled out, it is possible to do comparisons between families with the grant and others who are not yet receiving it. In the northeast, school attendance has increased and children in Bolsa Família families spend more time studying.[34]

Some cash transfer schemes, such as Bangladesh's Female Secondary School Stipend Programme, have explicitly focused on the goal of women's empowerment. One evaluation found "a wide range of positive impacts of the stipend programme on girls' lives, such as increase in age at marriage, greater birth spacing, positive attitude to smaller family size, and higher employment and earning levels." But Simeen Mahmud of the Bangladesh Institute of Development Studies also found that "there is unintended exclusion of the poorest girls because the amount of the stipend is too low to cover all costs of sending a girl to school [and] it has also failed to reach girls in under-served areas due to poor private investment in educational institutions in those areas."[35]

The main beneficiaries are not always girls. In Colombia girls are much more likely to go to school than boys, especially to secondary school. Primary school enrollment is already high, but the grant Familias en Acción increased secondary school attendance by almost 10%; both girls and boys were more likely to go to school, but boys were the biggest gainers.[36]

Reducing Inequality

Because cash transfers go the poor and poorest, they contribute to reducing inequality as well as poverty. Mexico, Brazil, and South Africa have all seen rapid reductions in inequality. These three countries have other social programs as well, so it is hard to disentangle the effects of different programs, and the specific impact of cash transfers on inequality is highly debated. In Brazil, for example, there was also a large increase in the minimum wage. A 2009 study of Brazil argues that one-third of the decline in inequality was directly due to cash transfers.[37] In turn, most of the cash transfer's contribution to reducing inequality comes from Bolsa Família and less from the social pension,[38] which together reach 39% of the population—74 million people. Researchers Degol Hailu and Sergei Soares argue that the second third of the inequality reduction derives from the "knock-on effects of better income distribution" and that the final third is from improved access to education after 1995.[39]

In Brazil, the share of people in poverty in 2003 was 28%, but this had fallen to 17% in 2008,[40] as measured by Brazil's own poverty line, or from 22% to below 13% using the World Bank $2-per-day poverty line— a record any government would be proud of (see Table 4.1). Inequality is sometimes measured by the Gini index, which is 0 if everyone has the same income and 100 for total inequality (one person has all the income). As Table 3.1 showed, the countries where income is most equally divided have a Gini index of around 25, whereas in unequal countries such as Brazil and South Africa, the Gini index is over 50. Cash transfers can be only one part of a package, but it is clear that if a government chooses to reduce inequality, it can do so. In Mexico the Gini index fell by 5 points in eight years,[41] in South Africa the Gini index declined by 3 points in five years,[42] and, as the table shows, Brazil's Gini index dropped 4 points in six years.

IMPACT ON WOMEN

Child benefit and family grants are paid preferentially to women in nearly all cash transfers. Jorge Morales Pablo lives in Yunuén, a tourist island in Lake Pátzcuaro, Mexico. He thinks it is better that the money is given to women, because "they are the ones to carry out the administration of the families. If the money was given to men they would spend it in the canteens with their friends—throw money around and say, 'Later I'll see how I'll manage.' With women, in contrast, the money is safer. Many women, when they get their benefits, get a good bunch of corn, beans, rice, and sugar. They buy enough so they don't have to worry about what to eat tomorrow or the day after tomorrow. I respect them for that."[43]

A study in northeast Brazil showed that paying cash transfers to women increased the bargaining power of women within the household, as shown by an increase in the decisions about spending made by women rather than men.[44] In Mexico, "men have increasingly accepted the nature of the transfers and the fact that women decide how to spend them. Women, on the

Table 4.1 World Bank Estimate of Poverty Reduction in Brazil

	2001	2003	2005	2007
Gini Index	59	58	56	55
Population under $2/day (PPP)[a]	22%	22%	18%	13%

Note: a. $2/day at World Bank purchasing power parity (PPP)
Source: World Bank World Development Indicators online database, accessed July 19, 2009.

other hand, feel they have gained an area of relative autonomy and power," explain Augustín Escobar Latapí and Mercedes González de la Rocha[45] of Mexico's Social Anthropology Investigation Centre (CIESAS) in Guadalajara. "On balance, most women see themselves in a better situation to fulfill their roles as care providers and, increasingly, as economic providers."

But Oportunidades is aimed at the next generation, and mothers are expected to sacrifice themselves. Oportunidades imposes on recipients many conditions, known as "co-responsibilities," and the burden of the program is entirely borne by women. Indeed, the program assumes that women do not do extensive work outside the house; most "co-responsibilities" need to be carried out during normal working hours, and interview teams intentionally arrive during the day without warning.[46]

This provoked harsh criticism by Maxine Molyneux of the Institute for the Study of the Americas, University of London. Daughters "are invested in as citizens, and their capabilities and life chances are expanded through education and health; the mothers, meanwhile, are treated as having responsibilities rather than needs and rights."[47]

Mothers' "co-responsibilities" became a key focus of the debate, because all studies agree that the classes (*pláticas*), meetings, voluntary labor, and other requirements add a substantial amount of time to women's already large burden. A detailed study on women's views of Oportunidades by a group headed by Michelle Adato[48] of IFPRI concluded that "almost all [women] felt that the benefits of participation outweighed the costs." The group's statement continues: "For some, through being able to leave the house more often without their husbands; by gathering in meetings and health *pláticas* and speaking to each other about concerns, problems and solutions; by developing more comfort with speaking out in groups; and through health, nutrition, sanitation, family planning and family care education they are receiving in the health *pláticas,* women say they have developed greater confidence, a greater awareness of their situation as women, and in general they know more."

Adato's team stresses that "because it is confronting longstanding gender biases, the program's success in the long-term depends to some extent on changing attitudes and beliefs among men and women." Thus women themselves stress the importance of educating their daughters. "Women also feel that by making them beneficiaries, the government is recognizing them."

Women feel that Oportunidades is personally empowering because it gives them more opportunities to leave the house and provides spaces in which to communicate with other women in new ways. The importance of this should not be underestimated, because research on Bolsa Família in Brazil, which has no similar required meetings and collective work, found that women felt a high degree of isolation and confinement to the house,[49] a pattern that is in some way broken in Mexico by the co-responsibilities.

But the Adato study also points to limitations. Although there is valuable personal empowerment, Oportunidades has no system of "collective empowerment" to "build . . . organizational capacity that could produce second-round social or economic benefits." Furthermore, although the women really appreciate and need the health talks, "we found that other types of adult education linked to productive activities would meet women's strongest aspirations. . . . They ask for government programs that will give them skills that will help them engage in productive activities and earn income. They also want to learn to read and write." And women said they would like Oportunidades to give similar talks to men on health care, family planning, and domestic relations in order to equip them to understand and help deal with the problems the women face at home. Escobar Latapí and Mercedes González de la Rocha confirm that Oportunidades has "no component designed to empower housewives"; instead, "the emphasis [is] on co-responsibility and investing in the future generation of citizen/workers."

Molyneux argues that women "may gain a sense of greater self-esteem or status without gaining any greater control over their lives."[50] Oportunidades reinforces a social policy that is "familial, patriarchal and paternalistic" and "creates a dependency on a subsidy which confirms mothering as women's primary role."[51]

Escobar Latapí and González de la Rocha respond that "although conditional cash transfer programmes do place a significant burden on women, and particularly on mothers, participation in these programs has nevertheless generated a number of positive outcomes for women of different age-groups."

The Oportunidades program itself has tried to refute the criticism via interviews with women who have been empowered by the program. Irma Huerta González lives in Emiliano Zapata los Molinos, in the municipality of Atlixco Puebla, Mexico. She was afraid of her husband, who would not let her out of the house. But then, after she signed up for Oportunidades, she left him. "I decided to act because I counted on some money from Oportunidades so I didn't have to depend on him economically and this way I could provide for my two daughters."[52]

Adela Alejandre Flores, from Capula in Michoacán state, Mexico, points to an indirect change brought about by Oportunidades. "Before Oportunidades there was a serious alcoholism problem. Men drank a lot and beat their women. . . . This has changed. Thanks to the conferences they give us we have decided not to cross our arms but to act to solve whatever worries us. We talked to the authorities to not allow them to sell wine late at night or to children." Women have learned not to let men beat them. "Now they defend themselves. Now all women go out to work, they do not stay doing nothing, because before they were not even allowed to go out. It all began because they had to go out to get their benefits, and their husbands, who were interested in the money, let them go. You should see how different our community is now! . . . We owe this all to the Oportunidades Program."[53]

NOT A MAGIC BULLET

Cash transfer programs "are as close as you can come to a magic bullet in development," said Nancy Birdsall, president of the Center for Global Development, a Washington-based research group. "They're creating an incentive for families to invest in their own children's futures. Every decade or so, we see something that can really make a difference, and this is one of those things."[54]

Birdsall was referring specifically to Brazil's Bolsa Família. Brazil is one of the most successful examples of cash transfers, but it also provides some key insight into why cash transfers are not a single "magic bullet" and cannot work on their own. Even the rapid reductions in poverty and inequality in Brazil are due not just to cash transfers but also to a doubling of the minimum wage over five years. This had a two-fold impact: Pensions and disability grants are at the minimum wage, and in the informal sector, wages do tend to rise in parallel with the minimum wage.

Although the grants do increase school attendance, there has not been an increase in children passing from one year to the next and graduating.[55] It appears that children from poor backgrounds attending school for the first time are not supported but are just dumped in the back of the classrooms. Without parallel improvements in education (in particular, training for teachers to help them support students from the poorest backgrounds), Bolsa Família on its own cannot improve educational outcomes. Similarly, Bolsa Família does not increase vaccinations or prenatal care for pregnant women, apparently because people living in the poorest areas lack access to health facilities. Thus there is clearly a need for parallel improvements in health care.

Improvements Yet to Be Made

What Bolsa Família shows is that a cash transfer, on its own, reduces poverty and inequality and improves the life chances of children. But the cash transfer is not sufficient. Government interventions to increase the minimum wage played an equal role. And action is needed to improve health and education and to reduce racial discrimination.

Many cash transfers, conditional or not, trigger a substantial increase in the demand for services. The first problem is simply to provide enough schools and clinics. "When I finished primary school, there was no high school in Tixmehuac; the closest one was 18 kilometers away in Tikax, it's too far to go and return by bicycle, therefore few of my friends were able to continue going to school," explained 16-year-old Wendy Canché, of Tixmehuac, Yucatán, Mexico.[56] A school had only just opened in Tixmehuac because of the increased demand, but it was too late for Wendy.

The second issue is ensuring quality and making certain that teachers and health workers have the training to deal with the problems of poorer people who have not used the services before. The failure of Bolsa Família and other cash transfers to improve educational outcomes is often attributed to teachers not paying special attention to children from poor families who joined their classes.

Data from the World Bank[57] show that simply sending a poor child to school is not very useful; the quality of the education offered must be high enough to ensure that the child learns. Nicaragua's Red de Protección Social had an interesting fillip to respond to this. Every schoolchild was given C$7 (US 50¢) per month to give to the teacher (called *bono a la oferta*); the teacher kept half, and half was given to the school. Thus both teacher and school gained from the extra children who arrived because of the program. And it seems to have made a difference; children in the program were 8% more likely to move up to the next grade than those in the control group.

Nicaragua's Red de Protección Social program included parallel increases in spending for both health and education in the whole area, for both program and control communities. The number of teachers and the number of school sessions each day were increased, and a school meals program introduced. The Ministry of Health increased distribution of vaccines and iron supplements, and there were other improvements in health services that decreased waiting time throughout the area. Nicaragua's program was introduced first in just some municipalities and only two years later in adjoining ones, which made it possible to compare people who were in the program with similar people who were not.[58] Nicaragua had relatively poor health and education systems. Primary school enrollment was just 72%, and it jumped to 93% in the second year of the program, but the control group also increased to 79%. Similarly, before the program only 74% of children under 3 had been taken for a health check in the previous six months; after two years of the program this jumped to 93%, but in the control group it also jumped to 84%. Thus one-third of the health improvements and half of the education improvements derived simply from better services, but the grant led to much greater increases, which shows that the lack of money had also been a major constraint.

Not Just Schools and Health Posts

In Namibia, Sister Mbangu, the nurse at Otjivero clinic, reported that attendance jumped fivefold when the basic income grant started—not because of an increase in ill health, but because more people could afford the N$4 (50¢) fee. Indeed, Sister Mbangu noted that after the grant started, she did not see a single case of malnutrition, and there was a sharp reduction in severe diarrhea because better nutrition had made people healthier.[59] Namibia already has a pension, and 14% of the pension is spent by pensioners on their own health. In Malawi 12% of the grant is spent on health.[60] Other cash transfer studies also report significant spending on medicines and clinic fees. This spending shows a real suppressed demand for health care that the poor cannot afford, and cash transfers play an important role in meeting this demand. But that raises a bigger issue: Is this what the cash should be used for? If health services were better and free to poorer families, this money could be invested in better housing and productive activities. Similarly, there is significant expenditure on secondary school fees and on textbooks, notebooks, and other education-related costs. Clearly, the grants are enabling children to go to school, but should income be a criterion for secondary school attendance? All things considered, this is a further argument that cash grants increase the demand for social services, including health and education, but that the grants should go hand-in-hand with increases in supply.

Finally, many people have trouble obtaining grants because of lack of documents: birth certificates, identity cards, marriage licenses, residence documents, and so on. And it is often the poorest people, who most need the grants, who have the most trouble obtaining documents. This is a problem reported in many countries, including Mozambique and South Africa. Thus the introduction of cash transfers must be accompanied by improved systems to issue key documents—and by rules that do not insist on so much documentation.

Santiago Levy, the architect of Mexico's Progresa-Oportunidades, comments that cash transfers "may be an essential component of the solution, [but] a single program cannot solve a problem that has multiple causes."[61]

REDUCING POVERTY KEY ISSUES

Cash transfers meet their first goal of reducing poverty. Typically, half of the grant is spent on more and better food, and the results are visible: children are taller and healthier. Key mental and physical development takes place in the first two years of life, and there is no way to compensate for losses in growth that children sustain then. Thus grants make a measurable difference to small children that stays with them for the rest of their lives. And all grants, including pensions, increase school attendance.

Most cash transfers go to women. They increase the workload of women, both because children who now go to school can do less around the house, and because the burden of meeting conditions falls on women. Nevertheless, women report that the increased money and responsibility enhance their self-esteem and status.

Cash transfers are not a magic bullet; they cannot accomplish everything on their own. Cash transfers help to reduce inequality, but other government programs also contribute. Children cannot attend school if there are no schools. And it is not just buildings. More children may attend school, but they do not do better unless the schooling is of high quality and is redesigned to give more support to children from poor families.

It is hardly surprising the money reduces poverty. But because poor families use the money wisely and well, the impact of cash transfers on nutrition, health, and education is dramatic.

NOTES

1. Magda Núcia Albuquerque Dias and Maria do Rosário de Fátima e Silva, "A Condição de Pobreza das Famílias Beneficiárias do Programa Bolsa Família no Município de Bacabal—MA: a Importância do Benefício" (Brasilia: UNDP International Poverty Centre, 2008), available at Biblioteca Virtual do Bolsa Família, http://www.ipc-undp.org/publications/mds/34P.pdf.

2. Diana Oya Sawyer, *Sumário Executivo—Avaliação de Impacto do Programa Bolsa Família,* Ministro do Desenvolvimento Social e Combate à Fome, 2007.

3. Orazio Attanasio and Alice Mesnard, "The Impact of a Conditional Cash Transfer Programme on Consumption in Colombia," *Fiscal Studies,* 27, no. 4 (2006): 421–42. See Ariel Fiszbein and Norbert Schady, *Conditional Cash Transfers: Reducing Present and Future Poverty* (Washington, DC: World Bank, 2009), p. 113, for a comparison table of five countries.

4. Jennifer Yablonski with Michael O'Donnell, *Lasting Benefits: The Role of Cash Transfers in Tackling Child Mortality* (London: Save the Children, 2009), available at http://www.savethechildren.org.uk/en/docs/Lasting_Benefits.pdf.

5. Aislinn Delany et al., *Review of the Child Support Grant: Uses, Implementation and Obstacles* (Johannesburg: Community Agency for Social Enquiry for UNICEF and The South African Social Security Agency, 2008).

6. Miriam Altman and Gerard Boyce, "Policy Options to Leverage the System of Social Grants for Improved Access to Economic Opportunity. Paper 1: Overview of Grant Beneficiary Households" (Pretoria: Human Sciences Research Council, 2008).

7. John Hoddinott and Emmanuel Skoufias, "The Impact of Progresa on Food Consumption" (Washington, DC: IFPRI, 2003), available at http://www.ifpri.org/divs/fcnd/dp/papers/fcndp150.pdf.

8. Emmanuel Skoufias, "PROGRESA and Its Impacts on the Welfare of Rural Households in Mexico" (Washington, DC: IFPRI, 2005), available at http://www.ifpri.org/pubs/abstract/139/rr139.pdf.

9. As noted in Chapter 1, Millennium Development Goal 4 is to "reduce by two thirds, between 1990 and 2015, the under-five mortality rate."

10. United Nations, *The Millennium Development Goals Report 2008* (New York: United Nations Department of Economic and Social Affairs, 2008), available at http://mdgs.un.org/unsd/mdg/Resources/Static/Products/Progress2008/MDG_Report_2008_En.pdf.

11. Sawyer, *Sumário Executivo.*

12. Sudhanshu Handa and Benjamin Davis, "The Experience of Conditional Cash Transfers in Latin America and the Caribbean," *Development Policy Review,* 24, no. 5 (2006): 513–36.

13. Jorge M. Agüero, Michael R. Carter, and Ingrid Woolard, "The Impact of Unconditional Cash Transfers on Nutrition: The South African Child Support Grant," Working Paper 39 (Brasilia: UNDP International Poverty Centre, 2007); and Esther Duflo, "Child Health and Household Resources in South Africa: Evidence from the Old Age Pension Program," *American Economic Review,* 90, no. 2 (2000): 393.

14. Yablonski, *Lasting Benefits,* p. 42.

15. Yablonski, *Lasting Benefits,* p. 10.

16. Lynette Neufeld et al., "Impacto de Oportunidades en el Crecimiento y Estado Nutricional de Ninos en Zonas Rurales," pp, 17–51. In *Alimentacion, Vol. 3, Evaluacion Externa de Impact al Programa Oportunidades 2004,* edited by Bernardo Hernandez Prado and Mauricio Hernandez Avila (Cuernavaca: Instituto Nacional de Salud Publica y CIESAS, 2005).

17. Yablonski, *Lasting Benefits,* p. 16.

18. Maribel Lozano Cortés, "Evaluación Cualitativa de los Impactos del Programa Oportunidades, en Alimentación, Salud y Educación en los Municipios del sur de Yucatán (2004–2005)" (Quintana Roo, México: Universidad de Quintana Roo, 2006), p. 25.

19. Christina Paxson and Norbert Schady, "Cognitive Development Among Young Children in Ecuador," *The Journal of Human Resources,* 42, no. 1 (2007): 49–84; and Christina Paxson and Norbert Schady, "Does Money Matter? The

Effects of Cash Transfers on Child Development in Rural Ecuador," World Bank Policy Research Paper No. 4226 (Washington, DC: World Bank, 2007).

20. Replaced in 2003 by Bono de Desarrollo Humano.

21. Fiszbein and Schady, *Conditional Cash Transfers,* p. 154.

22. Yablonski, *Lasting Benefits,* p. 13.

23. Yablonski, *Lasting Benefits,* pp. 40, 41.

24. Martin Williams, "The Social and Economic Impacts of South Africa's Child Support Grant (Extended Version)," Working Paper 39 (Cape Town: Economic Policy Research Institute, 2007), p. 19.

25. Martin Williams, "The Social and Economic Impacts of South Africa's Child Support Grant," Working Paper 40 (Cape Town: Economic Policy Research Institute, 2007), p. 40.

26. Cortés, "Evaluación Cualitativa," pp. 25, 27.

27. Mauricio Carrera, *Oportunidades: Historias de Éxito* (México, D.F: Secretaría de Desarrollo Social, Coordinación Nacional del Programa de Desarrollo Humano Oportunidades, 2008). Published in English as *Oportunidades: Stories of Success,* p. 21.

28. Dirección de Comunicación Social, Programa de Desarrollo Humano Oportunidades, "Oportunidades, un Programa de Resultados" (México: Sedesol—Secretaría de Desarrollo Social, 2008).

29. Cortés, "Evaluación Cualitativa," pp. 25, 27.

30. Augustín Escobar Latapí and Mercedes González de la Rocha, "Girls, Mothers and Poverty Reduction in Mexico: Evaluating Progresa-Oportunidades." In *The Gendered Impacts of Liberalisation: Towards "Embedded Liberalism"?* edited by Shahra Razavi (New York and Abingdon: Routledge/UNRISD, 2009).

31. Carrera, *Oportunidades,* p. 57.

32. Marcelo Medeiros, Tatiana Britto, and Fábio Veras Soares, "Targeted Cash Transfer Programmes in Brazil: BPC and the Bolsa Família," Working Paper 46 (Brasilia: International Poverty Centre, 2008).

33. "Indigent" means an income below that needed for a minimum food basket; "poor" in this study means below a poverty line set at double the minimum food basket. Francisco Ferreira, Peter Lanjouw, and Marcelo Neri, "A Robust Poverty Profile for Brazil Using Multiple Data Sources," *Revista Brasileira de Economia,* 57, no. 1 (2003): 59–92.

34. Sawyer, *Sumário Executivo.*

35. Simeen Mahmud, "Female Secondary School Stipend Programme in Bangladesh: A Critical Assessment" (Dhaka: Bangladesh Institute of Development Studies, 2003), available at http://portal.unesco.org/.

36. Orazio Attanasio, Emla Fitzsimons, and Ana Gomez, "The Impact of a Conditional Education Subsidy on School Enrollment in Colombia" (London: Institute of Fiscal Studies, 2005), available at http://www.ifs.org.uk/publications/3329.

37. Degol Hailu and Sergei Suarez Dillon Soares, "What Explains the Decline in Brazil's Inequality?" Institute for Applied Economic Research, One Pager 89 (Brasilia: International Policy Centre for Inclusive Growth, 2009).

38. Fabio Veras Soares et al., "Cash Transfer Programmes in Brazil: Impacts on Inequality and Poverty," Working Paper 21 (Brasilia: UNDP International Poverty Centre, 2006), available at http://www.ipc-undp.org/pub/IPCWorking Paper21.pdf.

39. Hailu and Soares, "What Explains the Decline in Brazil's Inequality?"

40. Marcelo Côrtes Neri, "Poverty, Inequality and Income Policies" (Rio de Janeiro: O Centro de Políticas Sociais, Fundação Getulio Vargas, 2007), available at http://www3.fgv.br/ibrecps/RET3/engl/index.htm; poverty defined as below R$125 per month per capita in 2006, then as 36% of the minimum wage. Updated to 2008 in "Evolução da Miséria" (Rio de Janeiro: O Centro de Políticas Sociais, Fundação Getulio Vargas), available at http://www.fgv.br/cps/pesquisas/miseria_queda_grafico_clicavel/.

41. Fábio Veras Soares, Rafael Perez Ribas, and Rafael Guerreiro Osório, "Evaluating the Impact of Brazil's Bolsa Família: Cash Transfer Programmes in Comparative Perspective," *IPC Evaluation Note 1* (Brasilia: International Poverty Centre, 2007).

42. Michael Samson et al., "Review of Targeting Mechanisms, Means Tests and Values for South Africa's Social Grants—Final Report" (Cape Town: Economic Policy Research Institute, 2007), available at http://www.wahenga.net/uploads/documents/news/Main%20Report%20Review%20of%20Targeting%20Mechanisms_Means%20Test%20and%20Values%20of%20SA%20Grants%20final.pdf.

43. Carrera, *Oportunidades*, p. 49.

44. Sawyer, *Sumário Executivo*.

45. Latapí and de la Rocha, "Girls, Mothers and Poverty Reduction."

46. Latapí and de la Rocha, "Girls, Mothers and Poverty Reduction."

47. Maxine Molyneux, *Conditional Cash Transfers and Women's Empowerment: Annotated Bibliography* (Waterloo, Ontario, Canada: IGLOO Network of the Centre for International Governance Innovation, 2008), available at www.igloo.org/pathways/download-nocache/currentdoc/conditiona.

48. Michelle Adato et al., *The Impact of PROGRESA on Women's Status and Intrahousehold Relations* (Washington, DC: IFPRI, 2008), available at http://www.ifpri.org/themes/progresa/pdf/Adato_intrahh.pdf.

49. Maxine Molyneux, "Conditional Cash Transfers: A 'Pathway to Women's Empowerment'?" Pathways of Women's Empowerment Working Paper 5 (Brighton, UK: Institute of Development Studies, 2009), available at http://www.pathwaysof empowerment.org/PathwaysWP5-website.pdf.

50. Molyneux, "Conditional Cash Transfers: A Pathway."

51. Molyneux, *Conditional Cash Transfers and Women's Empowerment.*

52. Carrera, *Oportunidades,* p. 42.

53. Carrera, *Oportunidades,* p. 71.

54. Celia W. Dugger, "To Help Poor Be Pupils, Not Wage Earners, Brazil Pays Parents," *New York Times,* January 3, 2004.

55. Sawyer, *Sumário Executivo.*

56. Cortés, "Evaluación Cualitativa," p. 27.

57. Fiszbein and Schady, *Conditional Cash Transfers.*

58. John A. Maluccio and Rafael Flores, "Impact Evaluation of a Conditional Cash Transfer Program—The Nicaraguan Red de Protección Social," Research Report 141 (Washington, DC: IFPRI, 2005).

59. Claudia Haarmann et al., *Towards a Basic Income Grant for All,* Basic Income Grant Pilot Project First Assessment Report (Windhoek, Namibia: Basic Income Grant Coalition, 2008), available at www.bignam.org.

60. Michelle Adato and Lucy Bassett, "What Is the Potential of Cash Transfers to Strengthen Families Affected by HIV and AIDS? A Review of the Evidence on Impacts and Key Policy Debates," Review for the Joint Learning Initiative on Children and HIV/AIDS (JLICA) (Washington, DC: IFPRI, 2008), available at http://programs.ifpri.org/renewal/pdf/JLICACashTransfers.pdf, citing C. Miller and M. Tsoka, "$13 a Month for Half a Year: Round 2 Impact of the Mchinji Cash Transfer," PowerPoint Presentation to the National Social Protection Steering Committee, Government of Malawi (Lilongwe, December 11, 2007).

61. Santiago Levy, *Progress Against Poverty: Sustaining Mexico's Progresa-Oportunidades Program* (Washington, DC: Brookings Institution, 2006), p. 20.

5

Pro-poor Growth:
Turning a $1 Grant into $2 Income

ECONOMIC GROWTH IS CENTRAL TO DEVELOPMENT, AND THE GOAL OF ANY developing country's finance minister must be to promote growth that benefits the poor, and especially the poorest. Although cash transfers are sometimes presented as charity or "social" spending, they are in fact an essential part of any pro-poor growth strategy. Historically, as we noted in Chapter 2, they created the conditions for economic growth in Europe. And the new generation of cash transfers instituted over the past decade have been shown to be capable of promoting growth. Individually, cash helps people out of the poverty trap and gives them the boots to lift themselves by their bootstraps. And the increased spending of the poor promotes local economic development by creating jobs and encouraging growth in a positive cycle; much more than the better off, poorer people spend locally, and they buy more locally produced goods.

"There is an interaction between low income and risk aversion," explains Santiago Levy, the main architect of Mexico's Progresa-Oportunidades:

> Living under the constant threat of a sudden drop in income—and hence consumption—probably makes poor families, on average, more risk averse than non-poor families. That affects their ability to participate in the labor market by searching for better jobs, or it may limit the possibility of migrating to other communities or of introducing new crops or improved technologies. Poor families may be induced to cling to small parcels of land or traditional farming methods that generate lower but safer returns, limiting the benefits that they may be able to obtain from

rural development programs or urban training programs. For those reasons, reducing poor households' uncertainty regarding food consumption
could allow them to engage in riskier productive projects or investments
with longer planning horizons.[1]

Studies show that in both Ethiopia and Maharashtra state in India,
cash transfer recipients buy more fertilizer and use higher-yielding seeds;
in India they took the risk of planting higher-yielding but less drought-
resistant crop varieties.[2] In Mexico a World Bank study found that "transfers
from the Oportunidades program to households in rural Mexico resulted
in increased investment in micro-enterprise and agricultural activities. For
each peso transferred, beneficiary households used 88 cents to purchase
consumption goods and services and invested the rest. The investments
improved the household's ability to generate income with an estimated
rate of return of 17.55%, suggesting that these households were both liquidity and credit constrained. By investing transfers to raise income, beneficiary households were able to increase their consumption by 34% after
five and a half years in the program."[3] Investments were highly profitable,
with a rate of return triple the real interest rate. The researchers continue:
"We find that beneficiaries invest in production and draft animals, and
that previously landless beneficiary households obtain land for agricultural
production. Furthermore, there are significant increases in the number of
households that operate micro-enterprises." In the economists' jargon, they
find that households are "liquidity constrained" and that "households face
imperfect credit markets."

In other words, without any advice from aid agencies, government, or
nongovernmental organizations (NGOs), poor people already knew how to
make profitable investments. They simply did not have the cash and could
not borrow the small amounts of money they needed.

Tiny Investments

An Oportunidades beneficiary in rural Mexico explained that with money
from the grant, "we saved 600 pesos [$50] to buy wood and the other ma-
terials for building a chicken coup, and with what was left we bought a
few chickens. Since then, we have raised many chickens which we sometimes sell, and we collect 10 to 15 eggs per week that we eat ourselves."[4]

Poor people live in an uncertain environment and face a range of shocks,
such as drought or pests in agricultural areas. With no insurance, to survive they must act in a risk-averse way and, if possible, save a bit of money

(which is not invested). The World Bank study found that people in Oportunidades actually reduced their precautionary saving. Knowing that they would have money coming from Oportunidades each month gave them a cushion to fall back on—and the option of saving less, investing more, and taking investment risks—exactly the behavior that should be encouraged as part of economic development.

In Mexico, evaluations found more improvements in housing, the regulation of land, and some asset accumulation in general; 7% of recipients were making productive investments (cattle, vehicles, machinery, small shops) compared to 5% of a similar group outside Oportunidades. This is believed to be due to higher income over the medium term, less vulnerability to shocks thanks to stable income, and improved family health. Shopkeepers saw recipients as more trustworthy and allowed them credit.[5]

The gains in Mexico were not unexpected. A study of the Procampo program in 1995–1997, a cash transfer for 3 million farmers to compensate for the negative effect of the North American Free Trade Agreement (NAFTA), showed that small farmers doubled the value of any cash they were given.[6] Farmers simply bought more of their current inputs; there was no technological change or introduction of new activities. The multiplier for all households was in the range of 1.5 to 2.6 and was highest for those with irrigated land. Farmers knew what to do profitably, but they lacked the cash and were caught in the poverty trap.

In South Africa, a small part of both pensions and child benefits is spent on widely varied ways to increase income. In urban areas this typically involves buying things that can be resold, ranging from sweets to beer to vegetables.[7]

Money is also saved for larger purchases. In South Africa, 42% of child benefit recipients have bank accounts, compared to 24% of eligible non-recipients, and 20% have some form of savings, compared to 11% of eligible non-recipients. Savings are in banks or informal saving clubs known as "stokvels." One recipient in Orange Farm, Gauteng province, commented that the grant "helps a lot in the home, not just for buying food. You can join a 'stokvel' and save the money. Maybe if they don't have beds, when you get that lump sum, then you can use it to buy them the beds."[8]

Bolivia has a universal pension, the only one in Latin America. A World Bank study[9] found that among pension beneficiaries in rural areas, overall consumption rises by almost twice the amount of the benefit. This is because of increased home production of meat and vegetables, which in turn results from increased use of land when pension money is available to spend on inputs and animals. Sebastian Martinez of the World Bank explains that thanks to agrarian reform following the 1952 revolution, 83% of households own land, but they cannot make the best use of it because they lack cash to invest; in economist-speak, they are "liquidity constrained." The social pension enables poor farmers to make essential investments, which they already know how to do but simply lack the money.

Starting the Upward Spiral

"Pension payday is when the wheel of the local economy goes round in rural Brazil," comments an International Labour Office study. The study adds that in small towns, it is frequently pension payments that keep local bank branches in business.[10] Bolsa Família has a similar effect. One shopkeeper commented, "We also depend on this program. Outside the period when people receive money, sales almost stop." Another said, "With Bolsa Família, things changed a lot. When people receive their grant, there is much more movement. If the program stopped, traders around here would lose 40% of their business."[11]

The cash transfer program in Mchinji district in Malawi shows the economic impact of even a relatively small program. An average grant of MK2,000 ($13) per month goes to the 10% of families who are both ultra-poor and labor constrained. Of this grant, more than 90% was spent locally on food, household goods, and services, and many local businesses reported increased sales.[12] But as would be expected for labor-constrained households, they spent part of the money to hire people, typically other members of their extended family, to till fields or repair their house. And of people in this very poor area who said they did day labor, 27% did it for those who received the grant; 12% of the families in the village reported that they did some work for the 10% receiving the grant. Thus even this small grant created a positive economic cycle. A study of a grant in Dowa district of Malawi showed that it had a local multiplier of more than 2. That is, each dollar received as a cash transfer was not simply spent by the recipient but was spent at least twice more by other local people before the dollar finally left the area. Thus the cash transfer clearly stimulated the local economy. And the study found that it was the small local farmers who gained most after all spending rounds were counted.[13]

This is not unexpected. The UN Conference on Trade and Development, in its *Least Developed Countries Report 2006,* argued that lack of domestic demand, especially in rural areas, was one of the biggest constraints on economic growth. The poor simply do not have enough money to buy basic goods, and if they do have more money, they tend to buy both food and non-agricultural goods produced by other poor people.[14]

Michael Samson, research director at Economic Policy Research Institute (EPRI), argues that cash transfers promote investment, economic growth, and job creation. He notes that "the poor spend more of their income on food—which in South Africa is produced domestically, and in a labour intensive manner. Upper income households spend more on transportation—often imported automobiles. Social transfers shift spending power from upper to lower income households—the composition of spending tends to shift from automobiles to food grains. In South Africa, the composition of spending tends to shift from imports to domestic goods, from capital intensive to labour intensive."[15] Social grants in South Africa are 3.5% of GDP, so the transfer of resources to lower-income households is not insignificant.

CASH DOES NOT MAKE PEOPLE LAZY

"Emerging data from cash transfer programmes, conditional or unconditional, largely dispel the counter arguments that these programmes prevent adults from seeking work or create a dependency culture which perpetuates intergenerational poverty," concludes the British medical journal *The Lancet*.[16] That giving people money promotes laziness and dependency is one of the arguments most often advanced against cash transfers, yet it is proving to be a huge myth. Because it is such a strong counter argument, it has been included in many research projects, and none has found any evidence for it. Indeed, the evidence is that, at least on average, people work harder because the cash helps them out of the poverty trap.

In this sense, the poor really are different from the better off. If you give money to a person who is relatively well off, such as one of the writers of this book, he or she is likely to take an extra holiday or buy better wine. The poor, on the other hand, find that the cash encourages them to work harder, because they are no longer caught in the poverty trap and can now see a way out. Thus, there is a serious danger that better-paid people in aid agencies, the World Bank, consultancies, and universities assume that the poor act as *they* would and will work less if given more money.

In Brazil, 3% more adults in Bolsa Família families were participating in the labor market, compared to similar households not in the program.[17] In Mexico, Oportunidades does not decrease or increase labor force participation.[18] But it does appear to increase migration to the United States, probably because families can afford to finance a riskier but potentially more profitable migration.[19] In high-emigration towns and villages of Mexico, Oportunidades may spur emigration by the male head through the regular income base that it provides, which reduces the risk posed by emigration.[20]

Namibia Bishop Dr. Zephania Kameeta points to concerns that a grant could create dependency and a culture of laziness. "Opponents said that if you give people money, and especially poor people, they will sit down and become lazy. If you receive manna from heaven, why should people work?" The research on grants refutes this claim. "Moreover, if you look in depth at Exodus 16, the people of Israel in the long journey out of slavery, they received manna from heaven. But it did not make them lazy; instead it enabled them to be on the move to travel through the desert. In Namibia, we know how harsh the circumstances of the desert can be. In this context nobody would say the manna made the Israelites dependent. To the contrary, it enabled them to move."[21]

South Africa: The Poor Are Different

Because the myth that grants make people reluctant to work is so strong there, South Africans have done an unusual number of studies of job seeking and employment. And the studies show that the response of very low-income South Africans to a small increase in their income is significantly different from the response of median-income South Africans. People on very low incomes try to use any extra money to leverage further gains, building on small extra income to try to find jobs or increase wages. Middle-income people are more likely to use extra money for leisure or to gain more spare time. South Africa has very high unemployment rates and a long history of labor migration from rural to urban and mining areas. Both pensions and child benefits promote work seeking, migration in search of jobs, and petty trade to try to increase income.

Pensions are important in South Africa because many households have three or four generations, and income tends to be shared. One study looked at the poorest quintile (fifth) of three-generation homes where no adult was working in 2004. During the year, in houses without pensions 13% of adults actively looked for work, whereas in pension households it was 15%. In the non-pension households 7% found jobs, compared to 9% in the pension households.[22] Thus the pension significantly increased the likelihood of looking for and finding a job.

Another study looked at three-generation African households and found that, on average, each household had one migrant working outside the home.[23] With the end of apartheid, female migration increased significantly. Financial and child care constraints limit migration. Poor households cannot afford the direct costs of initial migration and living costs during the job search, but these could now be funded through the child benefit or pension grants. Furthermore, pension income enables others, particularly grandmothers, to take over the care of children.[24] Thus cash transfers provide potential labor market participants with the resources and economic security necessary to invest in high-risk/high-reward job seeking.

A more recent study confirms this, finding that "large cash transfers to the elderly lead to increased employment among prime-aged adults, which occurs primarily through labor migration. The pension's impact is attributable to the increase in household resources it represents, which can be used to stake migrants until they become self-sufficient, and to the presence of pensioners who can care for small children, which allows prime-aged adults to look for work elsewhere."[25]

This study also notes that, in addition to prime-age adults being more likely to be working and to be labor migrants in a pension household, when the pension is lost because the pensioner dies then household members are significantly less likely to be employed or to be labor migrants.

Another piece of research showed that although women are significantly less likely than men to be migrants, a pension in the household significantly increased the number of women migrants, particularly in households with less access to land and fewer young children.[26]

A child benefit has a similar effect. The age of eligibility rose in steps from 7 in 2002 to 14 in 2005, so it was possible to compare families with and without the grant. And the study found a significant increase in women looking for and finding work.[27] What all these studies show is that grants provide a boost to help people out of the poverty trap.

The research also shows that grants increase men's participation in the labor market less than that of women. One explanation is the benefit trap—the median salary for women entering employment is well below the child benefit threshold, whereas the median salary for a married man is much closer—so the potential losses to the family for a man taking work are much greater.[28]

"There is no way you won't want to work in order to live on 190 Rand a month," explained a mother in Mdantsane, new East London. This was the size of a child benefit, about $25 per month, and "when you work, you earn more than that. Yes we are hungry, we are used to poverty, but there's no way you won't work only to depend on R190. By the time the R190 comes, your child needs a multitude of things from milk to shoes. You buy shoes and other small things and after that it's finished."[29] Group interviews with grant recipients in South Africa made it clear that it is not simply that the grant is too little to live on. Having a job was seen as central to self-worth and personal dignity. "Everyone would prefer to have a job—with a job you have a hope and a vision," said a disability grant recipient in Makhaza, Cape Town. The disability grant is enough to live on, but "it is more than just food and clothing. With a job you can keep your dreams alive." It was clear from group discussions that despite the huge unemployment levels in South Africa, joblessness had not become "normalized." Economic migration is common, and people in the groups largely supported extending the grants to cover all unemployed, because grants helped people travel to find work. Finally, in high-crime South Africa, it was repeatedly argued that there should be grants to the unemployed to reduce crime. "The reason why we have so much crime is because people are not working," explained a disabled man in Makhaza. With a grant, "at least people will be able to buy food. People do bad things, not that they want to buy drugs, but because they are starving."[30]

One of the other myths surrounding grants is that teenage girls will have babies in order to live on the child benefit. But a study in South Africa showed that just the opposite happened. Teenage mothers were actually less likely to apply for a child benefit than older mothers.[31]

Do Women and Children Work Harder?

The two exceptions to the general rule are that women in heavily conditional programs such as Oportunidades, and children in general, decrease their participation in formal labor. What appears to be happening is that going to school and studying, and (for mothers) meeting program co-responsibilities, take substantial amounts of time. Some of this time is taken from farm or other "productive" labor (which shows up as a decrease in formal labor participation), and some is taken from leisure time, which is also reduced. A key question for any cash program is whether this reduction of formal labor by women and children is desirable. Is it better for a mother to spend more time with her family and less time trying to earn money? Some programs, such as Bolsa Família in Brazil, have reduction of child labor as one of their goals. Both Bolsa Família and Oportunidades do significantly reduce children's participation in the labor force. South African pensions increase school attendance and significantly reduce the hours worked by schoolchildren.[32]

Despite cash transfers, people remain poor. Socorro Palma Cazabal in San Felipe Teotlancingo, in the state of Puebla, makes candles to sell to tourists. "We were surviving from what we sold, we couldn't afford to send our children to school or to take them to the doctor." She has seven children and now receives grants for five, so all go to school. But it is still hard. "They are not only good students, they also help us. My two older sons work. When they finish school, they go to cut some flowers. Later, at around five or six in the afternoons, we all gather to help with the candles. We all participate. My husband makes them, but each one has a task. Some of them pick up the pieces, some others place them in boxes, and some others pack them. This is good, because it teaches them to work and not only to conform to the benefits we receive."[33]

A study in Colombia showed that the cash transfer program Familias en Acción substantially increased school participation by 14- to 17-year-olds but did not decrease income-generating work. Instead, domestic work decreased and there was a reduction in children's leisure time.[34]

The position of women in the labor force is more complex. A survey in Brazil showed that in Bolsa Família families compared to similar non-beneficiary families, men were 3% more likely to participate in the labor market, but women were 4% more likely. Also, women were 6% less likely to quit their job. But the one group of women less likely to participate in the labor force were female heads of households.[35]

Studies of Oportunidades in Mexico show two problems. First, the "time demands on women associated with satisfying program obligations are significant," according to Augustín Escobar Latapí and Mercedes González de la Rocha[36] of Mexico's Social Anthropology Investigation Centre (CIESAS—Centro de Investigaciones y Estudios Superiores en Antropología Social) in Guadalajara. Women in Oportunidades

are more likely to report spending time in both taking household members to schools, clinics etc. as well as having a greater participation in community work. [They] must attend health talks and participate in locally defined *faenas* (collective tasks), which include cleaning the school or clinic, sweeping the streets or participating in sanitary campaigns. To this must be added the inevitable community meetings in which they are informed of news, changes in programme rules and so on. Our evaluations have found that some women find these burdens overbearing. They either drop out of the programme or drop a job in order to comply with their own and their family's obligations to the programme. This is particularly acute among households lacking an additional breadwinner."

A second problem is that there is clear evidence that increased school enrollment means reduced time spent in domestic work.[37]

All told, this means significant extra work for mothers, and there is clearly a negative impact on some women's ability to do paid work.

There is an even more serious problem with programs in India and Ethiopia that provide paid labor. Women in Ethiopia complained about the difficulties in managing domestic and child care responsibilities as well as laboring on the public works projects.[38]

LIMITATIONS

Education and motivation may be increasing, but a lack of new jobs is a serious problem. This issue has been examined most closely in Mexico. When families begin to receive the grants, both men and women use the opportunity to decrease their involvement in less lucrative non-salaried activities (such as agricultural work) and look for wage labor, but after a few months they return to the less profitable family enterprises, probably because of a lack of jobs.[39] Augustín Escobar Latapí and Mercedes González de la Rocha[40] of Mexico's Social Anthropology Investigation Centre (CIESAS) in Guadalajara point out that job opportunities in many parts of Mexico have been declining for 25 years, which has forced people increasingly to take refuge in "the informal sector and a sharply impoverished subsistence production" or in emigrating to the city or the United States. They continue: "One aim of the programme in its original design cannot be said to have succeeded (yet). Youths leaving school are not in general finding substantially better paid employment opportunities than their parents, due to the sluggish growth of employment and, possibly, the low quality of rural schools. This may provide negative incentives for their younger siblings, thus thwarting programme goals." In particular, "one trend visible in national statistics is the lower labour force participation of young men and women."

The Ceba household is one of the worst off in the already desperately poor area of Mount Frere in the Eastern Cape, South Africa. Two of their children have matriculated and moved to town but have been unable to secure anything but short-term jobs. In spite of this, the household passes on the lion's share of the three child support grants they do receive to their two daughters in grade 11. When asked why they continue to invest in their children's schooling when it has not paid off in the case of the older children,

Mrs. Ceba made clear the expectation that the children would help them and replied that she had not yet given up hope.[41] The faith in education remains strong, both among poor people themselves and among policy-makers who see education as the way to end poverty. But as more poor children with grants finish school and find there are no jobs, will this faith be retained?

There is some evidence, however, that social grants help people stay on the land and not migrate to the city to chase scarce jobs. In South Africa, households receiving the child support grant are significantly more likely to continue farming activities than households not receiving the grant.[42] An International Labour Office study showed that non-contributory pensions in Brazil reduced rural-to-urban migration: "Regular income, independent of weather—unlike income from agricultural production—allowed the acquisition of working instruments, seeds and the capitalization of the family production units, offering a basis on which the rural peasant economy subsisted" throughout the 1990s.[43]

The other issue that is raised by the slow creation of jobs is that it is important not to look at cash transfers as short-term or temporary. A study of Brazilian cash transfers for UNDP's International Poverty Centre warns that altering the labor market and the educational level of the labor force is not a quick or easy task. "Transfers, therefore, should not be regarded as a temporary solution."[44]

Micro-credit Is Not an Alternative

This chapter has highlighted the poverty traps that stop poor people from improving their lives and the pressing need that they have for small sums of cash to make investments or to reduce risk and vulnerability. But why give money to poor people? Why not lend it to them? Micro-credit has been one of the great successes of development policy in the last 20 years. Can't it meet the needs of the poor for cash?

The simple answer is "no," as one of us influentially argued back in the 1990s.[45] Micro-credit, or more accurately microfinance (which includes micro-loans, micro-savings, micro-insurance, and micro-transmission of remittances), is best understood as a platform that can help some poor people more adequately manage their complex livelihoods. It is not a "sky-hook" that lifts all micro-credit recipients out of poverty, as many people presented it in the 1990s. (These advocates included the Nobel laureate Professor Mohammad Yunus of the Grameen Bank, who has moderated his claims since that time.)[46] Microfinance can indeed help some poor people improve their condition,[47] but it is far from being the panacea for poverty reduction that the Micro-credit Summit Campaign used to claim. There are a number of reasons for this.

First, in most parts of the developing world, microfinance is not available. This is particularly the case in Sub-Saharan Africa and northern India. Despite decades of government and nongovernment activity, microfinance institutions (MFIs) have found it hard to establish viable programs where populations are dispersed and where economies are stagnant. Second, even where microfinance is functioning well, as in Bangladesh, many poor people are unable to access services, especially if they are extremely poor—or young or old or disabled. Self-exclusion (which occurs when people are worried about taking on the additional risk of being in debt), social exclusion (which occurs when MFI group members feel that some people are "not suitable" because of their ethnicity, religion, caste, or other factors), and MFI staff exclusion (which occurs when staff think people are "too risky or too poor") stop many people from using MFIs.[48] BRAC, one of the world's most successful microfinance providers, explicitly acknowledges this and has set up a Targeting the Ultrapoor Program (TUP) to help 800,000 extremely poor households in Bangladesh eventually access its microfinance. This involves an investment of around US$270 per household and the provision of cash grants, economic and social training, and an asset transfer.[49] Third is the cost of micro-credit. To stay viable, many MFIs charge interest rates of 36% to 120% per annum for their loans. While some borrowers can cover such costs, if they are involved in high turnover trading, many cannot. In particular, interest rates are much too high for poor farmers in Africa, who must take loans for several months if they are to borrow for improved seeds and fertilizer.

The assumptions of neoclassical economists, who view credit markets in poor countries as having "imperfections" that need to be overcome, simply do not match the realities people face on the ground. In the real world, "perfect credit markets" are unlikely to solve the problems of poor people. Rather, they need a web of services (formal and informal microfinance, basic health services, primary education, cash transfers, and other supports) to bulwark their personal efforts to improve their lives. Microfinance is one component of such services, but it is no panacea.

The poverty trap means that poor people need a minimum income before they can make use of micro-credit and other services. Furthermore, in many low-income contexts it may be more difficult, and perhaps more costly, to establish viable MFIs than to administer cash transfer programs.

So the starting point must be giving money to the poor to lift them out of the poverty trap.

THE UPWARD ECONOMIC SPIRAL: KEY ISSUES

Cash transfers promote economic growth. "We can safely argue that well designed and targeted social policies stimulate aggregate demand and consumption," concluded Hailu and Soares in their 2009 study of cash transfers in Brazil. "The transmission mechanism is straightforward. A virtuous cycle of increases in the income of poorer families, together with wage growth, has enlarged the domestic market. Greater consumption of mass-market goods has led to growing labor demand for these same families, spurring further increases in their income and purchasing power."

Initially, poor people spend the cash transfer locally, typically in local shops, or in rural areas buying locally produced food. This already helps to stimulate the economic cycle, supporting local farmers, tailors, and traders. Rural people who are older or disabled sometimes spend some of the money to hire local people to help in their fields.

Perhaps more important, however, is that even very poor people invest some of their small cash transfer in a way they hope will increase their income.[50] The fear of the rich is that giving money to the poor will make them lazy, but just the opposite happens. Small amounts of money loosen some of the constraints on poor people. In South Africa, pensioner households have more people working and more people looking for work than non-pensioner households. This is because the extra money helps to pay the expenses of looking for work, such as the costs of transport and food, and provides funds for child care. Typically, a grandmother with the pension will look after her grandchild, enabling her daughter to work in a town or city. Insurance is the second key factor; when a grant is guaranteed, poor people can risk going farther away to look for work or trying out a new crop, knowing that if the venture fails, at least some money will still be coming in and the family will not starve. Finally, from Mexico to South Africa, evidence is piling up that poor people know how to make small and profitable investments, and the main constraint is lack of cash. With a bit of extra money, they do buy fertilizer and better seeds, the raw materials for small local products, or goods they can sell in the community.

Cash transfers stimulate the economy and create conditions that enable people to search for work or to produce or trade more profitably. They do much more than simply reduce immediate poverty.

NOTES

1. Santiago Levy, *Progress Against Poverty: Sustaining Mexico's Progresa-Oportunidades Program* (Washington, DC: Brookings Institution, 2006), p. 11.

2. Rachel Sabates-Wheeler, Stephen Devereux, and Bruce Guenther, "Building Synergies Between Social Protection and Small-holder Policies," paper given at the conference "Social Protection for the Poorest in Africa: Learning from Experience," Kampala (September 3–10, 2008); and Daniel Gilligan, John Hoddinott, and Alemayehu Seyoum Taffesse, "The Impact of Ethiopia's Productive Safety Net Programme and Its Linkages," Discussion Paper 839 (Washington, DC: IFPRI, 2008).

3. Paul Gertler, Sebastian Martinez, and Marta Rubio-Codina, "Investing Cash Transfers to Raise Long-Term Living Standards," Report WPS3994-IE (Washington, DC: World Bank, 2006), available at http://go.worldbank.org/59S3O8JZP0.

4. Gertler, Martinez, and Rubio-Codina, "Investing Cash Transfers."

5. Augustín Escobar Latapí and Mercedes González de la Rocha, "Girls, Mothers and Poverty Reduction in Mexico: Evaluating Progresa-Oportunidades." In *The Gendered Impacts of Liberalisation: Towards "Embedded Liberalism?"* edited by Shahra Razavi (New York and Abingdon: Routledge/UNRISD, 2009).

6. Elisabeth Sadoulet, Alain de Janvry, and Benjamin Davis, "Cash Transfer Programs with Income Multipliers: Procampo in Mexico" (Washington, DC: IFPRI, 2001). The Procampo program itself was regressive, with only 10% of money going to the 45% of producers with farms smaller that five hectares.

7. Andries du Toit and David Neves, "Trading on a Grant: Integrating Formal and Informal Social Protection in Post-Apartheid Migrant Networks," Working Paper 75 (Manchester: Brooks World Poverty Institute, 2009).

8. Aislinn Delany, Zenobia Ismail, Lauren Graham, and Yuri Ramkissoon, *Review of the Child Support Grant: Uses, Implementation and Obstacles* (Johannesburg: Community Agency for Social Enquiry for UNICEF and South African Social Security Agency, 2008).

9. Sebastian Martinez, "Pensions, Poverty and Household Investments in Bolivia," paper presented at Perspectives on Impact Evaluation Conference, Cairo, Egypt (April 2009); and Sebastian Martinez, "Invertir el Bonosol para Aliviar la Pobreza: Retornos Económicos en los Hogares Beneficiarios." In *La Inversion Prudente. Impacto del Bonosol Sobre la Familia, la Equidad Social y el Crecimiento Economico,* edited by Guillermo Aponte et al. (La Paz: Fundacion Milenio, 2007), pp. 109–28.

10. Helmut Schwarzer and Ana Carolina Querino, "Non-contributory Pensions in Brazil: The Impact on Poverty Reduction," Extension of Social Security Working Paper 11 (Geneva: International Labour Organization, 2002).

11. Lucélia Luiz Pereira et al., *Efeitos do Programa Bolsa Família nas Condições de Vida de Beneficiários em Municípios de Muito Baixo IDH* (Brasilia: UNDP International Poverty Centre, 2008), available at http://www.ipc-undp.org/publications/mds/33M.pdf.

12. Candace Miller, "Economic Evaluation of the Mchinji Cash Transfer—Preliminary Findings" (Boston: Boston University School of Public Health, 2009), available at http://childresearchpolicy.org/images/Economic_Impacts_June_15.pdf.

13. Simon Davies, "Making the Most of It: A Regional Multiplier Approach to Estimating the Impact of Cash Transfers on the Market" (Malawi: Concern Worldwide, 2007).

14. Charles Gore et al., *The Least Developed Countries Report 2006: Developing Productive Capacities* (New York and Geneva: UNCTAD, 2006), ch. 7.

15. Michael Samson, "The Developmental Impact of Social Pensions in Southern Africa," presentation at the World Conference: Social Protection and Inclusion, Lisbon (October 4, 2006).

16. *The Lancet* Editorial, "Cash Transfers for Children—Investing into the Future," *The Lancet,* 373, no. 9682 (2009): 2172.

17. Jennifer Yablonski with Michael O'Donnell, *Lasting Benefits: The Role of Cash Transfers in Tackling Child Mortality* (London: Save the Children, 2009), p. 16, available at http://www.savethechildren.org.uk/en/docs/Lasting_Benefits.pdf.

18. Susan W. Parker and Emmanuel Skoufias, "The Impact of Progresa on Work, Leisure and Time Allocation" (Washington, DC: IFPRI, 2000).

19. Manuela Angelucci, "Aid and Migration: An Analysis of the Impact of Progresa on the Timing and Size of Labour Migration," Centre for the Evaluation of Development Policies Report EWP04.05 (London: Institute for Fiscal Studies, 2004).

20. Latapí and de la Rocha, "Girls, Mothers and Poverty Reduction."

21. Claudia Haarmann et al., *Making the Difference! The BIG in Namibia,* Basic Income Grant Pilot Project Assessment Report (Windhoek, Namibia: Namibian BIG Coalition, 2009), available at www.bignam.org.

22. Michael Samson, "The Social and Economic Impacts of South Africa's Social Grants," presentation at "Growing Up Free from Poverty Seminar," November 18, 2007 (London, Overseas Development Institute, 2007).

23. Dorrit Posel, James A. Fairburn, and Frances Lund, "Labour Migration and Households: A Reconsideration of the Effects of the Social Pension on Labour Supply in South Africa," *Economic Modelling,* 23, no. 5 (2006): 836–53.

24. Dorrit Posel and Danila Casale, "What Has Been Happening to Internal Labour Migration in South Africa, 1993–1999," *The South African Journal of Economics,* 71, no. 3 (September 2003): 455–79.

25. Cally Ardington, Anne Case, and Victoria Hosegood, "Labor Supply Responses to Large Social Transfers: Longitudinal Evidence from South Africa," *American Economic Journal: Applied Economics,* 1, no. 1 (2009): 22–48. An earlier version of this paper is available as NBER Working Paper No. 13442 (Cambridge, MA: National Bureau of Economic Research, 2007), available at http://www.nber.org/papers/w13442.

26. Posel, Fairburn, and Lund, "Labour Migration."

27. Martin Williams, "The Social and Economic Impacts of South Africa's Child Support Grant (Extended Version)," Working Paper 39 (Cape Town: EPRI (Economic Policy Research Institute, 2007).

28. Williams, "The Social and Economic Impacts."

29. Rebecca Surender, Michael Noble, Phakama Ntshongwana, and Gemma Wright, "Work and Welfare in South Africa: The Relationship Between Social Grants and Labour Market Activity" (Oxford: Centre for the Analysis of South African Social Policy, Oxford University, 2008), available at http://www.chronic poverty.org/socialprotectionconference/abstracts/Rebecca%20Surender.pdf.

30. Surender et al., "Work and Welfare."

31. Anne Case, Victoria Hosegood, and Frances Lund, "The Reach and Impact of Child Support Grants: Evidence from KwaZulu-Natal," *Development Southern Africa,* 22, no. 4 (2005): 467–82.

32. Williams, "The Social and Economic Impacts."

33. Mauricio Carrera, *Oportunidades: Historias de Éxito* (México, D.F.: Secretaría de Desarrollo Social, Coordinación Nacional del Programa de Desarrollo Humano Oportunidades, 2008), p. 21. Published in English as *Oportunidades: Stories of Success.*

34. Orazio Attanasio et al., "Child Education and Work Choices in the Presence of a Conditional Cash Transfer Programme in Rural Colombia," IFS Working Papers W06/13 (London: Institute for Fiscal Studies, 2006).

35. Marcelo Medeiros, Tatiana Britto, and Fábio Veras Soares, "Targeted Cash Transfer Programmes in Brazil: BPC and Bolsa Família," IPC Working Paper 46 (Brasilia: International Poverty Centre, 2008).

36. Latapí and de la Rocha, "Girls, Mothers and Poverty Reduction."

37. Parker and Skoufias, "The Impact of Progresa."

38. Sabates-Wheeler, Devereux, and Guenther, "Building Synergies."

39. Parker and Skoufias, "The Impact of Progresa."

40. Latapí and de la Rocha, "Girls, Mothers and Poverty Reduction."

41. Andries du Toit and David Neves, "Vulnerability and Social Protection at the Margins of the Formal Economy—Case Studies from Khyelitsha and the Eastern Cape," report prepared for USAID, 2006, available at http://www.plaas.org .za/publications/downloads/vulnerability.pdf.

42. Michael Samson et al., "Quantitative Analysis of the Impact of the Child Support Grant" (Cape Town: Economic Policy Research Institute, 2008).

43. Schwarzer and Carolina Querino, "Non-contributory Pensions."

44. Medeiros, Britto, and Soares, "Targeted Cash Transfer Programmes."

45. David Hulme and Paul Mosley, *Finance Against Poverty,* Vol. 1 (London: Routledge, 1996).

46. A report by International Development Support Services (1994) concluded that sections of the literature on the Grameen Bank at that time ranged from the adulatory to the sycophantic. See Hulme and Mosley, *Finance Against Poverty,* p. 137.

47. See Beatriz Armendariz and Jonathan Morduch, *The Economics of Microfinance* (Cambridge, MA: MIT Press, 2005) for a balanced review of the evidence.

48. Hulme and Mosley, *Finance Against Poverty,* pp. 130–31.

49. See David Hulme, Karen Moore, and Faisal Bin Seraj, "Reaching the People Whom Microfinance Cannot Reach: Learning from BRAC's Targeting the Ultra Poor Programme." In *The Handbook of Microfinance,* edited by Beatriz Armendariz and Marc Labie (Word Scientific Publishing, forthcoming 2010).

50. Armando Barrientos, "Social Protection and Growth: A Review," CPRC Working Paper 112 (Manchester: Brooks World Poverty Institute and CPRC, 2008).

6

To Everyone or Just a Few?
The Targeting Dilemma

"YES, I AM POOR. I HAVE TO WORK TWICE AS HARD TO EARN ENOUGH money," says Francisca. "I work today in order to eat tomorrow. I do laundry, I cook, I do whatever pays." In the same town, Maria Jose makes a distinction: "No, I am not poor. But I am needy. Being poor is a terrible thing." Isaura argues that being poor is "not having a house and living on the street, not having your daily bread. I am not poor because I have rice and beans every day, but I am not rich."

These three women live in the small city of Bacabal in northeastern Brazil, where more than half of families have income low enough to receive the Bolsa Família. Their discussion of "poor," "needy," and "not rich" is repeated everywhere, and it underlines an issue that arises in all cash transfer programs. If a central goal of cash transfers is poverty reduction, should the "poorest" people be targeted, and can they be identified?

If we apply Francisca's definition, then being poor is about not having enough money for food tomorrow; that is, it is about income. This is the most common definition. In Europe there are negative income tax programs, in which, instead of paying tax, people on low income receive money back through the tax system. But that would not work for Francisca, who is in the informal sector, is being paid in cash, and probably is not in the tax system at all. Brazil's Bolsa Família gives grants to families with low income from all sources.

But Isaura's view is that not having a house constitutes being poor. Both Mexico and South Africa use the family's assets, particularly a permanent house built of blocks or bricks and with a proper roof, as a defining crite-rion for not being poor.

Maria Jose raises another issue. She recognizes that she is not as poor as some other people in Bacabal, but she defines herself as "needy." Should she receive a cash transfer? In Brazil the Bolsa Família criteria mean that she does, but in some other countries she would not.

These three women demonstrate another issue as well. Informaliza-tion means that many people who appear in statistics as economically in-active, or as on a pension, or as disabled or going to school still do some kind of work—child care, cleaning, domestic service, selling by the road-side, or tending small plots of land. This income may be tiny, variable, and insecure, but for them and their family it is more than nothing. This small additional income makes it even harder for outsiders to define family in-come and poverty lines. On the other hand, having a low wage in the for-mal sector can exclude people who need assistance. Estate workers in Sri Lanka have some of the lowest incomes and worst health and education conditions in the country, but because they have formal income and hous-ing they are excluded from many social grants that people with much higher, but informal, incomes receive.[1]

The decision of who should receive money—the "targets" of the pro-gram—is political, social, financial, and economic. In different countries, the strength of social institutions will vary, and available funds will depend on the tax base, aid, and natural resources. Leadership matters; political elites will have more or less commitment to the plight of the poor, minis-ters of social welfare may be weak or strong, and finance ministers may or may not support social protection.

The first issue is about the goals of the program. Zambia and Malawi have embryonic social welfare programs aimed at the "ultra-poor" who cannot work. All three Bacabal women would probably not qualify for the Zambian grant, yet even if the goal is purely poverty reduction, at least some of these women deserve assistance.

Equally important will be the other goals of the cash transfer, as set out in Chapter 3. If an important goal is to reduce intergenerational transmis-sion of poverty, then more money will go to families with children, and per-haps even to the children themselves, to encourage them to attend school. The children will be relatively poor, but many will not be destitute or ultra-poor. In Bangladesh, the Stipend for Secondary Education program has sought to ensure that girls gain improved access to secondary education. It has been praised for its success with this goal but has also been criticized for supporting girls from lower-middle-class households rather than the poor.[2]

Growth is a target of many programs, which is interpreted to mean that money should go to those who can work and who have some assets. The World Bank comments that redistribution should not go just to the poorest of the poor, but also to those who are most likely to make productive investments. "It may be more effective to help people who are slightly richer, because with some help they may actually be able to start a business."[3] The working poor are a critical group. The United Nations 2009 report on the Millennium Development Goals[4] notes that in Sub-Saharan Africa and Southern Asia, 74% of working adults are self-employed or are working on family farms and businesses; in Southeast Asia it is 61%. These are people whose income is often very low but who could productively invest extra money from cash transfers. And for those who are employed, in Sub-Saharan Africa 64% are living on less than $1.25 per day.

Thus the mix of goals of the program will determine whether it is to assist just the destitute, to include the needy and the working poor, or to include slightly less poor school children and self-employed people who may be able to graduate from poverty permanently. Once goals have been agreed upon, the characteristics of each country will shape the design of the program.

Whichever mix of goals is selected, governments have limited budgets, and most programs will make some attempt to target poorer households, with a view to maximizing the poverty reduction impact of the cash transfer program. However, in developing countries it is not easy to identify poor and non-poor households or to characterize different categories of the poor. For countries with low administrative capacity, any such effort can be costly and still end up inaccurate. Countries may choose simpler but less accurate targeting.

The first step is to look more closely at poverty: Are most people poor or is there an identifiable smaller target group? An important indicator of poverty and ill health is child mortality. Most children die from a combination of malnutrition, poor water, and untreated diseases, conditions that are easily preventable at relatively low cost. A high child death rate usually indicates a much broader malnutrition problem, which in turn permanently impairs children's development; undernourished children of poor parents are highly likely to remain poor. Thus child mortality is an important indicator both of poverty and of intergenerational transmission of poverty.

The next step is to look at the distribution of child mortality by income group. Figure 6.1 compares Bangladesh and Indonesia in terms of the mortality of children under five. For the richest and poorest, the rates are similar, but for Bangladesh the mortality rate is high for more than half the population, whereas in Indonesia the rate falls off more quickly. As we noted in Chapter 3, Indonesia had a grant that went to 40% of the population but has moved to one targeted more carefully at the poorest 20%. Figure 6.1 supports the decision of Indonesia to concentrate only on the poorest fifth, but it suggests that any program in Bangladesh would need to target three-fifths of the population, and perhaps more.

Figure 6.2 shows three typical African countries. The mortality rate for the wealthiest is lower than for other groups, although wealthy African children are more likely to die than poor Indonesian children (see Figure 6.1). But what is most striking is how flat these graphs are; even children in the relatively well-off fourth quintile are almost as likely to die as the poorest. This is an indication of the extreme and generalized poverty in Africa.

A group writing in the UK Institute of Development Studies *Bulletin* distinguishes between what it calls "bottom inequity," in which a small minority is much worse off than everyone else, and "top inequity," in which a small minority is much better off than the broad mass of the population. Most Sub-Saharan countries are characterized by top inequity, and there is very little difference between families in the bottom half of the population, whereas Indonesia is characterized by bottom inequity.[5]

Figure 6.1 Child Mortality by Income Quintile in Bangladesh and Indonesia

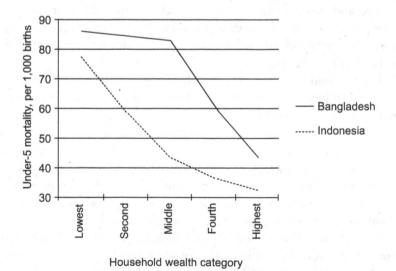

Household wealth category

Source: Demographic and Health Surveys project ("Measure DHS"), http://www.statcompiler.com/index.cfm, downloaded July 10, 2009.

Figure 6.2 Child Mortality by Income Quintile in Ghana, Malawi, and Mali

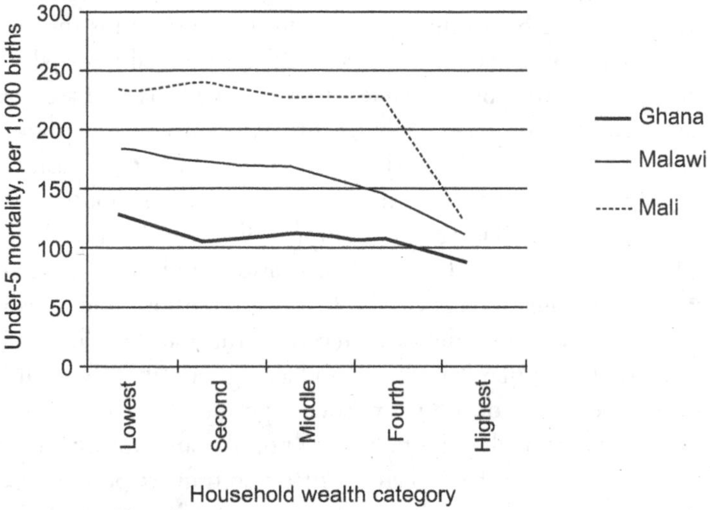

Source: Demographic and Health Surveys project ("Measure DHS"), http://www.statcompiler.com/index.cfm, downloaded July 10, 2009.

Instead of speaking just in terms of bottom and top inequity, one can divide countries into three groups. Many countries in Asia and Latin America are like Indonesia, where there is bottom inequity and a poor group that can be targeted. Another group is like Bangladesh, where roughly half the population is impoverished and at risk of ill health, and whose children will struggle to improve their lot. The third group consists of those countries with top inequity and poverty rates of 70% to 80%—most of Africa and a few countries in Latin America, the Caribbean, and Asia—and where it may make less sense to try to target the "poorest." It is necessary to think very differently about Africa. A study of targeting done for the Zambian government argues that "there is certainly no point in even attempting means testing . . . where over 75 percent of households are living in extreme poverty."[6] In such circumstances targeting may only serve to exclude poor but recently lucky households—those who had no sickness last year or sold a goat—and next year they will probably be poor again.

Politics Matters

Thus the choice of goals, government income, and the poverty distribution in the country will significantly affect how the target group is chosen. But the final decision will be political, based on a judgment of what will win support from the electorate and the taxpayers (and, in poor countries, what will be acceptable to the donors). On the one hand is the view that smaller amounts of money will be more effective if well targeted. On the other hand, voters may be more likely to support a broader-based transfer. Middle classes may be more likely to support a cash grant if they are included (as with the British child benefit) or could benefit easily if they needed help. In some contexts, the need to gain the support of middle-class voters could be a factor in designing a program. Finally, there is the intangible issue of fairness. Precise identification can be expensive and still may not be accurate; choices can be highly contentious and divisive. Do people feel that the right families are receiving the grant, or do they believe that they have been unfairly excluded and a neighbor unfairly included? As we will see later, non-contributory (social) pensions are not the best way to reach the poor, but they are politically popular and are seen as fair and transparent, so pensions have been the first cash transfer program to be introduced in many countries. Even though economists and technical specialists nearly always prefer complex targeting approaches, the public usually prefers very simple targeting of readily identifiable groups, such as the elderly or children.

Politics has played an important part in the differences between programs in Africa and Latin America. Tatiana Feitosa de Britto of the University of Brasilia notes that "electoral concerns seem to have been important in both Brazil and Mexico. Cash transfers establish a direct and regular link between the national government and beneficiaries. . . . The logic of the programme seems to have been to retain or win votes for the governing party through the maximization of the number of beneficiaries, even if the amount of the transfer was kept low."[7] She cites three other political factors as well. First, conditional cash transfers "appeared at a time of economic crisis in Latin America, when the need for social safety nets was widespread." This was linked to elites' fear of violence. Second, the programs were designed to be acceptable to the middle classes by putting emphasis on ending intergenerational poverty and improving national competitiveness in the world through increases in human capital. This is also linked to conditions, particularly in Mexico, so that grants are seen to help the "deserving poor." Third, there seems to be a broad consensus in Latin America about public goods and the state's responsibility for providing education and safeguarding health.

Sam Hickey of the University of Manchester (and colleague of two of the authors of this book) has studied the politics of cash transfer in Africa.

He finds promoters there of cash transfers struggling with a variety of political pressures.[8] The first source of pressure is the question (raised in Chapter 2 and Table 2.1) of why people are poor—and the related issues of whether to distinguish between deserving and undeserving poor and "whether the causes of poverty are linked to a perceived 'lack of effort' by the poor or to 'wider forces.'" Elite attitudes are particularly important, as are what Hickey calls "heated debates between elites." But on the other side are "popular perceptions of how 'people like them' will fare under a given programme."

A study of the Mongolian child benefit comments that it "provides a graphic example of the role of electoral politics and public attitudes in condemning a targeted programme to failure and substituting it with a far more popular universal programme."[9] Mongolia is a former socialist country that has been badly hit by the transition to a globalized market economy, and families still expect the government to provide social services. In the 2004 election both parties promised a child benefit, and a targeted one was introduced, but targeting was ineffective and unpopular. Donors and technocrats wanted to improve the targeting, but the political pressure was in the other direction. Families saw the grant as a way to ensure the well-being of all children, and politicians presented the child benefit as a way in which mineral wealth could be shared by all families. Thus the pressure to move to a larger and universal benefit was overwhelming, and spending jumped to nearly 4% of GDP.

Whatever the size of the budget, some choices have to be made about who receives money, and those choices are often more political than technical. As Mongolia, South Africa, and a number of Latin American countries show, it is not necessary to assume a fixed budget. Indeed, some countries have designed programs that can start small in a way and can be easily expanded if the program gains political support. For example, they may start with the very poorest districts or with just young children. When countries make the political choice to go ahead with a program, they are sometimes able to find very large amounts of money. And the pressure is often to increase the size of the grant or expand it to additional people. In a World Bank study, Johan Gelbach and Lant Pritchett developed a stylized model in which the poor, the middle-class, and the rich sectors are roughly equal in size, and all vote on the budget of a redistributive program. In these conditions, including the middle class in the program tends to persuade them not only to support the program but also to support increases in the program and higher taxes (largely paid by the rich).[10] But if a fixed amount is targeted to the poor alone, then both the middle class and the rich vote against taxes to pay for it, and the rich gain because they pay less taxes. Gelbach and Pritchett's intervention was partly tongue-in-cheek, but it made the important argument that politics matters, that the economists' perfect targeting may not be the most politically sensible, and that the size of the pie need not be fixed.

POPULIST OR MORE FOR THE POOR?

Not surprisingly, every country has established its cash transfer program differently, there is no obvious "best" way to do so, and a vigorous debate over targeting is raging in the academic and practitioner literature. We will not resolve that debate in this book, but we would like to give some flavor of the more outspoken arguments on the non-academic side. One group argues that it is unethical and improper to give money to the rich and that targeting and proxy means tests can be improved to a point where money can be given only to those who need it. Others prefer categorical and/or exclude-the-rich systems, on the grounds that no means tests has yet been found that really works, and means testing is socially divisive and ineffi-cient. Does a human rights perspective imply that all grants should be uni-versal? Or does it imply a poverty perspective in which transfers to the poorest must be maximized? This is a debate that mixes politics and tech-nical solutions in equal measure.

The donor-funded southern African Regional Hunger and Vulnera-bility Programme (RHVP) hosts the Wahenga website, which is intended to encourage policymakers and practitioners "to engage in the hunger and vulnerability debate." One such debate unfolded between Stephen Dev-ereux of IDS Sussex and Charles Knox of HelpAge International. Devereux dismisses untargeted benefits as "populist" and argues that

> universal programmes are more expensive by orders of magnitude than are targeted interventions. Giving a dollar a day to everyone costs five times as much as giving a dollar a day to the poorest 20%. Alternatively, . . . a given resource envelope will have five times more impact on poverty if it is disbursed to the poorest 20% than if it is thinly spread over an entire population. Poverty targeting may be tricky to do well, but it may also be the most cost-effective and equitable use of scarce public resources for achieving poverty reduction. Redistribution from rich to poor also narrows income gaps and reduces inequality, which is less "neoliberal" than is diverting public money from poor to rich people.[11]

"While Dr. Devereux doesn't want the rich to benefit from non-contributory pensions, there are strong arguments to the contrary. If by incorporating the rich, many more resources go to the poor, then isn't this a good thing? And, if the rich pay taxes, can't we argue that they could/should also benefit? We cannot divorce social protection financing from the politics of the real world," replies Knox. He adds that Devereux

> assumes perfect targeting, a situation that does not exist anywhere in the world. It's a great example of simplistic economics. . . . Let's try and base our discussion on evidence and realism. First of all, we need to recognize that no one knows how to do poverty targeting in poor countries with low administrative capacity. Let's stop pretending that it is possible. . . . In contrast, we know how to undertake universal categorical targeting. Look at the success of universal pensions in countries such as Namibia, Botswana, Lesotho, and Mauritius.[12]

John Rook, RHVP policy coordinator, summarized the debate by saying there is no perfect targeting approach. Targeting requires a realistic and pragmatic approach that reflects a national consensus:

> Where social transfer agendas are nationally owned and driven, the approach to targeting has been pragmatic and has usually favored categorical interventions such as old age pensions and child benefits. Conversely, where there has been a high degree of external engagement, targeting has become a protracted and even divisive issue, especially where countries have become the "battle ground" for external agencies to argue out their opposing approaches. The result of this has often been to further erode already weak national ownership and even to lead to disengagement and disillusion on the part of host governments.[13]

WE ARE ALL POOR HERE

Donor agencies have sponsored pilot programs in Zambia and Malawi explicitly targeting only 10% of the population. Zambia's Ministry of Community Development and Social Services,[14] the German agency GTZ, and Care run a program that is explicitly called the Social Safety Net Project. The ministry argues that the lack of social protection in Zambia necessitated the development of a "social safety net for the most vulnerable households in Zambia." The objective is to "reduce extreme poverty, hunger and starvation in the 10% most destitute and incapacitated (non-viable) households in the pilot region. The focus lies mainly—but not exclusively—on households that are headed by the elderly and are caring for OVC [orphans and vulnerable children] because the breadwinners are chronically sick or have died due to HIV/AIDS or other reasons." The 10% cutoff was chosen in Zambia and Malawi pilots because a study in Malawi showed that 22% of the population was "ultra-poor" (which typically means those who consume only one meal per day and own no valuable assets) and half of those did not have adequate labor in the family to feed their household (which usually means that each adult has more than three dependents).[15]

Zambia and Malawi are very poor countries with limited budgets. But because 70% of the population is poor, choosing just 10% has triggered an often angry debate. Measures of ultra-poverty and inadequate labor lie on a continuum, and neither of those cutoff points is precise. There are permanent insecurity and constant movement of income level in the bottom half of the pile. Good rains and the right crop can lift a poor family from the bottom for a few months; sickness or an insect attack can push a family from the middle to the bottom.

"The sentiment 'we are all poor here' accurately reflects the very small differences in personal and family circumstances separating everyone falling within the bottom 50–60 percent of per capita consumption in poor mainly rural SSA [Sub-Saharan African] countries," according to Frank Ellis, School of Development Studies, University of East Anglia, UK, whose studies lead him to argue against choosing just 10%.[16] He continues that beneficiary selection "occurs within a context of very close proximity in well-being, life styles, command over assets and income streams, and real material consumption of this proportion of the population." These are, he says, "wafer thin differences."

A study in Malawi showed poor rural communities in the central and southern part of the country opposed to targeting, fearing it would disrupt social harmony.[17] Where everyone feels they are poor, giving money to just some people raises questions of witchcraft and nepotism.

Even a small grant lifts people from the bottom 10% to the upper half, which means that anyone who is chosen jumps above her or his neighbors. The Malawi social protection team, Harry Mwamlima and Reagan Kaluluma, consider this outcome a "positive result" and are encouraged that such a poor household is able to improve its status by so much.[18] But Ellis finds it "ethically dubious" because the families that gain the grant leapfrog over very similar families, and it is hard to distinguish between them. Choices between families "often involve seeking tiny variations in circumstances that ordinary people do not perceive as real differences, in order to select a lucky few people as transfer recipients. This inevitably creates social tensions and division, as well as personal strategies to work around the selection criteria."[19]

Studies in both Zambia[20] and Malawi[21] found that more than 10% were ultra-poor and labor constrained, and called for the threshold to be raised to 15% or 20%. The Malawi study found households excluded by the 10% cutoff "in a desperate situation: eating one to two meals per day, wearing rags, lacking blankets and adequate housing."

It is a general experience of public works projects and distribution of food or seeds that if only some people in a poor community can benefit, then the community itself splits up the resources more equally among all community members.[22] An evaluation of the Mchinji cash transfer showed that it had clearly triggered some social changes, and 87% of those receiving grants shared them with other family members and neighbors in an average of 2.6 additional households.[23] Half of that sharing was in the form of employing labor to till fields or repair housing, as might be expected because by definition these are labor-constrained households. But the other half of the sharing was the sharing of food and money, and in 59% of cases, the recipients of this sharing begged for help. Clearly, these families who were once ultra-poor but are suddenly much better off than their neighbors feel strong social obligations. Indeed, 39% of non-beneficiary households borrowed from those who had grants. Of those who received grants, 13% report increased jealousy among neighbors, and 16% report increased begging.

But perhaps the core question about the 10% cutoff is one of the goals. Targeting 10%, as both Zambian and Malawian ministries state, is about providing social welfare to destitute and non-viable households. But the major goals of most cash transfers are developmental and intergenerational—to actually provide assistance to viable households so that they can invest and raise their productivity and income, and to raise the nutrition levels and school attendance of poor children. In Africa that means targeting more than half the population, rather than just 10%, and finding the money to reach a larger group may be more productive in the longer term.

PRINCIPLES AND EVIDENCE

Targeting is probably *the* most controversial issue surrounding cash transfers. Different individuals and agencies take different positions based on principles and interpretations of the growing empirical evidence. Technical specialists and researchers often argue for tight targeting to ensure that the poorest gain the benefits. Politicians in search of votes and rights-based NGOs argue for the broader provision of cash transfers to all people within a category or even to all citizens.

The dilemmas of targeting inspire both economic and political analysis. Economic analysis asks which program, targeted at which people, will best achieve the goals. Political analysis poses different questions, asking which form of targeting will be popular now. But the more far-reaching question is: What form of targeting will be politically and financially sustainable in the long term and will contribute to a fairer and more cohesive society in the future? Political leaders need to balance the political acceptability and sustainability of choices about who benefits now and how presently available funds are distributed with the knowledge that such decisions will determine the future of the program.

No targeting decisions are engraved in stone. "Old age" can first be defined as beginning at 70 years old and later reduced to 65; a target of the poorest 10% can be expanded to the poorest 20%. But once established, the shape of the program tends to be fixed.

Targeting decisions made in Brazil, Mexico, India, and South Africa have been radically different. Yet within their national political contexts, they have been popular and robust. Intense debate and shared experiences help. But when the technical and political meet, local context and history will determine the outcome.

NOTES

1. Meera Shekar, Aparnaa Somanathan, and Lidan Du, "Malnutrition in Sri Lanka: Scale, Scope, Causes and Potential Response," Report 40906-KL (Washington: World Bank, 2007).

2. Simeen Mahmud, "Female Secondary School Stipend Programme in Bangladesh: A Critical Assessment" (Dhaka: Bangladesh Institute of Development Studies, 2003), available at http://portal.unesco.org/.

3. World Bank, *World Development Report 2006: Equity and Development* (Washington, DC: World Bank and New York: Oxford University Press, 2005), p. 102.

4. United Nations, *The Millennium Development Goals Report 2009* (New York: United Nations, 2009), p. 9.

5. Rachel Sabates-Wheeler, Stephen Devereux, and Anthony Hodges, "Taking the Long View: What Does a Child Focus Add to Social Protection?" *IDS Bulletin,* 40, no. 1 (2009): pp. 109–19.

6. Ben Watkins, "Alternative Methods for Targeting Social Assistance to Highly Vulnerable Groups" (Washington, DC: Kimetrica International, 2008), for the Technical Working Group on Social Assistance, Zambia, p. 6.

7. Tatiana Feitosa de Britto, "The Emergence and Popularity of Conditional Cash Transfers in Latin America." In *Social Protection for the Poor and Poorest*, edited by Armando Barrientos and David Hulme (Basingstoke, UK: Palgrave Macmillan, 2008), p. 187.

8. Sam Hickey, "Conceptualising the Politics of Social Protection in Africa." In Barrientos and Hulme, *Social Protection*, pp. 253–56.

9. Anthony Hodges et al., "Child Benefits and Poverty Reduction: Evidence from Mongolia's Child Money Programme," Working Paper MGSoc/2007/WP002 (Maastricht: School of Governance, Maastricht University, 2007).

10. Jonath Gelbach and Lant Pritchett, "More for the Poor Is Less for the Poor—The Politics of Targeting," Policy Research Working Paper 1799 (Washington, DC: World Bank, 1997), available at http://go.worldbank.org/9BTYD9ZMT0.

11. Stephen Devereux, "Social Protection and the Global Crisis" (Johannesburg: Regional Hunger and Vulnerability Programme, 2009), available at http://www.wahenga.net/index.php/views/comments_view/social_protection_and_the_global_crisis/.

12. Charles Knox, "Response to Social Protection and the Global Crisis" (Johannesburg: Regional Hunger and Vulnerability Programme, 2009), available at http://www.wahenga.net/index.php/views/comments_view/response_to_social_protection_and_the_global_crisis.

13. John Rook, "Targeting: The Debate Goes on But What Does It Mean in Practice?" (Johannesburg: Regional Hunger and Vulnerability Programme, 2009), available at http://www.wahenga.net/index.php/views/comments_view/targeting_the_debate_goes_on_but_what_does_it_mean_in_practice.

14. Ministry of Community Development and Social Services (Zambia), "Social Cash Transfer Scheme" (2007), available at http://www.socialcashtransfers-zambia.org/social_cash_transfers_zambia.php.

15. Frank Ellis, "'We Are All Poor Here': Economic Difference, Social Divisiveness, and Targeting Cash Transfers in Sub-Saharan Africa," Paper presented at the conference on "Social Protection for the Poorest in Africa: Learning from Experience," Kampala, Uganda (September 8–10, 2008).

16. Ellis, "We Are All Poor Here."

17. Sarah Levy with Carlos Barahona and Blessings Chinsinga, "Food Security, Social Protection, Growth and Poverty Reduction Synergies: The Starter Pack Programme in Malawi," *Natural Resource Perspectives* (London: Overseas Development Institute, 2004), p. 95.

18. Harry Mwamlima and Reagan Kaluluma, "Malawi's Director of Social Protection Responds to 'One out of Ten' Comment" (Johannesburg: Regional Hunger and Vulnerability Programme, 2008), available at http://www.wahenga.net/

index.php/views/comments_view/malawis_director_of_social_protection_
responds_to_one_out_of_ten_comment/. The whole debate can be found at http://
www.wahenga.net/index.php/wahenga_comments/.

19. Ellis, "We Are All Poor Here."

20. Watkins, "Alternative Methods," p. 11.

21. Candace Miller, Maxton Tsoka, and Kathryn Reichert, "Targeting Cash
to Malawi's Ultra Poor: A Mixed Methods Evaluation," Center for International
Health and Development, Boston University School of Public Health, and The
Centre for Social Research, University of Malawi (2008), available at http://child
researchpolicy.org/images/Cash_Targeting_Evaluation.pdf.

22. Frank Ellis, Stephen Devereux, and Philip White, *Social Protection in Africa*
(Cheltenham, UK and Northampton, MA: Edward Elgar, 2009), p. 50.

23. Candace Miller, "Economic Evaluation of the Mchinji Cash Transfer—
Preliminary Findings" (Boston: Boston University School of Public Health, 2009),
available at http://childresearchpolicy.org/images/Economic_Impacts_June_15.pdf.

7

Identifying Recipients

IN UGANDA IN THE LATE 1990S, ONE OF US (DH) WAS INVOLVED IN EXAM-ining a scheme to share the income from tourists visiting national parks with "poor neighboring communities." At Lake Mburo civil servants drew up a complex and highly logical geographic targeting system based on the population size of each neighboring parish and on social and economic in-dicators. The bigger the population and the poorer the social and eco-nomic indicators, the greater the grant the parish would receive. Perfectly logical, but the parish leaders rejected this idea unanimously and agreed that each parish would get the same size grant, regardless of population and poverty indicators. William Othello, a parish chairman, explained this to us: "If we go for their system, then who can count the population with so many people moving about, where do the poverty figures come from, and who can check the sums? We will all be claiming to have big popula-tions and some people might bribe the civil servants to increase their poverty figures. If we share the grants out equally, we can all see what is happening and we shall not start quarreling with each other." The civil ser-vants thought this "crazy and unfair" but had to give way.[1]

Dividing pots of money is fraught with difficulties under any circum-stances. The main objective of cash transfer programs is usually to reduce poverty and vulnerability, so there is a strong desire to reach the poorest and most vulnerable. But transparency, politics, and different views of what is "fair" all come into play.

This is a technically complex area. Different countries have used many different ways of setting eligibility criteria; none is perfect, so most countries use a mix of methods. In this chapter we look in considerable detail at the targeting alternatives and at the experiences of cash transfer programs. The "bottom line" is to maximize the amount of money going to the poorest and most vulnerable, but, as at Lake Mburo, the context is political and social.

Selection Strategies

There are five main types of selection strategies:

Categorical. Selection is based on categories of households or individuals that are closely correlated with poverty and vulnerability, such as children, older people, and adults with disabilities.

Geographic. Communities that have high (or higher than average) poverty incidence, which is typically determined on the basis of census or survey data, are selected.

Household or individual means test. The poor or poorest individuals or families are identified by some sort of externally set criteria.

Community-based targeting. Neighbors decide who in the community needs help the most.

Self-selection. People are guaranteed the right to work, usually at physical labor for a minimum wage, and choose whether to accept the offer.

As we will see below, each of these methods has distinct advantages and disadvantages. For example, targeting the poorest households is theoretically a more effective way to reduce poverty, but applying selection strategies based on an assessment of households or individuals can be time-consuming and may tempt potential beneficiaries to adapt their circumstances to ensure eligibility. Often two or more methods are used together. There are categorical non-contributory pensions in Mauritius and Lesotho, and Britain has a universal child benefit; in both cases, benefits go to everyone in the category, rich or poor. But most categorical benefits are also means-tested.

Indeed, as we were writing this book there was a debate in Britain, where one group maintained that the country could not afford the grant and that it should be means-tested so that it would go only to the poor. The Child Poverty Action Group rejected this, arguing that the take-up rate of the child benefit is an incredible 98% only because it goes to everyone, which means it is easy to claim and carries no stigma. But the critics respond that the state should not be supplying "middle-class welfare" by giving grants to families that do not need them and will spend the money on luxuries.[2]

South Africa is an example of combining targeting methods. It starts with categorical grants—pensions and child benefits—but then uses means tests to exclude the better off. The pension goes, in effect, to every person over 63 who is not already receiving a private or civil service pension, and it goes to more than 85% of older people. But the child benefit has more complex targeting. Families are divided into three groups: families living in rural areas, families living in urban areas in an "informal dwelling," and families living in permanent housing in urban areas. Those in the first two groups are seen as more in need of help, so the grant goes to families with a family income under R1100 ($110) per month. Families in the third group receive a grant only if family income is under R800 ($80). Thus this categorical child benefit has a geographic component and two means tests: income and what is known as a "proxy test" to measure assets—in this case, the quality of the house.

Three of the five strategies rely on the government choosing a set of people to receive the grant, and this is still the most common approach. The other two strategies we have cited do not involve government choice. One is community-based selection, and the other is self-selection, usually in the form of workfare. One of the largest cash transfer schemes is the National Employment Guarantee Scheme in India, which guarantees 100 days of employment on demand to unemployed heads of households in rural India.

Finally, there is the option of not targeting at all. One such method is to give everyone a small amount of money, known as a citizen's income or basic income grant. There has been a strong campaign for this in South Africa, Namibia is running a pilot, and it has been seriously discussed in Brazil; Alaska distributes oil revenue equally to everyone living in the state. Another alternative is subsidies, particularly for the purchase of fertilizer. None of these programs is well targeted on the poorest, but all three have important developmental implications and can gain political support.

Political and Practical

Targeting has both political and practical dimensions. If immediate poverty reduction is the goal, it makes sense to try to make transfers to those who need money most. Figure 7.1 presents the results of a modeling exercise for Uganda. Under the assumptions applied in this simulation (see the figure

**Figure 7.1 Poverty Reduction from
Grants Allocating 1% of GDP in Different Ways**

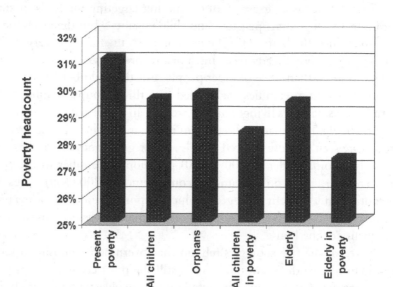

Note: These simulations using Uganda Household Survey data give grants worth 1% of GDP to different types of households. They assume perfect targeting and show the decrease in the percentage of people under the poverty line in each case.

Source: Uganda Social Protection Task Force, *Design of a Cash Transfer Pilot for Uganda, Final Report* (Kampala: Ministry of Gender, Labour and Social Development, 2007).

caption), either a child benefit or a pension will reduce poverty levels, and targeting the poor will reduce poverty further.

But targeting is complex and not always accurate, and it can be divisive. For example, excluded families may claim they are just as poor as included ones, leading to allegations of corruption, favoritism, or tribalism, as well as jealousy and even acts of sabotage. Targeting requires skilled administrative staff, who are more likely to exist in Latin America than in low-income countries in Africa. That staff must be paid, so targeting comes at a price. The greater the time and costs of targeting, the less funds remain in the budget for actual grants.

Finally, selection cannot be perfect. It is subject to "inclusion errors" or "leakage"—giving grants to people who do not have a right to them—and to "exclusion errors" or "under-coverage"—omitting from eligibility people who should receive the grant. To reduce errors, more sophisticated methods can be employed, but they are harder to implement, and they may lead to some of the poorest people being excluded because they do not have the right documents. How many people who should receive the grant can we afford to miss, and how many can be included who do not qualify?

A study[3] of a large number of targeted interventions found that of 33 cash transfers the investigators could evaluate, 20 seemed to have effective targeting, with poor people receiving at least 30% more money than they would have received from a universal grant. Of those interventions, 11— more than half—were child benefits, which seem from this study to be the most effective way of targeting poverty. Of those 11 child benefits, 8 also involved either a means test or geographic targeting. The effectiveness of child benefits should not be surprising, given that half the world's poor are children.[4] Of the remaining 9 successes, 8 involved means testing. The other important lesson was that a skilled civil service helps; half of the successes were in Europe. But others were administered in Jamaica, Costa Rica, Indonesia, Mexico, and Nicaragua, so it seems that developing countries can do successful targeting.

But it is also clear from the study that successful targeting is difficult. Of the remaining 13 programs, 3 were very regressive, meaning that the better off gained; the worst was a Vietnam pension program in which the poor gained only half of what they would have received as a universal benefit. Six had an impact similar to a universal benefit, and another 4 gave between 10% and 30% more to the poor than a universal benefit (probably not enough to cover the additional costs of targeting). Pensions proved very mixed; 3 of the top 20 were pensions, yet 6 of the poorly targeted 13 were also pensions. The same study notes that in South Africa, "targeting the elderly is an effective method for reaching poor children."[5]

CATEGORICAL—EASIER, BUT WHO IS LEFT OUT?

Traditionally, societies have readily accepted a responsibility to older people, children, and those who cannot work; such recipients are "deserving" of help, and all of us were young once, hope to be old, and fear we might be injured or disabled. Categorical grants are politically popular; "feeding children," "supporting the elderly," and "caring for the disabled" are ideal sound bites for politicians. But they are also very practical in terms of operation and outcomes. Identifying children, the elderly, and the physically disabled is relatively simple and is transparent to local communities. Investing in children to improve their health and increase their education makes them more productive adults. Because people die at different ages, collective pension systems reduce the risk that we will outlive our resources, and thus they reduce the amount that people must save or invest to provide for themselves in old age.

Poor people in developing countries have more children in the hope that at least one will survive to care for them in their old age.[6] Historically, state pensions have reduced fertility rates, because parents no longer need to depend on their children in old age. This, in turn, makes it possible to invest more in each child, thus boosting survival rates and education levels, so lower fertility rates promote broader economic development. State old-age benefits have existed for more than a century, but they were traditionally linked to payments made by employed workers. This discriminates against women and people in the informal sector who are not in pension-linked official jobs, and awareness of this inequity has led to a shift to categorical social pensions not linked to individual contributions over a working life.

Categorical grants, particularly pensions and child benefits, are easier to administer and are seen as fair. They also cover most low-income families. Combining grants to children, the old, and people with disabilities could reach a large majority of poor households, and there is convincing evidence from a range of countries to show that pensions—at least those paid to women—are used in large part to support children.

"Categorical targeting has the considerable added advantage of establishing a right to the social transfer for all those who meet the simple criterion that defines the category (such as an age threshold in the case of social pensions). Moreover, in the case of social pensions, social invidiousness does not occur because all citizens understand that if and when they reach the age threshold, they, too, will be entitled to the benefit," declares Frank Ellis in his study "We Are All Poor Here."[7] In countries where citizens do not trust the state or the civil service, most people prefer simple and "fair" targeting approaches to a theoretically better technical system that is controlled—and possibly manipulated—by bureaucrats and elites.

However, all studies show that not all households with older people are poor; categorical grants may give money to the children of the wealthy, and they exclude poor families without children or old people. South Africa excludes from social pensions the very small proportion of people who already have a private or civil service pension, and it also excludes the better off from the child benefit.

Categorical grants (those that go to everyone in the category, such as all elderly people) are the easiest to administer and the most transparent.

And they do effectively target the poorest if all three—pension, child benefit, and disability grant—are used in combination. But this can be an expensive mix. One way to reduce cost is to means-test the benefit. Another alternative is to try to target poorer families; broadly based family grants such as Bolsa Família in Brazil and Oportunidades in Mexico may be better at giving poorer people more money. Both face problems, as discussed below. But that takes us back to the political question of the previous chapter: Does one give a small amount of money to many people or try to give a larger amount to those who are poorer?

Larry Willmore, of the International Institute for Applied Systems Analysis (IIASA) in Austria, argues against means-testing pensions; rather, he supports giving smaller pensions to all elderly instead of larger pensions to the poorest, on both political and practical grounds.[8] First, such programs are politically attractive because they provide a guarantee of a basic income for *all* voters' old age, and for that of their parents and friends. Starting with a modest universal pension, the pressure from voters is to increase the size of the pension, as has happened in New Zealand and Mauritius. "Means tests promise fiscal savings, but tightly targeted benefits lack political appeal, so a means-tested benefit runs the risk of becoming smaller and smaller relative to wages and per capita GDP," Willmore warns. The second argument for avoiding means tests is that they send the wrong signals to workers. They discourage low-income workers from saving for their old age and from continuing to work, even on a part-time basis, beyond normal retirement age.

Geographic Choices

Choosing the three categories of children, the elderly, and people with disabilities is effective because it is relatively simple but includes most poor people. However, it spreads the money thinly and includes the better off in those categories. An alternative relatively simple method is to try to pick out the areas of the country with the highest concentrations of poor or marginalized people. Again, this gives grants to the better off living in those areas, but geographic targeting proves to be more accurate than one might expect. A study of Zambian targeting found that geographic targeting based on census wards is cheapest and most effective, even assuming the need to collect the sample data.[9] El Salvador opted for geographic targeting, simply selecting the 100 poorest municipalities and then all households with children.[10] Some countries, such as Malawi, use geographic criteria to pick the poorest places and then expanding to other areas. But the obvious objection to geographic targeting is that it excludes poor people in better-off areas, who can be a politically and socially important group. In Africa, it is often argued that rural people are poorer than those in urban areas. However, existing poverty measures are being criticized for not taking into account some of the higher costs of urban life, such as the costs of paying rent, buying water, and traveling to work. Also, poor urban youth can be a volatile and politically important group.

IDENTIFYING THE POOREST

Whether or not categorical and geographic criteria are used, many programs also try to identify poorer families. Informalization means that people's income is often very irregular and seasonal. It is difficult to take into account the small amounts that may be earned by children and elderly people, and it is hard to quantify the food that people raise for themselves.

A key question is how narrowly the cash transfer is to be targeted. Drawing boundary lines proves difficult, and there is an incentive to misreport income on simple means tests. Planners have looked for other ways to identify those most in need of grants, such as using "proxy means tests"—that is, indicators based on household characteristics other than income. The indicators used include the size and quality of the house, assets such a radios and bicycles, family size, number of children, and number of adults capable of working. Proxy means tests have another advantage in that they enable program managers to rank-order potential beneficiaries from poorest to moderately poor, and thus reach the poorest. Proxy means tests are used extensively and successfully in middle-income countries, but applying them is more challenging in low-income environments.

Proxy means tests have two other advantages because they are often based on assets and family members, rather than on income. Family incomes fluctuate, and it is not sensible or feasible to be taking people near the boundary on and off the list of beneficiaries. And there is the danger of an income line becoming a barrier and disincentive—the "benefit trap." If an income threshold is strictly enforced, people will not take day labor or small jobs that might push them over the line, causing them to lose more in benefits than they might gain from a week's work. But small shifts in income do not change the proxy values and thus do not lead to benefit loss.

Oportunidades and its predecessor Progresa in Mexico use a complex proxy means test. Once a community is selected via geographic criteria, a household census is conducted, and data are collected on household composition; literacy and education of members; economic activity and diverse sources of income; presence of handicapped persons; dwelling characteristics and availability of services; and possession of assets, including land and animals. A statistical technique is next used (separately for each geographic region) to identify the characteristics that best discriminate between poor and non-poor households, and an index is developed. Households are then identified along values of this index, and those below a predetermined threshold are selected as beneficiaries. Community validation is employed to adjust the final lists of beneficiaries.[11]

In Zambia, although geographic targeting worked best, the next best option was a complex proxy model that used six variables: household size, the number of orphans, the number of disabled people, the household head's age, the household head's education, and whether the household head is a woman. This model selected 61% of households below the poverty line.[12] World Bank studies found that proxy means tests excluded a quarter of the extreme poor in Panama but only 5% in Ecuador,[13] a very accurate outcome. Another study found that proxy means tests accurately identify extremely poor households, but that they make more errors identifying moderately poor households, and that the advantages over simple geographic targeting are small.[14] Recent studies in Bangladesh showed that a relatively simply proxy means test—land area, type of shelter, and main occupation—identified 95% of the income-poor.[15]

A broader study of targeting found that a whole range of targeting methods, including proxy means tests, were little better than just asking about household consumption, defined simply as the ability to purchase goods through markets. Other indicators may be better, but the targeting errors (both exclusion and inclusion errors) are highly concentrated around the poverty line, so they make little real difference to overall welfare. Thus more complex systems may not be worth the effort.[16]

The debate on narrow versus broad targeting continues. South Africa and Brazil attempt only to exclude the better off, and grants go to a majority of people in many areas. They have found that self-declaration of income, with limited verification and a measure of social control caused by better-off people not wanting to be seen to take the grant, has proved acceptably accurate. Mexico, Brazil, and Chile all have family grants that are considered to be quite well targeted on the poorest. An International Poverty Centre study concluded that "the Brazilian programmes' targeting results are almost as efficient as their counterparts in neighboring countries, frequently cited as best practices. Mexico and Chile, which use extensive and thorough questionnaires to identify beneficiaries, have reached an outcome similar to the highly decentralised targeting process used in Brazil."[17] Compared to Bolsa Família, Mexico's Oportunidades reaches fewer of those who should qualify but excludes more of those who should not. That is, Mexico has a higher exclusion error, or under-coverage, but a lower inclusion error, or leakage—the percentage of grants going to people who have no right to receive them.[18] However, the leakage of Brazil's Bolsa Família and the social pension, Benefício de Prestação Continuada (BPC) goes to families living near the poverty line,[19] and they are also poor.

Black Boxes and Other Problems

Although proxies have the potential to select those most in need, there are a range of problems with indicators. As the Lake Mburo, Uganda, example at the beginning of the chapter showed, a formula administered by outsiders is sometimes seen as an intrusive and impersonal "black box" that people do not understand and thus do not consider fair. Transparency can undermine a proxy means test because if households know the indicators, they can manipulate the results—for example, by hiding a radio or bicycle; thus the criteria for proxy means tests are sometimes kept secret. In Mexico beneficiaries and non-beneficiaries both attribute selection to luck or a lottery, and non-beneficiaries hope they will be luckier next time. "Some beneficiaries expressed guilt or discomfort because of their better luck."[20]

Michelle Adato did focus-group interviews with 70 communities in six states early in the development of the Mexican program.[21] She concludes that "the social cost of targeting at the household level may be high in these communities where the distinctions made by the program between poor and extreme poor, or needing assistance and not needing assistance, are not apparent in the view of the people who live there, who see themselves as 'all poor' and 'all in need.'"

Mexico has a skilled and experienced civil service, and the program has broad support, so these initial problems serve as a caution to any country trying to introduce a proxy means test. Nicaragua first did geographic targeting and then, within selected communities, used a proxy means test to identify beneficiaries. But that second stage had to be abandoned because it was widely perceived as unfair and created tensions in the community.[22] The proxy means test was not understood. One person in a geographically targeted area said, "Some people wonder why they weren't targeted even though they live in this same area. So we tell them that the Bible says that many are called but few are chosen."

Mongolia had to abandon its proxy means test and move to a universal child benefit.[23] The original proxy formula used 11 indicators ranging from household members to livestock and transport. But it was extremely inaccurate, and officials and applicants manipulating the process made matters worse. Leakage was 51%, so more than half of recipient children were not poor, and under-coverage—the proportion of poor children missed—was 21%. Donors wanted to improve the proxy formula and target more effectively, but the government instead decided to switch to a universal benefit, which increased leakage only to 58% but cut under-coverage to 8%.

Finally, proxy means tests are based on surveys, and this immediately introduces problems. In Vietnam, households colluded so that one could obtain a grant, and then the grant was shared; conflicts subsequently arose when the recipient household failed to honor its part of the bargain.[24] And proxy indicators can also be subjective; that is, responses may depend in part on how the question is asked. A Boston University team commented that "we found households that consumed pumpkin at mealtime but said they had no meals because, for Malawians, pumpkin alone does not count as a meal, which contrasts with households that do not even have pumpkin."[25]

South Africa Struggling to Target

South Africa has one of the largest and most effective social grants programs, but it is not without problems. It starts with categorical grants, and then its child benefit and pension are means-tested. But this has proved not to be straightforward. The child support is triply targeted; it is means-tested and also determined by geography (urban–rural) and a proxy (quality of housing). It currently reaches 55% of all children and has been highly effective as an anti-poverty and development program, as we have noted in previous chapters. But its targeting proved extremely controversial. South Africa found that means testing is extremely difficult when large numbers of people are working in the informal sector or are involved in casual or seasonal work. Less than one-half of 1% of applicants are rejected,[26] and there is substantial underestimation or under-declaration of income; however, most of those included incorrectly are quite close to the poverty line. On the other hand, a national survey of caregivers in 2006 shows that a significant number who did qualify had not applied because they were employed or thought they were not poor enough; the study argued that they had been put off by the complex means test.[27] Table 7.1 (where mn denotes "million") sets out some of the key issues.

Table 7.1 South Africa Child Benefit, 2007

Total children under 14	13.4 mn
Eligible to receive grant	8.3 mn
Percent eligible to receive grant	62%
Children receiving grant	5.8 mn
of whom eligible	4.5 mn
of whom ineligible	1.3 mn
Inclusion error = wrongly in, as percentage of those with grant	22%
Exclusion error = missed out, as percentage of those eligible	45%

Source: Michael Samson et al., "Review of Targeting Mechanisms, Means Tests and Values for South Africa's Social Grants—Final Report" (Cape Town: Economic Policy Research Institute, 2007).

Another issue involves farm workers.[28] If farm workers are paid the minimum wage, then their children are not eligible for the child support grant. Most farm workers are seasonal laborers in places where no other jobs are available. Yet South Africa does not allow their seasonal income to be averaged across the year, which would take them below the threshold, and instead requires farm workers to reapply each time the season ends, which is complex and time-consuming. Another problem is that many farms do not pay the minimum wage but are unwilling to admit it, making verification of income difficult.

South Africa has trouble with both its geographic (urban–rural) and its proxy (house with brick, concrete, or asbestos walls) indicators. A study by the Children's Institute of Cape Town University found that within the East London social security office, even senior officials disagreed about the definitions. The district office in Atlantis disagreed with the provincial department about whether farm villages (called *dorps*) were rural or urban.[29] The government agency Statistics South Africa abandoned an attempt to make the distinction between urban and rural explicit at a detailed level.[30]

The other issue for South Africa is that targeting makes the cash transfer process very bureaucratic, with 15 different social security officials involved in each decision. Applicants have to present a range of documents, including marriage and divorce certificates, proof of income, identity documents, evidence of occupancy of a house, and often bank statements, pay slips, rent books, and a host of other financial papers as part of the means test. Some offices require documents to be certified.[31] Collecting all the documents is difficult and time-consuming. A study in Western Cape province showed that it typically required more than four visits to benefit and other offices and the police, more than 12 hours of time, and R27 ($3) for travel costs and photocopying.[32] Lack of documents seems to be one of the main reasons why so many poor families do not claim the benefit.

South Africa's other grants also have problems. Its pension has a means test, but over time it has been considerably simplified. Originally there was an asset test, but this was dropped as too complex. Both child benefit and pension means tests are now being less rigidly enforced, which has increased the take-up by those who are eligible.[33] And there is a problem of corruption. One study found that in Mount Fere, Eastern Cape, "it appeared to be common knowledge" that it was possible to buy a disability grant.[34]

ASKING THE COMMUNITY

People tend to know their neighbors, so the community is often used as a way of checking eligibility, and many systems publish the list of recipients. For example, China's Di Bao program posts the names of all recipients in a public place for two weeks. In Bangladesh, BRAC's Targeting the Ultra-Poor program has the community draw up an initial list, to which the NGO then applies a means test.

Asking people to identify the most impoverished in their community had seemed a good way to target, but the results have proved less successful. Wahenga, the Regional Hunger and Vulnerability Programme in southern Africa, says baldly, "community based targeting of the poorest does not work."[35]

Malawi has had several pilot grants that aimed to find the 10% who were both ultra-poor and labor constrained. Recipients are selected through community-based targeting. A Community Social Protection Committee (CSPC) is elected and is trained by the District Social Cash Transfer Secretariat (DSCT) to rank households from the most to the least destitute. A community meeting is held to discuss the rankings, and the District Social Welfare Officer (DSWO) must then approve the list. The Mchinji district 2007 pilot was evaluated by a Boston University team headed by Candace Miller. It found that only two-thirds of eligible families were included (the exclusion error was 37%).[36] In terms of inclusion error, 24% of recipients did not meet the labor constraint criterion.[37]

Households in Mchinji were surveyed, and 32% said the program was not fair. Respondents maintained that people who were ineligible or wealthy were receiving the transfer, that too many people who are eligible were left out, and that nepotism was an important problem. There were particular complaints that benefits were given to families linked to chiefs and members of the CSPC.[38] An explicit program guideline is that village leaders are not allowed to serve on CSPCs because of the unfair influence they might have on committees. Nevertheless, headmen included themselves or their deputies.[39] The Boston University team notes that "we found cases where village leaders influenced CSPCs to include their family members" in the recipient lists. In total, 9% of household members in recipient households were "ghosts"; some households listed as many as five "ghost" children and two "ghost" adults or fake members. CSPC members themselves see a high risk of corruption and comment on the lack of monitoring.[40]

Another study in Malawi found communities unwilling to pass what they saw as life-or-death judgments on their neighbors; they said targeting went against the traditional spirit of *umodzi* (togetherness). Community-based targeting also led to charges of witchcraft and bred suspicion, hatred, and corruption.

Targeting costs 8% of the Malawi cash transfer program, and the Miller studies show that it is not enough. And this is just the cost to the government; it does not include community time. In Zambia the average committee member spent 60 hours on targeting. Zambia and Malawi pilots have also included substantial NGO time, which has not been included in the costs, and some district officials' time tends to be excluded as well. In a study of targeting in Zambia, Ben Watkins[41] notes that "no method is both cheap and accurately selected the poorest households." He argues that there is no reason why communities should be any better than outsiders at observing income and asset levels and that outsiders are actually less likely to exhibit bias and favoritism. To prevent bias, there are always more community members involved than outside evaluators, so community-based targeting is "generally more expensive than administrative targeting . . . because it involves more training, more steps, and more people. Unless community time is a great deal less valuable than official time, CBT [community-based targeting] will be more costly" than other targeting options. Thus it should be used only if it is significantly more accurate.[42]

In Zambia a study of community-based targeting in two districts revealed huge problems. In Chipata district, half of those targeted were non-poor, and 30% of the population believes that powerful households had preferential access. In Kazungula district, the poverty levels of the chosen group were no different from those of people who were not selected. In Kalomo district, community-based targeting was combined with proxy and administrative elements, and there were very high supervision costs. This approach was better at targeting the neediest, but despite high supervision, there was also evidence of elite capture, and high-income households were included. In Zambia, 87% of Community Welfare Assistance Committee (CWAC) members said they came under pressure from family or friends, and 47% experienced pressure from headmen or local chairpeople.[43] And when the Kolomo program was expanded with less intensive supervision and fewer external resources, it proved to be less accurate in targeting the poorest.[44] In Malawi, village headmen took a cut from recipients' cash transfers, justifying this practice by claiming they should be paid for the time they spent organizing the program.[45]

Discretion Begets Corruption

Systems that are characterized by a high degree of administrative discretion or based on small differences or survey data are all subject to manipulation. Political and social elites can include their own friends and family. Party membership cards can be required. And bribes can be demanded. In Varanasi district, Uttar Pradesh, older people applying for the pension of 125 rupees ($2) per month reported that bribes are often expected and paid at various stages of the application process. With 85% illiteracy among older people in this area, the requirement for written application forms and supporting documents presents a considerable hurdle and creates opportunities for manipulation.[46] In the late 1990s, in response to the Asian financial crisis, Indonesia introduced a scholarship program for poor children. But as a study found in West Java and Lombok, the children who received scholarships were from well-off families. "The poor were unaware of the criteria by which children were being selected. Village and school authorities told them only that the lists of recipients was decided 'from above' (by authorities outside the village) or that their children were not clever enough to qualify. In reality the Social Safety Net scholarships had no merit-based criteria and were meant to help the neediest of children."[47]

ALTERNATIVES TO ADMINISTRATIVE CHOICE

All of the targeting systems discussed so far involve some degree of administrative and government choice. Three alternatives that do not involve administrative choice, but have other shortcomings, are also in use.

For centuries, projects have been created to give work to willing laborers, and this practice continues in many parts of the world. Often called workfare, it satisfies a basic demand of the better off that the poor should work for their money, and it is self-targeting because people have the opportunity to choose whether to do hard labor for a minimum wage. The most important change in policy, which makes these programs equivalent to cash transfers, is that India and Ethiopia are guaranteeing work to anyone who wants it. Both of these programs are very large. India's National Rural Employment Guarantee Scheme (NREGS) guarantees each rural household 100 days of unskilled wage labor per year. It involves 44 million households as a cost of $4 billion per year. Ethiopia's Productive Safety Nets Programme (PSNP) has reached more than 7 million people with an annual budget of $500 million (this is 2% of GDP, which makes PSNP the largest program in Sub-Saharan Africa, after South Africa's).

The shift to *guaranteeing* work means that these schemes offer the advantages of other cash transfers: The assured additional income not only improves the diet but also makes investment and risk taking possible. And they are self-targeting (available to all without any administrative targeting), which ensures fairness. Labor schemes also have one more general benefit. They effectively set a wage floor, which can buoy up the very low wages paid in the informal sector and for day labor, because otherwise people will choose the government scheme instead. But labor schemes have four problems that mean they are less widely used: (1) They have very high design, administration, and supervision costs. (2) They specifically exclude those who cannot work—the young, old, ill, and disabled, as well as mothers of small children—who are often a target of cash transfers. (3) There is an opportunity cost; working on labor schemes means forgoing the often small income from other activities. (4) Although they are self-targeting, they are not well targeted on the poor. In Amhara, Ethiopia, vulnerable non-poor and moderately poor households were more likely to be included than the poorest.[48] In Maharastra, India, the poor made up only half the workers, and only 15% of poor adults participated.[49]

Both Ethiopia and India have faced problems with slow payment; payments were delayed an average of 39 days in Ethiopia[50] and up to four months in Andra Pradesh, India.[51] If you are hungry, that's a long time to wait.

Administration costs and costs to the poor themselves are high. Work sites are often far from where poor people live, imposing hidden transportation costs. A World Bank modeling exercise for India compared a workfare scheme with a universal grant that would give the same amount to everyone.[52] The study found that an untargeted grant to everyone "has a greater impact on poverty" than a labor scheme that spends the same amount of money. "The greater cost in terms of leakage to the non-poor from untargeted transfers is not enough to outweigh the extra costs (to both the poor directly and the government)" of labor schemes. Yet just as in many technical arguments surrounding grants, the finding may be accurate but politics may be more important, and in India political support is much greater for "workfare" than for unconditional grants.

Basic Income Grant

The idea of providing a minimum or basic income to everyone, unconditionally and as a right, has been around for at least two centuries without gaining much traction. But the concept of a Basic Income Grant (BIG) has been taken most seriously in South Africa and neighboring Namibia. High unemployment led the Congress of South Africa Trade Unions (COSATU) to back the BIG, and it has gained support from government commissions.[53] The government-appointed Taylor Committee[54] looked at a grant at the destitution level, R100 (then $9) per month, going to everyone, rich and poor, and found that "a Basic Income Grant is most able to eliminate destitution and have a developmental impact on the poorest." And the committee called for a "solidarity grant," effectively a BIG, to go to all South Africans within three years. This was not accepted by the government. The BIG has also been promoted in Namibia, where a three-year (2007–2010) pilot project is being conducted. Two issues are central to the debate: cost and the ethics of giving a grant to the rich. Proponents argue that income tax and value-added tax (sales tax) can be adjusted to take the grant back from the better off, and perhaps to pay for the whole program. A "solidarity grant" for all can be financed by a "solidarity tax" on the rich.

Subsidies

Subsidies, typically on the purchase of food or fuel, have been popular with many governments, but they tend to benefit the better off who consume more; cash transfers benefit those who are poorer or at least benefit everyone equally (in the case of categorical or universal benefits). In several countries, including Indonesia and Mexico, cash transfers have been funded by ending regressive subsidies. Subsidies direct consumers toward certain goods, whereas cash transfers enable people to make their own choices.

Malawi's fertilizer subsidy scheme has been widely discussed. First introduced for the 2004–2005 season, it dramatically increased maize production and turned Malawi from an importer of maize into an exporter. The program is intended to give able-bodied farmers who cannot afford fertilizer two vouchers authorizing the purchase of 50-kg bags of fertilizer for MK 950 (about $7).[55] The program reaches 1.7 million households; 70% of Malawi smallholders receive the vouchers.[56] In 2007–2008, the subsidized price was 28% of the market price. The cost rose from 1.4% of GDP in 2004–2005 to 2.8% of GDP in 2007–2008; unusually high fertilizer prices made it 4.7% of GDP in 2008–2009.

A study of 170 households in Mlomba, Machinga district, for the 2007–2008 maize season found that the average subsidy was MK 2871 ($20) but the average increase in income was MK 5096 ($36), which meant that household income increased by MK 2225 ($16) more than the subsidy cost.[57] The Mlomba study argues that without the subsidy, few households would have been able to buy fertilizer. But even at the subsidized price, the poorest households could not use all the vouchers; in the poorest 40% of the households, 70% used only one voucher and 19% used only half a voucher. All farmers gained something; better-off farmers gained more, but this is a poor area, so "better-off" farmers are still poor.

Nicaragua has a similar program, Zero Hunger, which gives farmers a loan of $1,500 to buy animals and feed and to plant fruit trees. To participate, however, households must have 1.4 hectares (3.5 acres) of land, a condition that excludes many poor Nicaraguans.[58]

There is a potential link between Malawi's fertilizer subsidy and its cash transfer program. Fertilizer vouchers go to households with farms, whereas the cash transfer goes to ultra-poor households without adequate labor. Thus the cash transfer goes to households without farms, and for those with farms, it provides the means to purchase fertilizer and hire labor. Thus the two programs can be seen as compatible, not competitive.

MAKING CHOICES: KEY ISSUES

Cash transfers inevitably involve choices about who should receive money and who should not. Should the grants be concentrated on a small percentage of households or thinly spread across more families? This choice is highly political, but it is also about allocation of scarce resources, administrative capacity, and goals. Fairness and transparency are always important. And the human right to a decent standard of living is an idea that is increasingly coming to the fore.

Categorical grants—grants to children, to the elderly, and to disabled people—satisfy a broadly felt social responsibility to support the young, the old, and those too weak to support themselves. They speak directly to us, because we all have been young and hope to be old. They also have the obvious advantages of being seen as fair and transparent and of being easier to administer. Most poor households contain elderly people and/or children, and there is strong evidence that grants are shared throughout the family. Political pressure can sometimes push the payment level high enough to provide real lifelines for poor families, and wealth cutoffs can be introduced. Thus there are strong administrative, social, and political reasons for preferring categorical grants.

However, categorical grants face two interrelated problems. First, not all poor adults live in households with children or older people, so they miss out on the grants. Second, categorical grants give money to better-off people who may not be as needy as others who are not receiving grants, and money is spread across the entire category of people instead of being given to the poorest. Because children in such better-off homes receive a child benefit, those in poorer homes receive less. Categorical grants can have wealth cutoffs, as in South Africa, to exclude those who manifestly do not need the grant. Many countries have opted to target the grants on smaller numbers of people, who are seen as most needy or most likely to benefit—especially when foreign aid is involved. Proxy means tests require a civil service that can do good surveys and administer complex systems, but at their best, such tests can better identify the poorest. However, one study of Africa argued that "some broad targeting measures, such as targeting rural children only, give results almost as good as income-linked targeting and, given their low administration costs, are to be preferred."[59]

The simplest choice is geographic: selecting the poorest wards or districts. But that excludes poor people elsewhere. There are other simpler choices. South Africa's social pension excludes those with other pensions. Brazil's Bolsa Família tries to exclude the better off and expects people to identify themselves; it largely trusts people and makes only the most limited checks, and research suggests that people have responded to that show of trust by not registering if they do not need the grant.

Other countries have tried to target more precisely and often to select smaller groups, hoping to make spending more effective and efficient in reducing poverty. Various methods have been used, including simple means tests, simple proxy tests based on characteristics such as housing quality, more complex proxy means tests, and additional requirements such as too few able-bodied adults to support the family. Means testing is difficult to do accurately, and proxies are not straightforward: Is a family counted as having a radio if it has no batteries and so does not work? Furthermore, people's income and assets are on a continuum without sharp dividing lines, and a person's income rank can change dramatically when a job is gained or lost, or when there is a good crop or poor rains.

Each option has advantages and problems. Four factors come into play in targeting choices, and they are different in each country:

ADMINISTRATIVE CAPACITY: Can the civil service carry out more complex targeting, and can it be trusted to act honestly and objectively?

GOALS: Is the program just a safety net, or is it to be broader and more rights-based? Are other goals coming into play? For example, giving a higher priority to gender might raise the importance of a universal pension because of the way women are discriminated against in work-based pensions. An emphasis on trying to reduce the intergenerational transmission of poverty and on building human capital will give priority to children over other groups.

INCOME DISTRIBUTION plays a central role. If nearly everyone is poor and there is little difference within the poorest half or two-thirds of the population, then strict targeting will be inaccurate and unpopular, and it also is not likely to meet program goals. However, if there is a clearly identifiable poor group, it is sensible to target.

POPULAR PERCEPTION: The public's sense of fairness plays a role, as do electoral judgments about what will be popular with voters, and elite opinions matter.

Deciding who is to receive a cash transfer—and thus who will not—will always be fraught with difficulty. Each country will need to look at a host of factors, make its own choices, and design its own program, and then it must be willing to modify that program in response to subsequent events and oucomes. But a decade of development and the very wide range of choices made by different countries offer a wealth of experience to draw on. Targeting techniques have been finely honed, and the political tradeoffs are better understood. Perhaps most important, countries are learning to mix and match, choosing several targeting techniques and combining them in ways that satisfy local conditions—and thus ensuring that millions of poor people (and their children) benefit from cash transfers.

NOTES

1. David Hulme and Mark Infield, "Park-People Relationships: A Study of Lake Mburo National Park, Uganda." In *African Wildlife & Livelihoods: The Promise and Performance of Community Conservation,* edited by David Hulme and Marshall Murphree (Oxford: James Currey, 2001).

2. See, for example, Kate Green, "Means Testing Child Benefits Will Hit the Poor, Not the Rich," *Guardian,* London, September 30, 2009.

3. David Coady, Margaret Grosh, and John Hoddinott, "Targeting Outcomes Redux" (Washington, DC: IFPRI, 2002), available at http://www.ifpri.org/divs/fcnd/dp/papers/fcndp144.pdf.

4. Carol Bellamy, "Commentary: The 6 Billionth Baby," in *The Progress of Nations 1999* (New York: UNICEF, 1999). Carol Bellamy was then executive director of UNICEF.

5. Coady, Grosh, and Hoddinott, "Targeting Outcomes Redux."

6. Stephen Kidd, "Equal Pensions, Equal Rights: Achieving Universal Pension Coverage for Older Women and Men in Developing Countries" (London: HelpAge International).

7. Frank Ellis, "'We Are All Poor Here': Economic Difference, Social Divisiveness, and Targeting Cash Transfers in Sub-Saharan Africa," Paper presented at the conference on "Social Protection for the Poorest in Africa: Learning from Experience," Kampala, Uganda, September 8–10, 2008.

8. Larry Willmore, "Universal Pensions for Developing Countries," *World Development,* 35, no. 1 (2007): 24–51.

9. Ben Watkins, "Alternative Methods for Targeting Social Assistance to Highly Vulnerable Groups" (Washington, DC: Kimetrica International, for the Technical Working Group on Social Assistance, Zambia, 2008), pp. 24, 45.

10. Jennifer Yablonski with Michael O'Donnell, *Lasting Benefits: The Role of Cash Transfers in Tackling Child Mortality* (London: Save the Children, 2009), available at http://www.savethechildren.org.uk/en/docs/Lasting_Benefits.pdf.

11. Michelle Adato, *The Impact of PROGRESA on Community Social Relationships: Final Report* (Washington, DC: IFPRI, 2000), available at http://www.ifpri.org/sites/default/files/publications/adato_community.pdf.

12. Watkins, "Alternative Methods," pp. 24, 45.

13. Ariel Fiszbein and Norbert Schady, *Conditional Cash Transfers: Reducing Present and Future Poverty* (Washington, DC: World Bank, 2009), pp. 76–77.

14. Emmanuel Skoufias, Benjamin Davis, and Sergio de la Vega, "Targeting the Poor in Mexico: An Evaluation of the Selection of Households for

PROGRESA" (Washington, DC: IFPRI, 2001), available at http://www
.ifpri.org/divs/fcnd/dp/papers/fcndp103.pdf.

15. Sharifa Begum and Binayak Sen, "Maternal Health, Child Well-being
and Intergenerationally Transmitted Chronic Poverty: Does Women's Agency Matter?" Working Paper 8 (Manchester, UK: Chronic Poverty Research Centre, 2005).

16. Emmanuel Skoufias and David Coady, "Are the Welfare Losses from Imperfect Targeting Important?" (Washington, DC: IFPRI, 2001), available at
http://www.ifpri.org/divs/fcnd/dp/papers/fcndp125.pdf.

17. Marcelo Medeiros, Tatiana Britto, and Fábio Veras Soares, "Targeted
Cash Transfer Programmes in Brazil: BPC and the Bolsa Família," Working Paper
46 (Brasilia: International Poverty Centre, 2008).

18. Fábio Veras Soares, Rafael Perez Ribas, and Rafael Guerreiro Osório, "Evaluating the Impact of Brazil's Bolsa Família: Cash Transfer Programmes in Comparative Perspective," *IPC Evaluation Note 1* (Brasilia: International Poverty Centre,
2007).

19. Fabio Veras Soares et al., "Cash Transfer Programmes in Brazil: Impacts on
Inequality and Poverty," Working Paper 21 (Brasilia: UNDP International Poverty
Centre, 2006).

20. Adato, *The Impact*.

21. Adato, *The Impact*.

22. Michelle Adato and Terry Roopnaraine, "A Social Analysis of the Red de
Protección Social (RPS) in Nicaragua" (Washington, DC: IFPRI, 2004).

23. Anthony Hodges et al., "Child Benefits and Poverty Reduction: Evidence
from Mongolia's Child Money Programme," Working Paper MGSoc/2007/
WP002 (Maastricht: School of Governance, Maastricht University, 2007).

24. Peter Chaudhry, "Unconditional Direct Cash Transfers to the Very Poor
in Central Vietnam," Paper presented at the conference "What Works for the Poorest?" (BRAC and CPRC), December 3, 2006, Dhaka, Bangladesh.

25. Candace Miller, Maxton Tsoka, and Kathryn Reichert, "Targeting Report—External Evaluation of the Mchinji Social Cash Transfer Pilot" (Boston,
MA: Center for International Health and Development, Boston University School
of Public Health, and The Centre for Social Research, University of Malawi,
2008), available at http://childresearchpolicy.org/images/Targeting_Evaluation_
Final_August.pdf.

26. Solange Rosa, Annie Leatt, and Katharine Hall, "Does the Means Justify
the End? Targeting the Child Support Grant" (Cape Town: Children's Institute,
University of Cape Town, 2005).

27. Michael Samson et al., "Review of Targeting Mechanisms, Means Tests
and Values for South Africa's Social Grants—Final Report" (Cape Town: Economic
Policy Research Institute, 2007).

28. Rosa, Leatt, and Hall, "Does the Means Justify the End?"

29. Rosa, Leatt, and Hall, "Does the Means Justify the End?"

30. Michael Samson et al., "Final Report: The Social and Economic Impact of South Africa's Social Security System," Report commissioned by the South Africa Department of Social Development, EPRI Research Paper 37 (Cape Town: Economic Policy Research Institute, 2004), available at http://www.epri.org.za/rp37.htm, p. 9.

31. Rosa, Leatt, and Hall, "Does the Means Justify the End?"

32. Debbie Budlender, Solange Rosa, and Katharine Hall, "At All Costs? Applying the Means Test for the Child Support Grant" (Cape Town: Children's Institute and Centre for Actuarial Research, University of Cape Town, 2005).

33. Michael Samson et al., "Review."

34. Andries du Toit and David Neves, "Vulnerability and Social Protection at the Margins of the Formal Economy—Case Studies from Khyelitsha and the Eastern Cape" (Cape Town: USAID and Programme for Land and Agrarian Studies, 2006).

35. Wahenga, "One out of Ten: Social Cash Transfer Pilots in Malawi and Zambia," 2008, http://www.wahenga.net/index.php/views/comments_view/one_out_of_ten_social_cash_transfer_pilots_in_malawi_and_zambia/.

36. Candace Miller, Maxton Tsoka, and Kathryn Reichert, "Targeting Cash to Malawi's Ultra Poor: A Mixed Methods Evaluation" (Boston, MA: Center for International Health and Development, Boston University School of Public Health, and The Centre for Social Research, University of Malawi, 2008), available at http://childresearchpolicy.org/images/Cash_Targeting_Evaluation.pdf.

37. Miller, Tsoka, and Reichert, "Targeting Report"

38. Miller, Tsoka, and Reichert, "Targeting Report"

39. Miller, Tsoka, and Reichert, "Targeting Report"

40. Miller, Tsoka, and Reichert, "Targeting Cash to Malawi's Ultra Poor."

41. Watkins, "Alternative Methods," p. 6.

42. Watkins, "Alternative Methods," pp. 6, 50.

43. Watkins, "Alternative Methods," pp. 28, 35.

44. Wahengo, "One out of Ten."

45. Frank Ellis, Stephen Devereux, and Philip White, *Social Protection in Africa* (Cheltenham, UK and Northampton, MA: Edward Elgar, 2009), p. 65.

46. HelpAge International, "Old Age Pensions in India," *Ageing and Development* 15 (London: HelpAge International, 2003).

47. Nilanjana Mukherjee, Joan Hardjono, and Elizabeth Carriere, "People, Poverty and Livelihoods: Links for Sustainable Poverty Reduction in Indonesia," World Bank Report 25289 (Washington, DC: World Bank, 2002).

48. Stephen Devereux et al., "Ethiopia's Productive Safety Net Programme (PSNP)" (Brighton, UK: Institute of Development Studies and Addis Ababa: Indak International, 2006).

49. Raghav Gaiha and Katsushi Imai, "The Maharastra Employment Guarantee Scheme," Policy Brief 6 (London: Overseas Development Institute, 2006).

50. Daniel Gilligan, John Hoddinott, and Alemayehu Taffese, "The Impact of Ethiopia's Productive Safety Net Programme and Its Linkages," Discussion Paper 839 (Washington, DC: IFPRI, 2008).

51. India Together, "NREGA: A Fine Balance," July 13, 2008, available at www.indiatogether.org/2008/jul/psa-finebal.htm.

52. Rinku Murgai and Martin Ravallion, "Is a Guaranteed Living Wage a Good Anti-poverty Policy?" Policy Research Working Paper 3640 (Washington, DC: World Bank, 2005).

53. Stefaan Marysse and Joris Verschueren, "South Africa's BIG Debate in Comparative Perspective," Discussion Paper 2007.03 (Antwerp: University of Antwerp, 2007).

54. Viviene Taylor, *Transforming the Present—Protecting the Future: Report of the Committee of Inquiry into a Comprehensive System of Social Security for South Africa* (Pretoria: Taylor Committee, 2002).

55. In 2008–2009 reduced to MK 800 ($6).

56. Blessings Chinsinga and Aoiffe O'Brien, *Planting Ideas—How Agricultural Subsidies Are Working in Malawi* (London: Africa Research Institute, 2008); Philip White et al., "Fertiliser Subsidies and Social Cash Transfers," Frontiers of Social Protection Brief 1 (Johannesburg: Regional Hunger and Vulnerability Programme, 2009), available at http://www.wahenga.net/uploads/documents/reba_studies/FOSP_Brief_1.pdf.

57. John Seaman, Celia Petty, and Patrick Kambewa. "The Impact on Household Income and Welfare of the Pilot Social Cash Transfer and Agricultural Input Subsidy Programmes in Mlomba TA, Machinga District, Malawi." Lilongwe: Malawi Vulnerability Assessment Committee, 2008, available at www.wahenga.net/uploads/documents/comments/sct/EvDev_Mlomba_Survey_2008_Report.pdf.

58. Charity Moore, "Nicaragua's Red de Protección Social: An Exemplary But Short-Lived Conditional Cash Transfer Programme," Country Study 17 (Brasilia: UNDP International Policy Centre for Inclusive Growth, 2009), available at http://www.ipc-undp.org/pub/IPCCountryStudy17.pdf.

59. John Farrington and Rachel Slater, "Introduction: Cash Transfers: Panacea for Poverty Reduction or Money Down the Drain?" *Development Policy Review,* 24, no. 5 (2006): 499–510, referring to Nanak Kakwani, Fabio Soares, and Hyun Son, "Cash Transfers for School-age Children in Africa," *Development Policy Review,* 24, no. 5 (2006): 553–70.

8

Co-responsibility and Services: The Conditionality Dilemma

"My two boys were expelled from school 7 months ago, because I could not pay their school fees. It hurts me to see my children out of school. They used to ask me, 'mummy when are we going back to school?'" This was recorded in an interview with Willemina Gawises, a single mother in Namibia, before she started to receive a cash transfer.[1] Evidence from many studies shows that people without money want to attend clinics and send their children to school, and that the biggest constraint is lack of funds; cash transfers substantially increase school attendance and health service use. Willemina sent her children to school and used her grant to pay the fees and buy the school uniforms.

Her story raises two important issues. First, Willemina wanted to send her children to school, but should she have been forced to? Many countries have compulsory primary school, and very often children must attend school until they are 16 or even 18 years old. But programs such as Oportunidades in Mexico make school attendance a condition of receiving the grant. Compulsory school attendance is widely considered correct and useful. But is it right to impose on poor people even a reasonable condition that is not imposed on others? Does Willemina have fewer rights than people who are better off?

The second issue raised by Willemina is that cash transfers increase demand for services. Thus cash transfers need to be matched with more and better schools and health centers. Mexico speaks in terms of "co-responsibilities"—the government takes responsibility for providing the grant and improving services, while the recipient takes responsibility for actions such as going to school that will help to pull the family out of poverty.

This chapter examines co-responsibilities.

Options for Conditions

The Universal Declaration of Human Rights commitment to an adequate standard of living is unconditional; it does not exclude the "undeserving" poor or bad parents. A South African team writes, "Conditional social security, based on assumptions that poor parents are in some way culpable if their children fail to attend school or attend clinic, is inconsistent with the structural explanations of poverty which are implicit in the [South Africa] Constitution."[2] There is also an issue of power: Who sets the conditions and who has the power to restrict the rights of the poorer and less powerful?[3] On the other hand, the human rights declaration also says that "everyone has the right to work" (Article 23), which implies that work is the norm, and that "everyone has duties to the community" (Article 20). Not surprisingly, cash transfer programs exhibit a tension between rights and responsibilities.

Cash transfers in developing countries are new; many countries are still experimenting, and programs are changing. There is also a lively intercontinental interchange, with countries trading ideas and experiences. Four models of cash transfers are emerging. All transfers have a mix of goals, but the first two models put more stress on reducing immediate poverty, and the second two place more emphasis on preventing intergenerational transmission of poverty—helping the children of poorer parents not to become poor adults.

WORKFARE. India, with one of the largest cash transfers in the world, and Ethiopia guarantee work to all who demand it. Manual labor is therefore a condition of the grant, although this scheme is sometimes paired with grants for those who cannot work.

UNCONDITIONAL. Social pensions are largely unconditional; there is not much point in asking elderly people to carry out activities, although in developed countries there is sometimes a requirement that recipients of social pensions no longer be working. South Africa has the largest unconditional child benefit. Unconditional grants are evolving in southern Africa, where poverty is widespread and civil services are weak, and there is a preference for systems that are easier to administer. Advocates of unconditional grants argue that the main problem for poor people is lack of money, not lack of knowledge or will.

CONDITIONS OR CO-RESPONSIBILITIES. Family grants and those targeted at children often require that small children be vaccinated and attend health clinics, and that older children attend school; mothers sometimes are expected to attend parenting lessons. Oportunidades in Mexico initially required voluntary labor. Latin America, with more experienced civil services to administer more complex systems, has led in programs based on this model. The conditions imposed can be "hard," where a family loses all or part of the grant when conditions are violated. In Nicaragua, 10% of households failed on some conditions and lost some money.[4] Or they can be "soft," as in Brazil, where families who violate the conditions are given additional support by social services and other government agencies. Justin Lin, World Bank chief economist, and Joy Phumaphi, vice president for human development, actually define conditional cash transfers as programs that "transfer cash while asking beneficiaries to make prespecified investments in child education and health."[5] Confusingly, they go on to call these "safety net programs." Mexico's Oportunidades fits the model best; it puts its main stress on human capital formation and on reducing the intergenerational transmission of poverty.

Many countries give student grants, bursaries, and scholarships (*bolsa de estudo* in Portuguese, *beca* in Spanish). In practice, these are conditional cash transfers. But instead of evoking the pejorative connotation of "conditions," they recognize that secondary school students and college students are young adults old enough to take paid work and make some decisions for themselves. Thus the scholarship is seen as a social payment that enables the teenager to continue in education rather than starting employment. In poorer families, young adults who want to contribute to the family may see themselves as being paid to go to school rather than as satisfying a condition. Payments to the students themselves are often part of a family grant that includes money for parents.

BEHAVIOR CHANGE OR PERFORMANCE BONUSES. Money is given for children passing exams or progressing to the next school year, for babies being the appropriate weight, or for adults attending classes. This relatively uncommon and controversial practice is discussed below.

All four models are evolving, and, as we have noted, some countries have programs that include features drawn from more than one model.

WHY CONDITIONS?

Reasons for conditions on transfers are as varied and overlapping as the different goals for transfers identified in Chapter 3. Proponents of conditions give three justifications, which Ariel Fiszbein and Norbert Schady address in their World Bank report *Conditional Cash Transfers.*[6] "Essentially, there are two broad sets of arguments for attaching conditions to cash transfers," they explain. The first argument is that parents' investment in the human capital of their children is too low. "Paternalism will be justified if the individuals in question hold persistently erroneous beliefs" and "somehow are not capable of choosing what is in their best interests" or in the best interests of their children or the broader society.[7]

"The second argument applies if political economy reasons mean that there is little support for redistribution, unless it is seen to be conditioned on 'good behavior' by the 'deserving poor.'" They add, "People who object to targeted transfers as 'pure handouts' might support them if they are part of a 'social contract' that requires the recipients to take a number of concrete steps to improve their lives or those of their children."[8]

If there is "little evidence" for under-investment in human capital, or that voters do not need the appeal of "co-responsibilities," then unconditional cash transfers may be preferable, Fizbein and Schady conclude.

They then cite a third justification for conditions and point to its different ideological and attitudinal underpinnings. In Brazil "the conditions fundamentally are viewed as *encouraging* beneficiaries to take up and exercise their right to free education and free health care, so noncompliance is taken to be a manifestation of some kind of obstacle that the family cannot overcome to access the service rather than an unwillingness to comply."[9] Chile Solidario is a unique program in which the main purpose of the cash transfer is to pay people to make use of social workers.[10]

The World Bank's Norbert Schady is a strong advocate of conditions. He told a London meeting[11] that there is a problem with "persistently misguided beliefs" on the part of the poor that means their children remain poor. Some poor people do not act in the best interests of their children, either because they see no point to schooling, particularly for girls, or because the adults want to use the money for themselves. To reduce intergenerational poverty, sometimes "we must compel the family to make the necessary investment in human capital that they would not otherwise make." He accepted that this is "old school paternalism," and he argued that governments know better than low-income people how they should raise their children.

Attitudes toward poverty, as shown in Table 2.1, are again significant. In the United States, where people tend to blame the poor for their poverty, conditions may be more important, but in countries where this is less true, it may be better to put less stress on blame and behavior modification. Conditions and an emphasis on the next generation, rather than on present poverty, have been particularly important in Latin America because of the key role there of the Washington-based institutions, the World Bank and the Inter-American Development Bank, which have been financing some of the cash transfer programs with human-capital investment loans.[12]

But even the World Bank is divided on the issue. Fiszbein and Schady's book is called *Conditional Cash Transfers*,[13] and it hardly mentions South Africa because cash transfers there are unconditional. But in *For Protection & Promotion: The Design and Implementation of Effective Safety Nets*, also published by the World Bank in 2008, Margaret Grosh and colleagues take a much more nuanced view of conditions.[14] While arguing that "donors and the public prefer to provide transfers to the deserving poor with children while being reassured that beneficiaries will do the right things for their children," they accept that there are also situations in which conditions are inappropriate.

Why Impose Conditions?

As we showed in Chapters 4 and 5, there is substantial evidence that people with little money do know how to make good use of additional funds. It also seems that most people can learn more about health, sanitation, and parenting and that many people are eager to attend health promotion talks. The issue, then, is about the usefulness of compelling only those poor enough to be eligible for cash transfers to change their behavior. Conditions are often criticized as demeaning because they apply only to poor people receiving grants (unlike, for example, compulsory school attendance laws, which apply to everyone) and because they imply that recipients are irrational or incapable of acting in their own best interests.

Linking conditions to inadequate parents who need compulsion creates two important perception issues. First, "most people believe that they are not bad parents," admit Fiszbein and Schady.[15] This leads them to argue that because most parents think they are good parents, inadequate parents "are unlikely to respond either to an information campaign or to home-visiting programs in which social workers teach them how to be better parents." Compulsion is necessary to force them to attend meetings and lectures. But there is a danger of the opposite occurring—that people who think they are good parents may be eager to learn more but will avoid the lectures aimed at inadequate parents.

Second, from a political economy standpoint, as we noted in Chapter 6, targeting a program on the poor who are bad parents (precisely the "undeserving poor") means that the vast majority who think they are good parents are told the program is not for them, and thus the cash transfer program is unlikely to gain widespread public support.

Whereas some in the World Bank and elsewhere in Washington—and often among local elites in poor countries—believe the undeserving poor must be compelled to act in the best interests of their children, there are several more subtle reasons why conditions are drawing some public support in the South. Perhaps most important is that most conditions, notably attending clinics and seeing that children go to school, are not a burden because they are what most poor parents already want to do—and are able to do because of the extra money. On the other hand, most would accept that there are a few feckless and incompetent parents (rich and poor), and conditions may be justified to reach that small group. An increase in school attendance of 1% or 2% may seem small, but that change at the margin can have far-reaching effects. This is a justification of compulsory schooling, for instance.

As with compulsory education, there may be a need to put pressure on older children, rather than on their parents, to continue attending school. For older, secondary school children, a conditional grant means that they are effectively being paid a wage to attend school—and thus are doing productive work and contributing to the family. Genaro Poot, of Chaksinkin, Yucatán, Mexico, comments that "these are hard times, many children disobey their parents, and the fact that the schools are so far away means that parents do not check how their children are doing in school. . . . The parents are left clueless about what time the kids leave school; many students do not go to school at all, instead they spend the day in town. . . . The truth is that young people do not want to study, who knows why, all they want now is to look good, they have nice shoes and clothes, but they don't do anything."[16]

Finally, under certain circumstances, conditions can enhance dignity and self-respect. Women often receive the money and must satisfy the conditions, which, as we noted in Chapter 4, is a highly contested issue. But in many cases, satisfying the conditions does increase the power of women within the household. Conditions in Mexico that require mothers to go to meetings and do communal labor force husbands to let their wives leave the house.

Do Conditions Work?

Despite the importance of conditions, their effectiveness has not been studied separately from the programs that include them, and it tends simply to be assumed that they work. In fact, there is almost no evidence that conditions make any major difference. Bernd Schubert and Rachel Slater comment that "Latin American countries assisted by the World Bank and the Inter-American Development Bank are spending millions of dollars on administering conditionality without ever having analysed how much the conditions contribute to the impact of social cash transfer programmes and whether this contribution is worth the costs involved."[17]

It is very difficult to distinguish between the effects of conditions and those of the grant itself. Norbert Schady and Maria Caridad Araugo of the World Bank looked at four provinces in Ecuador when the Bono de Desarrollo Humano was introduced.[18] It had been announced that the grant would be conditional on school attendance, but this condition was not enforced. Within the sample, one-quarter believed attendance was compulsory and one-quarter did not; the first group was significantly more likely to send their children to school. Perhaps this is proof that conditions really do have an effect. However, the first group was also better educated, and parents with more schooling usually are more likely to send children to school.

Alan de Brauw and John Hoddinott report that in Mexico, the requirement of school attendance increased the number of children making the transition from primary to secondary school, although conditions made no difference in primary school attendance.[19] But this is contested, and it may be that the carrot can work as well as the stick. Two other studies of Mexico put much greater weight on the fact that secondary students receive larger grants and showed that increasing the size of the grant would cause more students to stay in school.[20] This does not argue against the condition claim, because to receive the larger grant, children had to attend school. But in Nicaragua, where enrollment in fifth grade or higher was not a condition, the grant had the unanticipated result of greatly increasing the number of children who passed from fourth to fifth and sixth grades. Further evidence for the carrot, also from Mexico, is that a higher grant for girls has brought about a gender balance in secondary schools.

Paying by Results

The most extreme type of condition is payment for results. In Argentina, Becas recipients not only had to attend school but also had to pass and receive adequate marks.[21] This reflects another level of condition: Program administrators are not simply ticking a box to indicate that someone was present but, rather, are paying for performance. This is significantly more controversial.

New York City is now running a three-year pilot of performance payments that breaks with most precedents.[22] New York City Mayor Michael Bloomberg set up a Commission for Economic Opportunity; in a meeting after its report was presented, a commission member who had worked in South Africa suggested that country's model of unconditional cash transfers for New York. Bloomberg was intrigued and went to Mexico in 2007 to look at Oportunidades. The result was Opportunities NYC, which is explicitly called a conditional cash transfer and cites Mexico as the model, but which is, in fact, radically different from any southern cash transfer, because it consists entirely of payment for actions and results. It is a three-year $53 million pilot program funded entirely with private donations, including money from the wealthy mayor himself. It largely bypasses government structures and the city council, has few community links, and has not attempted to build a political base. Opportunity NYC is based on the belief that the root of low educational achievement in poor families rests entirely in the family and is caused by lack of role models; it rejects all traditional ideas about education being seen as liberating. Instead, education is a job, and children should be paid in accordance with the results achieved. Payments range from $25 for attending parent–teacher conferences to $600 for passing one of the state final high school exams. Further, the program makes no attempt to improve services or change the supply side of education, and it largely ignores schools and teachers.

Fiszbein and Schady suggest that New York will serve as a model for the South: "serious thought should be given to the possibility of paying parents not only for school enrollment, but also for their children's performance on standardized tests."[23] Laura Rawlings of the World Bank supports performance payments and has suggested that parents of small children might be given extra money if the children's growth met WHO norms.[24] Something similar was tried in Nicaragua, where one version of the cash transfer was conditional on children's maintaining a healthful weight. The result was that the poorest households with ill children were punished,[25] and some households stuffed their children with food and water on growth-monitoring days to avoid penalties.[26]

Distortions

Satisfying the conditions of a grant can produce a range of distortions. In Argentina the Programa Nacional de Becas Estudiantiles gave grants to poor parents of secondary school pupils, but continuation of the grant into the second year was dependent on performance. Some teachers relaxed standards and promoted Becas students into the next year so that poor families would not lose their grants.[27]

A study of Mexico warns that "conditionality can create an opportunity for corruption, as individuals responsible for certifying that conditions have been met, demand payments for doing so."[28] In Mozambique and many other African countries, there are particular problems. Teachers often force students to perform chores for them, such as fetching wood and water, and some demand money or sexual favors in exchange for passing grades; asking teachers to sign forms for grants would make the process much worse. Other studies have shown political interference and corruption in programs in Argentina, Nicaragua, and India. "One time I lost my benefit because of the teacher," complained a beneficiary from La Gloria, Nicaragua. "He just reported that she [my daughter] didn't go to class, and that was a lie."[29] Indeed, any program that increases administrative discretion is open to corruption and influence, and this needs to be taken into account.

Punitive conditions penalize those who need help most. The households that are often in the most desperate straits are the ones that cannot meet all the conditions and lose their grant. Augustín Escobar Latapí and Mercedes González de la Rocha[30] of Mexico's Social Anthropology Investigation Centre (CIESAS—Centro de Investigaciones y Estudios Superiores en Antropología Social) in Guadalajara found that there was a serious problem with co-responsibility for the poorest households, especially those where the mother was the main earner. "Some particularly poor households, nevertheless, are in fact excluded from the programme due to non-compliance with their co-responsibilities, and this is worrying." A grant in Honduras required women to participate for 6–8 hours each week of training sessions for six months, but many poor women did not have the time.[31]

CO-RESPONSIBILITY AND EXPANDING SERVICES

Many of the programs in Latin American and increasingly in some parts of Africa are best understood as cash transfers *plus* services—health, education, and information. There is a synergy: Services make a major difference for poor people, while the cash makes it possible to use the services. Nutrition lectures for mothers are useful only if mothers can buy better food for their children. Seen in this way, co-responsibility really is a joint commitment. The government commits itself to giving a grant and improving services, while the recipients commit themselves to using those services. Nicaragua, for example, increased the number of teachers, introduced a school meals program, and sent more vaccines to clinics.[32]

When a team was investigating a possible conditional cash transfer pilot in Chipata, Zambia, it found that primary schools were already turning away applicants and would have no new places for additional children from cash transfer families.[33] Two attempts to introduce very simple health conditions on the child benefit were defeated because of a lack of clinics. In Brazil, too, there are complaints that many municipalities do not have available the basic social services that recipients would need to seek out in order to satisfy the conditions of Bolsa Família.[34]

A report from Britain's Overseas Development Institute found that in West Africa and Central Africa, the main obstacles that women encountered in trying to access health services were difficulty finding the money for treatment, distance to the clinic, and cost of transport.[35] User fees introduced in the 1980s under pressure from the World Bank are still widely collected in Africa. Cash transfers are used to pay fees and transport costs, but more and better clinics are needed as well.

Not Just Sitting in School

Behavior with respect to education is perhaps the area most often cited by World Bank and other economists as an example of how poor people undervalue investment in their children. Specifically, they take children out of school to work and earn small amounts of money to keep the family alive, but this is a wrong choice in the long run because, it is claimed, these children would earn much more over their lifetimes with a higher level of education. The economists justify their view by citing a myriad of studies showing that the greater one's education, the higher one's income. But the economists are making an unwarranted assumption about cause and effect, and they are ignoring class, social capital, and the quality of education. Merely pushing more poor children into overcrowded schools does not produce better-educated adults with jobs. Rather, education must be accompanied by a job-creating growth strategy.

In many countries universal primary education remains a dream, secondary school is still for the privileged few, quality is appalling, and there is huge pressure for more practical education that includes farming and nutrition information. In South Africa, which is wealthier than its neighbors, education is described as "parlous" with "poor teaching and lack of leadership in under-resourced schools."[36] Even in Asia and Latin America, low quality and limited access remain serious problems, reducing the gains of cash transfers and making it harder to meet conditions.

Many studies show that better schools improve attendance. A study in Mozambique showed that distance to school was critical, especially for poor families, who apparently could not afford the lost labor time if children had to walk long distances to school. Three other factors affected primary school enrollment: school quality, household income, and adult literacy.[37] In Mexico, children were much more likely to enroll if the secondary school was within the community, and enrollment dropped off rapidly if the school was more than 3 kilometers away.[38] Two studies in Honduras showed similar effects. Two-thirds of school days missed were due to the school being closed, and days open varied from the official school year of 172 days down to as little as 110 days.[39] And there was a significant increase in enrollment if the school quality was perceived as high.[40]

The World Bank's Fiszbein and Schady note that although there is clear evidence of increased attendance at school as a consequence of cash transfers, "there is little evidence of improvements in learning outcomes"; indeed, in many places children sit in school but learn hardly anything.[41] The problem would appear to be poor-quality education, and particularly an inability to support children who are brought into school by cash transfer programs and tend to be poorer. These children often seem less able, because parents have already sacrificed to send to school those who appear brighter.[42] Ariel Fiszbein noted that in Chile, schools seem unable to deal with the new pupils, who are just told to sit at the back of the class.[43] Schools often have large classes, and teachers tend to focus their attention on the children who have had a head start by coming from less impoverished backgrounds. Conditional cash transfers may overcome the social discrimination that keeps the poorest children out of school, but other processes and actions will be needed to tackle the day-to-day discrimination that occurs within the classroom. Children from the poorest families already have a large gap in cognitive development before they reach school, and without special support, they are unlikely to catch up. Several studies show improved learning outcomes only for better-off students or when the quality of education is higher, especially with a more experienced teacher. But cash transfers are often geographically targeted, and schools in poor areas are often worse than average.[44]

It will be important to consider what kinds of opportunities children have when they eventually leave school; some worry that pupils supported by cash transfers will not gain better jobs. Three factors come into play. First, despite extra schooling, such students are not better educated. Second, most countries are not creating new jobs rapidly enough to match the increases in the numbers of students who are completing their schooling. Third, as a consequence, success in job seeking depends increasingly on contacts (what economists call social capital) and on knowing people in the place of employment. This circumstance, of course, discriminates against young people from very poor backgrounds. Nevertheless, the handful of studies that have been completed on the long-term impact of schooling-related transfers support a moderately optimistic judgment on this issue.[45]

On the other hand, improved service provision can make a difference. A study of the Programa Nacional de Becas Estudiantiles, a conditional cash transfer to families of pupils in secondary school in Argentina, showed that after the program began, more students stayed on and received higher grades in better schools with more supportive teachers.[46] Also, many of the schools had special programs to integrate Becas students and to focus on the priorities of low-income students. In Brazil, one of the precursors to Bolsa Família was the Eradication of Child Labour Programme, which combined a cash transfer with an extended school day, mixing culture, play, art, and sports with an average of two hours extra for tasks related to regular education. The Brazilian Court of Audit evaluated the program and found that by broadening knowledge and skills, it effected a significant improvement in school performance, social life, and self-esteem.[47]

If cash transfers are to work, co-responsibilities must be real. Grant recipients should attend schools and clinics. But at the same time, governments must raise the quality and quantity of health and education services and must take other actions to promote the creation of jobs for new school graduates.

BALANCING POLITICS AND ADMINISTRATION

Conditions substantially increase the administrative burden on civil servants, service providers, and parents and grant recipients. Teachers and health workers have to fill in special attendance sheets, and other administrators have to verify compliance. In countries, particularly in Africa, where schools and administrations are already overextended, there may not be the capacity to administer conditions.

Conditions exist because of an implicit or explicit assumption that poor people do not act in the best interests of themselves and their children and must be pressured to do so. But the shift to the term "co-responsibilities" reflects a more nuanced understanding of the social contract. Children must go to school, but the state must provide schools. Babies must go to clinics and be vaccinated, but the government must ensure that there are adequate health services. This underlines the realization that cash transfers do not work on their own; they require the expansion of basic services, and those who provide these services must take into account the fact that the poorest people start from a disadvantaged position.

Each country must analyze the political and administrative questions involved and make its own choice about whether to impose hard conditions, soft conditions, or no conditions. Politically, the middle class is key. Will conditions win them over because the poor must take "co-responsibility"? Or will the middle class be lost because they think they themselves are not bad parents and thus will never be able to use the benefit? Are conditions worth imposing at all? Can health, education, and social services be provided to those who must meet conditions? And does the country have the administrative capacity to administer conditions successfully?

A study of Oportunidades in Mexico set out the costs quite well:

> The administrative costs employed in getting transfers to poor households appear to be small relative to the costs incurred in previous programs and for targeted programs in other countries. According to the program cost analysis, for every 100 pesos allocated to the program, 8.9 pesos are "absorbed" by administration costs. Dropping household targeting would reduce program costs from 8.9 pesos to 6.2 pesos per 100 pesos transferred, while dropping conditioning would reduce the program costs from 8.9 pesos to 6.6 pesos per 100 pesos transferred. Dropping both would reduce these costs to 3.9 pesos per 100 pesos transferred.[48]

Each country designs its own cash transfer program, and each has to decide whether targeting and imposing conditions are worth the cost.

NOTES

1. Claudia Haarmann et al., *Towards a Basic Income Grant for All*, Basic Income Grant Pilot Project First Assessment Report (Windhoek, Namibia: Basic Income Grant Coalition, 2008), available at www.bignam.org.

2. Frances Lund et al., "Is There a Rationale for Conditional Cash Transfers for Children in South Africa?" Working Paper 53 (Durban: School of Development Studies, University of KwaZulu-Natal, 2008), available at http://sds.ukzn.ac.za/files/WP%2053%20web.pdf.

3. John Veit-Wilson, "Who Set the Conditions? Conditionality, Reciprocity, Human Rights and Inclusion in Society," *Global Social Policy,* 9, no. 2 (2009): 171–74.

4. Charity Moore, "Nicaragua's Red de Protección Social: An Exemplary But Short Lived Conditional Cash Transfer Programme," Country Study 17 (Brasilia: International Policy Centre for Inclusive Growth, 2009), available at http://www.ipc-undp.org/pub/IPCCountryStudy17.pdf.

5. Justin Lin and Joy Phumaphi, "Foreword." In *Conditional Cash Transfers,* edited by Ariel Fiszbein and Norbert Schady (Washington, DC: World Bank, 2009), p. xii.

6. Fiszbein and Schady, *Conditional Cash Transfers,* pp. 10, 66.

7. Fiszbein and Schady, *Conditional Cash Transfers,* p. 51.

8. Fiszbein and Schady, *Conditional Cash Transfers,* p. 66.

9. Fiszbein and Schady, *Conditional Cash Transfers,* p. 89.

10. Fiszbein and Schady, *Conditional Cash Transfers,* p. 6.

11. May 26, 2009.

12. Sudhanshu Handa and Benjamin Davis, "The Experience of Conditional Cash Transfers in Latin America and the Caribbean," *Development Policy Review,* 24, no. 5 (2006): 513–36.

13. Fiszbein and Schady, *Conditional Cash Transfers.*

14. Margaret Grosh et al., *For Protection and Promotion: The Design and Implementation of Effective Safety Nets* (Washington, DC: World Bank, 2008), pp. 312–24.

15. Fiszbein and Schady, *Conditional Cash Transfers,* p. 55.

16. Maribel Lozano Cortés, "Evaluación Cualitativa de los Impactos del Programa Oportunidades, en Alimentación, Salud y Educación en los Municipios del Sur de Yucatán (2004–2005)" (Quintana Roo, México: Universidad de Quintana Roo, 2006), p. 28.

17. Bernd Schubert and Rachel Slater, "Social Cash Transfers in Low-Income African Countries: Conditional or Unconditional?" *Development Policy Review,* 24, no. 5 (2006): 571–78.

18. Norbert Schady and Maria Caridad Araujo, "Cash Transfers, Conditions and School Enrollment in Ecuador," *Economia,* 8, no. 2 (2008): 43–70.

19. Alan de Brauw and John Hoddinott, "Must Conditional Cash Transfer Programs Be Conditional to Be Effective?" Discussion Paper 757 (Washington, DC: IFPRI, 2008).

20. Orazio Attanasio, Costas Meghir, and Ana Santiago, "Education Choices in Mexico: Using a Structural Model and a Randomized Experiment to Evaluate

Progresa" (London: Centre for the Evaluation of Development Policies, Institute for Fiscal Studies, 2005), available at http://www.ifs.org.uk/projects/301; Alain de Janvry and Elisabeth Sadoulet, "Making Conditional Cash Transfer Programs More Efficient: Designing for Maximum Effect of the Conditionality," *World Bank Economic Review*, 20, no. 1 (2006): 1–29.

21. Carolyn Heinrich, "Demand and Supply-Side Determinants of Conditional Cash Transfer Program Effectiveness," *World Development* 35, no. 1 (2007): 121–43.

22. Michelle Morais de Sá e Silva, "Opportunity NYC: A Performance-based Conditional Cash Transfer Programme: A Qualitative Analysis," Working Paper 49 (Brasilia: International Poverty Centre, 2008). See also http://www.nyc.gov/html/ceo/html/programs/opportunity_nyc.shtml and http://opportunitynyc.org/.

23. Fiszbein and Schady, *Conditional Cash Transfers*, p. 143.

24. Laura Rawlings, speaking at a meeting on conditional cash transfers at the Renaissance Chancery Court Hotel, London, May 26, 2009.

25. Charity Moore, "Nicaragua's Red de Protección Social."

26. Michelle Adato and Lucy Bassett, "What Is the Potential of Cash Transfers to Strengthen Families Affected by HIV and AIDS? A Review of the Evidence on Impacts and Key Policy Debates" (Washington, DC: IFPRI, 2008), citing Michelle Adato and Terry Roopnaraine, "Un Analysis Social de la 'Red de Protección Social' en Nicaragua" (Washington, DC: IFPRI, 2004).

27. Heinrich, "Demand and Supply-Side Determinants."

28. Alan de Brauw and John Hoddinott, "Is the Conditionality Necessary in Conditional Cash Transfer Programmes? Evidence from Mexico," One Pager 64 (Brasilia: International Poverty Centre, 2008).

29. Michelle Adato and Terry Roopnaraine, "A Social Analysis of the Red de Protección Social (RPS) in Nicaragua" (Washington, DC: IFPRI, 2004).

30. Augustín Escobar Latapí and Mercedes González de la Rocha, "Girls, Mothers and Poverty Reduction in Mexico: Evaluating Progresa-Oportunidades." In *The Gendered Impacts of Liberalisation: Towards "Embedded Liberalism"?* edited by Shahra Razavi (New York and Abingdon: Routledge/UNRISD, 2009).

31. Charity Moore, "Assessing Honduras' CCT Programme PRAF, Programa de Asignación Familiar: Expected and Unexpected Results," Country Study 15 (Brasilia: UNDP International Poverty Centre, 2008).

32. John A. Maluccio and Rafael Flores, "Impact Evaluation of a Conditional Cash Transfer Program—The Nicaraguan Red de Protección Social," Research Report 141 (Washington, DC: IFPRI, 2005).

33. Bernd Schubert and Rachel Slater, "Social Cash Transfers in Low-Income African Countries: Conditional or Unconditional?" *Development Policy Review*, 24, no. 5 (2006): 571–78.

34. See, for example, Fábio Veras Soares, Rafael Perez Ribas, and Rafael Guerreiro Osório, "Evaluating the Impact of Brazil's Bolsa Família: Cash Transfer

Programmes in Comparative Perspective," IPC Evaluation Note 1 (Brasilia: International Poverty Centre, 2007); Magda Núcia Albuquerque Dias and Maria do Rosário de Fátima e Silva, "O Programa Bolsa Família no Município de Bacabal—MA: Avaliação de Implementação com o Foco nas Condicionalidades" (Brasilia: UNDP International Poverty Centre, 2008), available at the Biblioteca Virtual do Bolsa Família, http://www.ipc-undp.org/publications/mds/29M.pdf.

35. Cora Walsh and Nicola Jones, "Alternative Approaches to Social Protection for Health in West and Central Africa" (London: Overseas Development Institute, 2009), available at http://www.odi.org.uk/events/2009/06/16/1885-presentation-cora-walsh-nicola-jones.pdf.

36. Frances Lund, Michael Noble, Helen Barnes, and Gemma Wright, "Is There a Rationale for Conditional Cash Transfers for Children in South Africa?" Working Paper 53 (Durban: School of Development Studies, University of KwaZulu-Natal, 2008), available at http://sds.ukzn.ac.za/files/WP%2053%20web.pdf.

37. Sudhanshu Handa, "Raising Primary School Enrolment in Developing Countries—The Relative Importance of Supply and Demand," *Journal of Development Economics*, 69, no. 1 (2002): 103–28.

38. Alain de Janvry and Elisabeth Sadoulet, "Making Conditional Cash Transfer Programs More Efficient: Designing for Maximum Effect of the Conditionality," *World Bank Economic Review*, 20, no. 1 (2006): 1–29.

39. Arjun S. Bedia and Jeffery H. Marshall, "Primary School Attendance in Honduras," *Journal of Development Economics*, 69, no. 1 (2002): 129–53.

40. Sudhanshu Handa and Benjamin Davis, "The Experience of Conditional Cash Transfers in Latin America and the Caribbean," *Development Policy Review*, 24, no. 5 (2006): 513–36.

41. Fiszbein and Schady, *Conditional Cash Transfers*, pp. 3, 142.

42. Fiszbein and Schady, *Conditional Cash Transfers*, p. 143. Also, with specific reference to a study of Cambodia, Norbert Schady speaking at a meeting on conditional cash transfers at the Renaissance Chancery Court Hotel, London, May 26, 2009.

43. Ariel Fiszbein, speaking at a meeting on conditional cash transfers at the Renaissance Chancery Court Hotel, London, May 26, 2009.

44. Fiszbein and Schady, *Conditional Cash Transfers*, p. 164.

45. Augustín Escobar Latapí and Mercedes González de la Rocha, "Evaluacion Qualitativa del Programa Oportunidades. Etapa urbana 2003" (Mexico City: CIESAS—Occidente, 2009).

46. Heinrich, "Demand and Supply-Side Determinants."

47. Adylson Motta (rapporteur), *TCU Evaluation of the Child Labor Eradication Program*, Official translation of *Avaliação do TCU sobre o Progama de Erradicação do Trabalho Infantil* (Brasilia: Brazilian Court of Audit [Tribunal de Contas de União], 2003), available at http://portal2.tcu.gov.br/portal/page/

portal/TCU/english/publications/institucional_publications/EXECUTIVE_
SUMMARIES_3.PDF.

48. Emmanuel Skoufias, "PROGRESA and Its Impacts on the Welfare of
Rural Households in Mexico" (Washington, DC: IFPRI, 2005), available at http://
www.ifpri.org/pubs/abstract/139/rr139.pdf.

9

Cash Transfers Are
Practical in Poor Countries

THE WAVE OF INTEREST IN CASH TRANSFERS HAS REACHED SOME OF THE least developed countries. But they face many more difficulties than larger and wealthier states such as Brazil, Mexico, and South Africa, which began the "revolution from the South" of giving money to the poor. Low-income countries usually have a majority of the population below the poverty line. These people are typically in the "informal" economy or are involved in low-technology peasant agriculture. Thus they are outside any employment-related pension or social insurance schemes, which have been limited to the civil service, the military, and a few highly paid private sector workers. The least developed countries also have weaker civil services and, partly because of informalization, less ability to collect taxes. They generally lack health and education infrastructure. Low-income countries, like poor people, are caught in a poverty trap; they lack the money to pull themselves out of the hole so that they can start developing.

We argued in Chapter 1 that aid has failed to promote development in the poorest countries because it has been misdirected by donors—particularly by being channeled through thousands of projects—and because it has come tied to conditions that actually retarded development. International financial institutions argued that low-income countries should concentrate on market-based economic growth because countries had to grow before they could start redistributing wealth and combating poverty. But the failure of that approach has led to a broader understanding that equity and social protection are essential prerequisites to growth and development.

143

This perspective more accurately reflects the experience of developed economies, where the establishment and extension of social protection featured prominently in facilitating economic growth and in strengthening state financial and administrative capacity.

After a decade of success of the big cash transfer programs, governments in poorer countries are looking to cash transfers as a way to kickstart a rising development spiral and pull themselves out of the poverty trap. Some donors, the World Bank, and international studies are increasingly backing cash transfers. The independent and eminent Joint Learning Initiative on Children and HIV/AIDS (JLICA) advocated cash transfers in its final report.[1] It argues that "while elaborate, multisectoral strategies may appear desirable, . . . the most fruitful approach is to 'get the basics right'—focus first on doing a few relatively simple things well." The report goes on to conclude that "economic strengthening for families affected by AIDS is crucial to improving outcomes for children" and points to "the most effective actions that countries can take to provide vulnerable families with basic economic security. [The study] argues that national social protection policies are the best tools for this task and shows that income transfers can be an especially effective approach." The JLICA report also cites six reasons for supporting income transfers as a priority: They "are efficient and direct," "do not require families to have pre-existing capacities," "empower women and reduce gender inequalities," "serve as a springboard to other services," "are relatively simple to administer," and "are AIDS-sensitive."

In this chapter we argue that cash transfers are practical in even the poorest countries, but only if governments take control, design their own programs, and pay for them largely out of government revenue.

This is increasingly possible because of changing attitudes. Building a domestic political constituency is discussed further in the next chapter. But several points are central. Democratization has given the poor a greater voice, though it is still constrained in many countries. There has been a backlash against the corruption fostered by the "greed is good" attitudes promoted by the international financial institutions. Elites both are frightened by rising crime and violence among unemployed youths and again are promoting the concept of developmental states. The southern alternative of cash transfers fits well in these new politics.

South–South cooperation and learning from neighbors have become another driver. Brazil is advising Ghana; Mexico is assisting Indonesia; the South African pension model is spreading throughout southern Africa. This affects both the thinking around cash transfers and, sometimes more important, the mechanics—how to do registration, targeting, and handing out the money.

Donors and NGOs continue to promote pilot studies. But the distinguished British medical journal *The Lancet* commented that "family poverty and undernutrition can be addressed through income-transfer programmes, such as Mexico's Oportunidades programme or South Africa's child support grants." It goes on to argue that "any developing country, no matter how poor, can afford social protection packages for children." And it concludes that "the positive effect of this policy is now established beyond doubt and no further pilot studies are needed."[2]

NEW TECHNOLOGY MAKES IT POSSIBLE

New technology is transforming the administration of cash transfers, making it practical in even the poorest countries, and with a significant number of cash transfer systems in operation, there is a lot of experience to learn from. No cash transfer system is simple, but new computer and electronic communications systems make registration, distribution of funds, and audits much more practical than even a decade ago.

In this chapter we examine practical issues surrounding registration, handing out the money, and verification. Then we look at costs and consider where low-income countries might acquire the money.

Registration

The process starts with registration. For countries that already have a good identity card system, such as South Africa, that system can be the basis. Chile and Brazil already had registers of potential recipients of a range of benefits. But if a new registration is required, the technology already developed for electoral registration is effective, easy to use, and inexpensive. Indeed, in many countries more people have photo voters cards than have ID documents, and in Lesotho, voters cards were successfully used for initial identification for pensions.

A widely used voter registration system is based on a briefcase containing everything needed for registration: a laptop computer, camera, fingerprint reader, and card printer. The ID card is printed out and sealed in plastic and then handed to the person registering. The card usually has the person's name, address, photo, and fingerprint; an identification number; and often a machine-readable barcode. The process takes just minutes, and the system is robust enough to be carried into remote areas. It runs all day with a pair of batteries, which can be recharged overnight. Data are stored on a CD-ROM or memory stick and taken back to the provincial or national capital for processing, where basic fingerprint reading and other software can be used to reduce multiple registrations. Registration is not expensive; Mozambique in 2007–2008 registered 9 million voters at a cost of $4 each.[3]

The system can also be adapted. Lesotho allows other people to collect pensions for incapacitated elderly people, and this option is chosen by 15% of pensioners, but a photo of the person collecting the pension must also appear on the ID card.[4]

Other identification systems have developed around electoral registration, so that when people have no identity documents of any sort, respected individuals in the community (such as elders, religious leaders, teachers, or even neighbors who do have documents) can confirm that the registrant is who he or she claims to be and can give some estimate of age.

Child and family benefits need birth registration, which is already promoted by UNICEF as one of the rights of the child. All primary healthcare programs and the Millennium Development Goals are linked to efforts to ensure that pregnant women attend clinics and give birth in some structured framework, even if it is at home with a traditional birth attendant. Thus there is a need to link pre- and post-natal care to birth registration, which should be made possible locally.

Registering potential recipients is the easiest part. The next step depends on the type of grant and on the program's goals and targeting. For a pension, the identity card is sufficient. For a family grant or child benefit, the adult receiving the grant will need a card. Older children should also be given cards, because the fingerprint limits multiple registration and will also facilitate school registration and record keeping, especially for a conditional grant. Young children would need a birth certificate or at least a receipt indicating that a birth certificate had been applied for and where the application was filed.

Disability grants have another level of complexity. They usually require certification by a health worker, and they may require the registration of a caregiver who will collect the grant; in this case a double photo card may be issued, as with the Lesotho pension. The identification of some disabilities (such as loss of limbs, blindness, paralysis, and Down syndrome) is relatively straightforward, but other forms of disability (such as learning difficulties and chronic mental health problems) are more difficult to identify, and administrative capacities need to be developed over time.

Up to this point, registration can be done—as is common in electoral registration—with temporary teams or brigades. These teams are often made up of school teachers during the holiday period, and their members need only a few days of training. Many grants also involve a means test, however, and that more complex approach requires a larger administrative system. Very simple means tests can be verified locally. For a social pension that simply requires that the beneficiary not be a recipient of another pension, a respected person in the community can confirm that the person did not work for the government, in the mines, or for a big employer. A simple cutoff for a child or family benefit is that the family earns too little to pay taxes, which can be verified via a check with the tax office and confirmation by a respected person that the registrant is not regularly employed and is not earning significant amounts from trade. This verification also can be done by brigades or teams with limited training. The results may not be perfect, but the overall goal—getting cash to priority households—should be achievable with limited leakage to the better off and limited exclusion of families that should qualify.

It is useful to remember the Brazilian means test, which is self-declaring with only the most rudimentary checks. When the cutoff line is high enough to include all those seen locally as poor, people seem to be relatively honest and do not claim benefits when they should not.

If a more precise means test is required, either because it is politically necessary or because the cutoff is very low and thus divides people who think "we are all poor here," then applying much more complex means tests will require more and better-trained officials. Both direct means tests and proxy means tests require interviews and site visits, although the balance is different. If there is a straight means test, then staff need to be trained in interview techniques and in completing what might be quite complex forms or questionnaires. Usually there is a follow-up visit, at least on a sample basis, to confirm that assets do not vastly exceed those associated with the income claimed. If a proxy means test is used, then survey teams tend to visit the household, and they need to be trained how to make distinctions about assets, such as the quality of a house. Some interviewing will also be required to establish household characteristics, such as family composition and education of household head. Eligibility derived on the basis of means tests or proxy means tests is often assessed centrally.

The final step is often to post the list of recipients. This allows neighbors to say, "She really doesn't have seven children" or "I remember when he was born and he is not 70"—or, conversely, to identify poor or indigent people who were omitted from the list, perhaps because they did not apply. Knowing that lists will be posted is in itself a strong deterrent to making improper applications. Of course, posting lists increases the risk that some applicants will stay away because they fear stigma, especially where the cutoff is low and people are being labeled as indigent or as living in non-viable households. But the community will know in any case when the person or family receives money, and it is hoped that the prospect of improved circumstances will carry more weight than possible embarrassment.

Handing Out Money

Most transfers require that the recipient collect the money. From Indonesia to Lesotho, the most common pay point is the post office, because most medium-sized towns have post offices. But a wide range of institutions that already handle money are also used for payments; these include bank branches, shops, lottery sales offices, and local government offices. Usually the recipient needs no more than the identity card; often there is a small electronic point-of-sale terminal that can read the barcode. A number of countries, however, have moved to machine-readable cards such as credit or debit cards. Some require the user to remember a PIN (personal identification number), and others require a fingerprint. Reliable, low-cost technologies now mean that these "high-tech" mechanisms can be widely accessible.

Several countries where security is a problem use armored cars with cash machines to drive around the country, arriving at the same place on the same day each month. For very sparsely populated countries such as Namibia, this proves more effective than using shops or post offices. Mexico contracts with the post office to make payments. In rural areas, armored cars take money to pay points in community centers and other local facilities; in urban areas, banks are used. Nicaragua contracted with security companies that went to municipal centers and distributed the money to recipients.

Brazil subcontracted distribution to a state bank, Caixa Económica Federal, which offers a simplified current account and has more than 15,000 banking points in lottery sales offices, supermarkets, and petrol (gas) stations. The outlets are linked electronically by point-of-sale terminals (as used for credit cards). Two-thirds of Bolsa Família beneficiaries collect their grant from lottery sales points.[5] Bangladesh recently stopped paying social pensions through municipal offices and now uses banks; this has been shown to be more convenient for recipients and to reduce corruption.

A pilot in Kenya contracted with Equity Bank but made grant payments through shopkeepers and local traders, who paid mainly from their own cash; thus large amounts of money did not need to be transported.[6] Recipients could access grants easily—and they often spent some of the money in the shop.

Ethiopia makes its payments from municipal and government offices. There have been various experiments with vouchers or coupons, which work if they are accepted by a large number of traders and banks but do not work if recipients have to sell them at a discount in order to obtain cash.

Problems can occur when many people are paid in the same place on the same day; there were complaints in Honduras, for example, of people waiting more than nine hours to collect their grant.[7] Either there must be enough pay points, or payment days need to be spread out.

Some countries offer the option of depositing the money into a bank account. This is controversial in three ways. First, forcing people to collect the money has the helpful effect of discouraging those who do not really need it from registering. Second, depositing the money into an account encourages saving, which is good if a goal of the grant is to promote investment, but bad if the grant is intended to promote immediate consumption, notably of food. Third, automatic transfers to banks facilitate fraudulent transfers to "ghosts" on grantee lists.

Finally, mobile telephone technology is advancing rapidly, and phones are already being used for banking and money transfer. It is already possible to deposit the grant in a mobile telephone account and to use text messages to transfer the money—for example, to make payments in shops. Mobile telephone banking began in the Philippines in 2005, and the Kenya M-Pesa scheme started in 2007. Money is transferred by text message, and cash can be deposited by giving money to a registered agent, typically a local shop, which credits the account.

These standard methods cover most people, and experience suggests that people are prepared to travel for a day or two to collect grants large enough to be important. Nevertheless, there are remote areas that are hard to reach, and in many parts of Africa there are no shops, and basic goods are sold only by traveling traders. In the rainy season, these areas may become completely cut off and inaccessible. Often a prominent local person—a chief or elder or teacher—is designated to hand out the money. The money may be delivered to recipients, or they may have to go to the nearest town with a post office to collect their grant—perhaps only every two or three months.

Several countries, including Mozambique and Tanzania, use community representatives to make payments. This arrangement is more complex and expensive, but it increases the likelihood that the poorest households will benefit from cash transfers.

Administration

Administration of an income transfer system is usually entrusted to a special government agency, either a new agency created for the program or one already established to deal with government pensions or social welfare.[8] Some countries, such as Mexico, do all the administration centrally, whereas others, such as Brazil, delegate a large part of the administration to municipalities and local governments.

Means tests and conditions demand a substantial increase in administrative capacity, and they usually entail the hiring of extra staff and the creation of specialized units at the national or local level. In poorer countries with a weaker civil service, this can be a serious problem. The conditions themselves often require an expansion of health and education services, and where work is being guaranteed, projects must be identified and overseen. In countries such as Brazil and Chile where, in different ways, cash transfers are seen as part of broader social support for the poorest, there is a need to expand social services departments. Conditional grants also require that the ministries of education and health be incorporated into the program, which may be hard to do in a country with weak and competing ministries. The design of the program and the choices made must take into account capacity. In Colombia, the program Familias en Acción was restricted to municipalities that had a bank and an adequate health and education apparatus.[9] This simplified administration of the program, but it also left out poor people in more remote and war-affected areas; other countries may opt for a cash transfer system that requires less administration and fewer facilities.

Finally, it is necessary to verify that the conditions have been met. This requires special forms and procedures. It can be handled centrally, or recipients can be required to obtain the necessary certificates and signatures and hand them in to a cash transfers administration office. Sometimes existing documents can be used; for example, the widely used "road-to-health" card already records a child's immunizations and health center visits, as required by many grant conditions.

Updating and Auditing

To function effectively, transfer systems require regular updating: People are born and die, move and marry, and get and lose jobs. Some cash transfers, especially means-tested ones, are for a specific period—typically three years; most allow people to remain in the system for another period if they still qualify. Child benefits normally assume that the grant will be given until the child reaches a certain age, and social pensions are for life, but some young children and the elderly die, at which point their grants should be stopped. Even in industrialized countries there are cases of deaths not being registered so that families can continue to collect pensions, often for many years. This problem is particularly hard to address when benefits are deposited directly into a bank account rather than collected in person.

Many of the same problems apply to electoral registers, which are usually updated annually or every two years via a combination of advertising campaigns and registration brigades traveling around the country. Similar systems can be used for benefit registration, where people need to provide their fingerprint to prove they are still alive and living in the area.

One of the more difficult administrative problems is dealing with changes, such as a move to another town, the births of children, the loss of ID cards, and a change of caretaker. In South Africa, the child grant follows the child but is given to the adult caretaker; if a mother goes out in search of work and the grandmother becomes the caretaker, then the grant should be transferred, but in some cases this process has proved slow. Moves to a new town are often a problem in decentralized systems where records are kept at the municipal level and have to be transferred.

Last but not least, and of particular importance to taxpayers and donors, are transparency and audits. Accounting systems need to be clear enough for money to be traced from the central level down to the beneficiary. Independent auditors are essential. Spot checks of recipients are also needed. One common fraud is the creation of "ghost" recipients who do not really exist, such as extra family members or entirely nonexistent families; this fraud is sometimes perpetrated by middle-level administrators who siphon off the money. Unfortunately, the drive to lower program costs and discourage local corruption by using information technology has created opportunities for centralized theft by "white-collar" criminals. Another common fraud is to give grants to people who manifestly do not qualify, such as families of chiefs, healthy people who have "bought" (that is, bribed someone to issue) a disability certificate, or others who pay the administrator or doctor a share of an improper grant. These frauds are combated both by spot checks and by the publication of lists of beneficiaries. Spot checks are also important to ensure that recipients are receiving their full benefit and that "commissions" have not been extracted or payments missed.

Having active local councilors can make a difference. In Kapashia, Bangladesh, one of us (DH) found Shahida, an elected councilor, waging an effective campaign against a councilor who took "commissions" from widows with pensions. One widow, Muhira Noore, told us, "I used to get Taka 1000 [$15] every few months but it is now Taka 1500 since Shahida talked to the *parishad* [council]." Shahida threatened to expose her male colleague: "I told him, I shall tell the *parishad* meeting you steal from old women."

Maintaining the credibility of a cash transfer system requires ensuring that payments are regular and correct, that lists are accurate and up to date, that honest people can make changes easily, and that the system can be independently audited to prevent misconduct.

HOW MUCH WILL IT COST?

Cash transfers are rarely enough to lift a family out of poverty. But as we noted in Chapter 4, most of the money is spent on food, and it can make a huge difference to a poor family. Mexico's Oportunidades increases purchased consumption levels by an average of 20%.[10] An alternative way to measure the grant is as a proportion of the poverty line, and in both Latin America and Africa, transfers range from 5% to 30% of the national poverty line.[11]

Mozambique gives a social pension ranging from $45 to $135 per year to 150,000 older people.[12] That may not seem like much money in Manchester (England or New Hampshire), but the average cash income in rural Mozambique is only $30 per person per year, and for the poorest 40% of families, cash income averages $12 per person per year,[13] so this pension makes a huge contribution to family consumption. By contrast, the family grant in Honduras amounted to only 4% of a rural family's expenditures, which was not even sufficient to buy enough food to improve nutrition outcomes,[14] so it was too small to have any real impact or to be worth much effort on the part of recipients.

It appears that grants need to increase family consumption by at least 10% to be seen by recipients as useful (as in China, Ecuador, Jamaica, and Brazil's Bolsa Família) and by 15–20% (as Mexico and Colombia) for substantial impacts to be achieved.

That, in turn, is directly linked to the targeting question. Money is inevitably limited, and if the cash is spread too thin, the grant becomes ineffective.

The cost of a program is best estimated as a percentage of GDP (gross domestic product), which is the country's output of goods and services, excluding income from abroad such as aid. As noted in Chapter 3, South Africa is one of the biggest spenders, with 3.5% of GDP (12% of the total national budget) spent on child benefits and social pensions. Brazil spends 1.5% of GDP on pensions and only 0.3% on Bolsa Família; similarly, Mexico spends 0.3% of GDP on Oportunidades.

One question is whether the grant should be indexed and, if so, to what. There is a tendency to set the grant level, leave it at that level (which means that as inflation increases, the grant's value declines), and then perhaps raise the grant level at election time. Brazil has been very progressive and indexes its grants to the minimum wage, which in recent years has been rising more rapidly than inflation. Stephen Devereux[15] of IDS Sussex warns that protecting poor people against rising food and fuel bills requires that cash transfers be index-linked to the price of a basket of basic goods or to the consumer price index (CPI).

The UN's International Labour Organization (ILO) has looked at the cost of basic social protection. It estimates that a universal old-age and disability pension would cost between 0.5% of GDP (for richer countries such as India) and 1.5% of GDP for poorer countries (such as Tanzania and Nepal). Lesotho is one of the very poor countries that already has a pension, and it costs 1.4% of GDP. ILO estimates that a universal child benefit would cost between 1.5% and 3.5% of GDP.

Although this can be a big chunk of a government budget, there are two other ways to assess this. First, we must remember that *not* providing grants entails a cost—a cost measured not directly in GDP but in preventable deaths, stunted children, family breakdown, and weakened social cohesion. Second, and surprisingly, the World Bank notes that "the idea that governments cannot afford to redistribute income to the poor must be contrasted with the evidence that they regularly redistribute income to the nonpoor."[16] Energy subsidies go largely to the better off; Egypt spent 8% of GDP and Indonesia 4% of GDP on such subsidies. Pension subsidies are quite large and often go to the better off. "Another example of where governments have found money to assist the rich but not the poor is the bailouts made to financial sectors," notes the World Bank. After the Asian financial crisis, Indonesia's bank bailout cost 50% of GDP, whereas spending on the poor was under 3%; Korea spent 27% of GDP on banks and 2% on the poor.

And How to Pay

The countries that have started cash transfers have paid for them largely through their own tax revenues, in some cases supplemented by loans from international financial institutions.[17] Not all such arrangements involved tax increases. Initial programs in Indonesia and Mexico replaced fuel and food subsidies that tended to benefit the better off; in many poor countries it should be possible to retarget some subsidies to cash transfer programs. Ghana is initially funding its LEAP (Livelihoods Empowerment Against Poverty) program with money saved from debt service payments after debts were canceled under the HIPC (Heavily Indebted Poor Countries) initiative.

Counties with high levels of cash transfers tend to have higher tax collections. Britain and South Africa, for example, both collect 28% of GDP as tax, Ghana 23%. By contrast, two countries with much less social protection, the United States and India, both collect only 12% of GDP as tax.[18] Chile uses the proceeds from an extra 1% of value-added tax (VAT) and tobacco taxes to finance social programs. Namibia is currently discussing a program costing 3% of GDP that would be funded by a 2% increase in VAT plus a small increase in the highest rate of income tax. Even though they would pay higher levels of VAT, those with lower income would be net gainers.[19]

One problem is the very different revenue structures in the South. The United States may collect only 12% of GDP in taxes, but it collects more than that from employers and employees in social security insurance payments, which in turn fund most of its cash transfers. Most poor countries collect more than 12% of GDP in taxes, but the whole point of adopting cash transfer systems is that so few people are in formal-sector employment on which insurance payments can be made. In many poor countries, customs duties on imports were once an important source of government revenue, but the pressure for free trade and removal of tariff barriers has largely ended duties. And taxes on corporations have been kept low to encourage foreign investment. All that is left is higher taxes on consumption or income. Poor countries tend also to have low tax collection because of badly functioning and sometimes corrupt tax offices. Increasing tax revenue is essential, and there have been experiments with semi-autonomous revenue authorities, where there is close cooperation with the Ministry of Finance, but ministry officials and politicians are not involved in day-to-day operations. These approaches are sometimes linked to group bonus systems, where bonuses are paid to staff in departments (Customs, VAT, Income Tax, and so on) that exceed revenue targets.[20]

Finally, many poor countries have substantial mineral and energy reserves; oil and gas discoveries from Mozambique to Uganda to Ghana, diamonds in Zimbabwe, and a wide range of minerals in Congo promise new streams of revenue. Notorious and blatant corruption in the handling of mineral revenues has led many countries, often induced by domestic or foreign pressure, to join the Extractive Industries Transparency Initiative (EITI) under which mining and energy companies publish what they pay and governments disclose what they receive. Some low-income countries may follow the examples of Alaska and Bolivia and pay for grants directly out of earnings from mineral and energy exports.

What Is the Responsibility of the North?

The gap between the world's rich and its poor is increasing. Yale University philosophy professor Thomas Pogge's views on global justice are widely respected, and he argues that "If the global economic order plays a major role in the persistence of severe poverty worldwide and if our governments, acting in our name, are prominently involved in shaping and upholding this order, then the deprivation of the distant needy may well engage not merely positive duties to assist but also more stringent negative duties not to harm."[21] He continues that "in the real world, the global poverty problem—though it involves one third of all human deaths—is quite small in economic terms."

Nearly 3 billion people live below the international poverty line of $2 per day. It would take $900 billion per year to bring them up to the poverty line, but that is under 3% of the incomes of the billion people in the high-income economies. Similarly, ILO estimates that it would cost only 2% of global GDP to provide basic cash transfers for the world's poor. World military spending reached $1.5 trillion in 2008 (of which 42% was by the United States).[22] This is 2.4% of world GDP and is equivalent to $2.25 per day for every child in the world under 15 years old. As Pogge concludes, "Clearly, we could eradicate severe poverty—through a reform of the global order or through other initiatives designed to compensate for its effects on the global poor—without 'sacrificing' the fulfilment of our own needs or even mildly serious interests."

Some international donors are committed to increasing aid. The G20 wealthiest countries, meeting in London on April 2, 2009, promised substantially increased aid for "social protection" and "income support,"[23] which includes cash transfers. Donors are rarely able to make long-term commitments and money is often tied to projects, while poor countries cannot sustain permanent programs without an assured revenue stream. But it is sometimes possible to use external money for some of the start-up costs. Brazil, for example, used World Bank funds to establish its *cadastro único,* which is a centralized register used for all social programs, including Bolsa Família.

Donors are increasingly giving aid as "general budget support," in which money goes directly into government coffers. Although budget details must be agreed upon with donors, the money can be spent just like tax revenue and other income, and it can be used to fund cash transfers, as is done in Ghana, Pakistan, and Mozambique.

For a number of years there have been calls for global redistribution, and global taxes and alternative global transfers outside the formal aid system are increasingly under discussion. Taxes on financial transactions, airline tickets, and carbon use are being promoted more widely to satisfy two goals at the same time: to slow speculative banking transactions and slow global warming, while also generating revenue that might be used to reduce poverty or create a global child benefit. There would probably be some initial disquiet about money going directly into the government budget, but national cash transfer systems are usually run by a semi-autonomous agency with transparent accounting systems, and thus they already exist as possible recipients of external funds outside the normal donor and NGO system. If necessary, it might be possible to restructure the board of a cash transfer agency to include national government and civil society representatives, preferably ensuring a national majority, but to have bankers or other international representatives on it as well. In that way, taxpayers of rich countries could be assured that their carbon or other tax was assisting poor people. This may still seem a long way off, but governments and donors might start in pairs or groups by making a long-term pledge to fund a benefit in a single country or region.

Keeping Donors on Board But Not in Control

Donors retain overweening power in the policies of the least developed countries. The poorest countries will be dependent on aid for decades to come, and tensions about who is driving the policy agenda will continue. Donors are moving away from food aid and from emergency aid programs and shifting toward support for cash transfers, although often with quite strong agendas, particularly to concentrate on human capital development or safety nets, rather than using cash transfers for redistribution and to promote long-term economic development. Donors and international NGOs often demand eternal pilots or excessive complexity to satisfy their own accounting demands. There is a long history of donor fads: several years of pushing a priority and then dropping it suddenly and moving on to something else. Least developed countries cannot be dependent on the whims of donors if they are to make long-term commitments to cash transfers. Rather, they must have locally designed and politically owned programs that can be funded from government revenue (which may include donor budget support but should include donor project funds only if those projects are unusually long-term.)

Where there is strong domestic political support, donor-dependent governments can act. This is illustrated by three examples of policies introduced recently in southern Africa over strong donor objections. Lesotho introduced its pension in 2004 at a cost of 1.4% of GDP. In 2005 Malawi began a fertilizer subsidy that originally cost 2% of GDP but was quickly increased to 5%. Mozambique in 2006 introduced a decentralized district development program costing 0.6% of GDP. In Asia, donors to Bangladesh said they were enthusiastic about non-contributory social protection but did not support non-contributory old-age pensions, so the government went ahead with a domestically funded social pension.

Although the administrative costs of cash transfers are relatively low, start-up costs (including registration) can be significant, and it is tempting to turn to donors for initial support. But that can give donors too much power over the design of the program, while excluding local interests. Zambia has been reluctant to extend four pilot programs that were pushed, financed, and largely managed by international partners.[24] In Nicaragua, a development bank–driven program was abandoned because it failed to gain local support.

Even for the poorest countries, it may make more sense to start the program locally, funded from the state budget, and try to bring donors on board to expand.

MAKING THE HARDEST CHOICES

Many successful cash transfer programs start out in the range of 0.5% to 1.5% of GDP—large enough to have an impact but small enough to be fundable and politically acceptable both domestically and to donors. Many start small and expand. South Africa's child benefit began with children under 7 and was expanded slowly to children under 15. The Bangladesh pension started with just 5 elderly people in each ward (local administrative unit); later this was increased to 10, and there are plans for further increases. India's rural employment guarantee scheme began in just one state, Maharashtra. Several programs started with the poorest districts. If a program is successful, domestic political and voter pressure often drives its expansion.

Any program must be politically, administratively, and financially feasible. Politically, it must be seen to be fair and useful. It must be within the administrative capacity of the civil service and contractors. In middle-income countries, quite large programs are not terribly expensive; Bolsa Família in Brazil and Oportunidades in Mexico cost 0.3% of GDP (and there are much larger subsidies to pension and social insurance schemes that benefit the better off). But in the least developed countries with large percentages of poor people, even 1% of GDP will not fund a large program of grants. It has to start somewhere—but where?

Returning to Chapter 3 and the discussion of goals, three choices have to be made. First, what is to be the balance between reducing current poverty (the southern Africa preference) and reducing future poverty by investing in the next generation (the Latin American option)? Second, does one target the poor (a majority in the least developed countries) or only the poorest and indigent (perhaps 10% or 15%)? Third, is this program to be seen as purely social welfare (thus targeting only economically inactive households, as in Zambia) or is it to be developmental (and therefore designed to support households that will use the grant to invest in or support job seeking)? These are political as well as practical choices.

Different countries have followed a variety of paths. After several donor-supported pilots, Ethiopia is moving to its Productive Safety Net Programme, which combines dry season labor-intensive public works with direct support for labor-deficient households. More than 7 million people were benefiting in 2008. But this program has a number of problems. Its seasonal nature means it does not provide a guaranteed income. All public works require a high level of administration and management, and if the quality is not good, this may mean high maintenance costs in the future.

In 2006 Malawi launched a program in Mchinji district that attempts to identify the 10% of poorest, non-viable households. By early 2009, the program had reached 7 districts and 23,561 households. Because of the limited capacity of the district and national administration, it will take the program at least until 2013 to reach all 28 districts. By then it will reach 273,000 households, including 1.2 million people, 720,000 of whom are children. On average, households receive $14 per month, and the cost will be 1.4% of GDP.[25] But even then the program will reach only the ultra-poor in labor-constrained households, which means half of the ultra-poor and all the rest of the poor will not be included. Although the program does have some developmental impact (labor-constrained households hire people, and money is spent locally, particularly on food), this is still a social welfare and not a development program. However, this social welfare program for labor-constrained households complements the fertilizer subsidy, which helps those families that are not labor constrained, so the two programs together probably reach most poor households.

Categorical Targeting

There are also serious debates about the ability to target poverty and to correctly identify just 10% or even 20% of people. Even developed countries have problems with means-tested benefits, and many poor people miss out. The most common response to difficulties in targeting poor families is instead to target categories with high proportions of poor people—the old, the young, and the disabled. Pensions have proved to be the preferred starting point in many countries, both in Latin America and southern Africa. Pensions have a strong social resonance, because we feel a responsibility to our elders, and we all hope to be cared for in our old age; in low-income countries, older people are disproportionately poor. Administratively, categorical targeting is one of the easiest cash transfers to operate; pensions have a clear target group, and payments can be transparent. Pensions avoid debates about creating dependency. And there is anecdotal evidence that pension administration suffers less corruption, because even the most venal bureaucrats have consciences: "Who would rob a grandmother?" fieldworkers in southern India asked us. Often disability grants are given by the same agency as old-age grants. Pensions work developmentally because so many elderly people live in multi-generation households, and the money supports many people who invest, look for work, and go to school. The biggest problem is that some very poor households do not have a pensioner, which means they are not helped. But social pensions, once established, tend to generate sufficient political support to ensure their continuation, so they make a good starting point and can be a springboard for other cash transfers. The ILO estimates that a pension would cost 0.5% to 1.5% of GDP, which is exactly in the range for starting a cash transfer. Cost can be reduced by setting the starting age high— the Lesotho pension is for those over 70. It is easy to exclude the small group already receiving pensions (about 4% in Lesotho).

A child benefit is the alternative.[26] Most poor households have children, so this approach is better at responding to current poverty, while also explicitly combating the intergenerational transmission of poverty. In Africa the HIV/AIDS pandemic has battered entire communities and hits families hard because it is precisely the working-age adults who are dying, leaving orphans to be cared for by grandparents or other relatives, so child grants provide direct support. A child benefit is relatively easy to administer, but means testing makes it much more complex. A Brazilian-style self-declaring means test aimed only at excluding the better off, plus publication of lists, would probably exclude the top third of the population in many countries without increasing administration costs significantly. The following three alternatives have been proposed to provide reduced child benefits, which would probably start below the 1.5%-of-GDP threshold but could be expanded later.

- The ILO suggests limiting the benefit to two children per household.
- Save the Children UK argues that "cash transfer programmes should prioritize children under 5 and pregnant women, expanding to older ages as possible."[27] It goes on to add that "the size of the transfer must be sufficient to allow families to invest beyond their immediate consumption needs." This is the model followed by South Africa. It is important because it supports children in that critical first two years of life.
- The ILO has done some modeling on a cash transfer only for school children aged 7–14. For Tanzania and Senegal the cost would be 2.1% of GDP if the grant went to all school children, and it would still have a significant effect on poverty.[28] The most important advantage of this plan is that the grants apparently encourage children to stay in secondary school. An administrative advantage is that the children are old enough to have their own registration cards, and benefits can be linked to schools. Bolivia has a grant of $25 per year for primary school pupils (grades 1–5), but it is paid only to pupils of state schools, a constraint that automatically excludes the better off.

Geographic targeting is yet another option. One choice is to start only with the poorest districts or villages. In most African countries, rural areas are poorer and most poor people are rural; a study for the UNDP's International Poverty Centre in Brasilia concluded that "targeting only rural children is not a bad option to achieve a better poverty outcome."[29] But any kind of geographic targeting can lead to ethnic or political tensions if one groups feels that it is disadvantaged.

And Services

Cash transfers do not end poverty and do not work on their own. Health and education services are essential, and if grants are to be made conditional, services must be in place before the grant starts. Indeed, the lack of essential services leads many to argue that conditions cannot be applied in Africa, because it is impossible for either governments or people to meet them. The cost of basic health care is greater than the cost of cash transfers, going from 1.5% of GDP to as high as 5.5%, the ILO found. An entire package ranges from 4% to 10% of GDP, which would require significant increases in revenues for many countries.

There is also a question of priorities. Even many advocates of cash transfers would argue that a first step is to eliminate user fees; there seems to be no point in giving people money just so they can pay it back to the government for schools and health visits. Ghana first ended school fees, leading to a 20% rise in enrollment in two years. It had already created a National Health Insurance Scheme, but this proved too expensive for poor people, so it was made free to all children under 18. Only then did Ghana introduce LEAP, a program that is conditional on school attendance and on registration with the National Health Insurance Scheme.[30]

LOW-INCOME COUNTRIES
NEED CASH TRANSFERS: KEY ISSUES

There is growing evidence that cash transfers are an essential component of an effective development strategy. Rather than a luxury that comes after development, they are central to helping the poor to climb out of the poverty trap and join an upward development spiral. By their very nature, the informal and peasant economies that dominate most lower-income countries demand cash transfers both as an income guarantee and as a way to promote broad-based economic growth. Cash transfers must be more than social welfare. They also need to be productive, going to poor people who can invest some of the money or use it to fund job searches—and they must be large enough to make a difference to poor families. This is a radical, and southern-driven, change in thinking that explicitly challenges the dominant view in the North that economic growth must come first. Yet it builds on northern history of a century ago, when cash transfers, pensions, and basic social security came first and were the foundation of economic growth and development.

But setting a new agenda means that to be effective, cash transfers must be domestically driven and must have clear local political credibility; they also must be designed in such a way as to strengthen government institutions. Simplicity and transparency in design are likely to lead to greater acceptability and buy-in by the middle classes and elites. These programs will also be easier for weak civil services to administer—an advantage that may make it worthwhile to sacrifice more complex conditions and targeting that might theoretically lead to better outcomes. Finally, cash transfers will not survive if they are donor- and project-based alone; a domestic political constituency is also essential.

This chapter has shown that even the poorest countries can afford cash transfers and can take the lead, designing the program themselves, learning from the experiences of other southern countries, and paying for initial phases from government revenues. Poverty always means that hard choices must be made. But many avenues are available to enable each country to create a national, developmental cash transfer program that can be expanded and extended to make a significant difference to poor households and to the prospects for local and even national economic growth and longer-term social cohesion.

NOTES

1. Alec Irwin, Alayne Adams, and Anne Winter, *Home Truths: Facing the Facts on Children, AIDS, and Poverty,* Final Report (Boston and Geneva: Joint Learning Initiative on Children and HIV/AIDS, 2009), especially Chapter 4, "The Critical Lever: Investing in Social Protection," available at http://www.jlica.org/protected/pdf-feb09/Final%20JLICA%20Report-final.pdf.

2. *The Lancet* Editorial, "A New Agenda for Children Affected by HIV/AIDS," *The Lancet,* 373, no. 9663 (2009); also citing Irwin, Adams, and Winter, *Home Truths.*

3. *Mozambique Political Process Bulletin,* 36, August 18, 2008.

4. Frank Ellis, Stephen Devereux, and Philip White, *Social Protection in Africa* (Cheltenham, UK and Northampton, MA: Edward Elgar, 2009), p. 135.

5. Margaret Grosh et al., *For Protection and Promotion* (Washington, DC: World Bank, 2008), pp. 159–65. Box 5.14, on pages 164 and 165 of the book, has a good discussion of the contracting process.

6. Ellis, Devereux, and White, *Social Protection,* pp. 59–62.

7. Charity Moore, "Assessing Honduras' CCT Programme PRAF, Programa de Asignación Familiar: Expected and Unexpected Realities," Country Study 15 (Brasilia: International Poverty Centre, 2008).

8. Armando Barrientos, "Introducing Basic Social Protection in Low Income Countries: Lessons from Existing Programmes." In *Building Decent Societies. Rethinking the Role of Social Security in Development,* edited by Peter Townsend (London: Palgrave Macmillan and ILO, 2009) 253–73.

9. Orazio Attanasio et al., "How Effective Are Conditional Cash Transfers? Evidence from Colombia," Briefing Note 54 (London: Institute of Fiscal Studies, 2005); and Orazio Attanasio and Alice Mesnard, "The Impact of a Conditional Cash Transfer Programme on Consumption in Colombia," *Fiscal Studies,* 27, no. 4 (2006): 421–42.

10. Emmanuel Skoufias, "PROGRESA and Its Impacts on the Welfare of Rural Households in Mexico" (Washington, DC: IFPRI, 2005), available at http://www.ifpri.org/pubs/abstract/139/rr139.pdf.

11. Jennifer Yablonski with Michael O'Donnell, *Lasting Benefits: The Role of Cash Transfers in Tackling Child Mortality* (London: Save the Children, 2009), available at http://www.savethechildren.org.uk/en/docs/Lasting_Benefits.pdf.

12. D. Matabele and F. Sidumo, "Centena e Meia mil de Idosos Recebe Assistência Social no País," *MediaFax,* Maputo, August 27, 2009.

13. David Mather, Benedito Cunguara, and Duncan Boughton, "Household Income and Assets in Rural Mozambique, 2002–2005," Research Report 66 (Maputo: Ministério da Agricultura and Michigan State University, 2008). Data for 2005 are from Trabalho de Inquérito Agrícola. Cash income per person is for adult equivalents. This is cash income; for all but the best-off quintile (20%), more than half of total income is production for self-consumption.

14. Moore, "Assessing."

15. Stephen Devereux, "Social Protection and the Global Crisis" (Johannesburg: Regional Hunger and Vulnerability Programme, 2009), available at http://www.wahenga.net/index.php/views/comments_view/social_protection_and_the_global_crisis/.

16. Grosh et al., *For Protection and Promotion,* pp. 32–34.

17. Armando Barrientos, "Financing Social Protection." In *Social Protection for the Poor and Poorest: Concepts, Policies and Politics,* edited by Armando Barrientos and David Hulme (London: Palgrave, 2008), pp. 300–12.

18. Figures for 2007 are from World Bank World Development Indicators online, downloaded August 31, 2009. These figures exclude social security contributions by employers and employees. If those are included, then government revenue in the US rises to 28%, well below the OECD average of 36%. From OECD, *OECD Factbook 2009: Economic, Environmental and Social Statistics* (Paris: OECD, 2009).

19. Claudia Haarmann et al., *Making the Difference! The BIG in Namibia* (Windhoek, Namibia: Basic Income Grant Coalition, 2009), available at www.bignam.org.

20. See, for example, the U4 Anti-Corruption Resource Centre at the Chr. Michelsen Institute (CMI), Bergen, Norway. In particular, see "Revenue

Administration and Corruption: 5. What Works?" at http://www.u4.no/themes/pfm/Revenueissue/revenue5.cfm#7.

21. Thomas Pogge, "'Assisting' the Global Poor." In *The Ethics of Assistance: Morality and the Distant Needy,* edited by Deen K. Chaterjee (Cambridge, UK: CUP, 2004), pp. 260–88.

22. Stockholm International Peace Research Institute, *SIPRI Yearbook.*

23. G20, "The Global Plan for Recovery and Reform, 2 April 2009," London, 2009, available at http://www.g20.org/Documents/final-communique.pdf. The pledge is in paragraph 25, headed "Ensuring a fair and sustainable recovery for all," and says, "the actions and decisions we have taken today will provide $50 billion to support social protection, boost trade and safeguard development in low income countries" and "we are making available resources for social protection for the poorest countries." In paragraph 26, the G20 leaders add, "We commit to support those affected by the crisis by creating employment opportunities and through income support measures."

24. Armando Barrientos, David Hulme, and Miguel Nino-Zarazua, "Will the Green Shoots Blossom? A New Wave of Social Protection in Sub-Saharan Africa" (Manchester, UK: Brooks World Poverty Institute, University of Manchester, 2009).

25. Bernd Schubert, "Targeting Social Cash Transfers," Wahenga Comments (2009), http://www.wahenga.net/index.php/views/comments_view/targeting_social_cash_transfers/.

26. Armando Barrientos, and J. DeJong, "Reducing Child Poverty with Cash Transfers: A Sure Thing?" *Development Policy Review,* 24, no. 5 (2006): 537–52.

27. Yablonski with O'Donnell, *Lasting Benefits,* p. 30.

28. Franziska Gassmann and Christina Behrendt, "Cash Benefits in Low-income Countries: Simulating the Effects on Poverty Reduction for Senegal and Tanzania," Issues in Social Protection Discussion Paper 15 (Geneva: International Labour Organization, 2006).

29. Nanak Kakwani, Fabio Soares, and Hyun Son, "Cash Transfers for School-age Children in African Countries: Simulation of Impacts on Poverty and School Attendance," *Development Policy Review,* 24, no. 5 (2006): 555–69.

30. Sonya Sultan and Tamar Schrofer, "Building Support to Have Targeted Social Protection Interventions for the Poorest—the Case of Ghana," Paper delivered at the conference "Social Protection for the Poorest in Africa: Learning from Experience," Kampala, September 8–10, 2008.

10

The Way Forward

CASH TRANSFERS ARE SPREADING ACROSS THE GLOBAL SOUTH AND INCREASingly becoming part of national development strategies. In the short term they reduce poverty levels and ameliorate suffering. In the medium term, they enable many poor people to exercise their agency and pursue microlevel plans to increase their productivity and incomes. In the longer term, they create a generation of healthier and better educated people who can seize economic opportunities and contribute to broad-based economic growth. And when sudden crises spread across the world—such as the recent triple whammy of global food, fuel, and financial crises—they help poor families cope with the consequences of globalization.

Expanding across the South is a heterodox analysis that sees welldesigned cash transfers as contributing to the achievement of several goals at the same time. Brazil, Mexico, South Africa, India, Indonesia, and China are leading the way, but the idea is spreading in a genuinely southern revolution. The focus is on trusting the poor to use money wisely and on emphasizing what poor people already want to do: send their children to school, improve their diet, and make small investments to increase their income. Cash transfers work especially well when money is targeted at a relatively large, easily identified group of people and is seen as developmental.

Recognizing that cash transfers have become an important part of social protection, the rich countries of the North have responded, but they have not yet accepted such transfers as developmental, and they have much less trust in the poor. The North tends to use phrases such as "safety nets" and "social welfare" and to see transfers as temporary or short-term. The attitude of the United States, where the poor are blamed for their poverty (as Table 2.1 shows), is to insist on hard conditions—withdrawing money if children do not attend school or making recipients take jobs with public works projects. Norbert Schady, one of the authors of the 2009 World Bank report *Conditional Cash Transfers*,[1] is a strong advocate of conditions because he is convinced that the problem is the "persistently misguided beliefs" of the poor.[2]

In Europe, and especially among European donors, there is less suspicion of the poor and greater support for cash transfers, but also more of a tendency to view cash transfers as largely welfare or anti-poverty programs. The emphasis is on targeting to keep expenditures down and ensure that the ultra-poor are the main (or only) beneficiaries, because poverty reduction, rather than national development, is the goal.

A century ago, Britain and the rest of Europe shifted from a behavioral to a structural explanation of poverty[3]—from blaming the poor to understanding the poverty trap. By contrast, the United States has clung to the myth that anyone can succeed through hard work alone and, hence, still subscribes to the behavioral explanation of poverty. This still marks the fault line between the two northern tendencies.

These three tendencies (southern, US, and European) reflect different responses both to recent economic crises and to the centrality of market-led development. Back in 1944, the renowned economic historian Karl Polanyi outlined what he called the "double movement" in the development of modern capitalism. The "self-regulating market" was promoted by governments with a wave of special legislation, and it did bring growth. But this free market could not work for labor and the environment. Low wages and unemployment created poverty and misery on a large scale. This led to the counter-movement for "social protection," which was increasingly supported in society, forcing governments to constrain the free market.[4] This double movement can be seen in recent history. The US-driven model of the last three decades of the 20th century (known variously as Reaganism, neoliberalism, and the Washington Consensus) was predicated on the belief that a totally free global market would create rapid and sustained growth and would be the "tide that lifts all boats," especially in poor countries. Structural adjustment in the 1980s was part of an attempt by the North to force the South to promote the "self-regulating market." Yet even in the United States the model has not worked; most people have made no economic gains over the last 20 years, and many have become poorer. The model has also failed in the South, and the last three decades have been lost decades in most developing countries. The lack of development and the growth of poverty outside of China and India, culminating in the 1997 Asian financial crisis, demonstrated the failure of neoliberalism and the Washington Consensus, and it brought about the second part of the double movement: the push for social protection. The northern response was the Millennium Development Goals. These were characterized by a real increase in social spending and strict social targets for health and schools, but they still kept governments at arm's length from the economy. The southern response has been cash transfers, which shift the emphasis to providing poor people with the money they need to take action to end their own poverty and to make full use of economic opportunities.

During the late 1990s Mexico, Brazil, and South Africa introduced big programs in a clearly Polanyian response to the harm being done by the free market. And they were challenging neoliberalism, because the programs are redistributive and involve governments reallocating resources within the country. The initial response from the North was disbelief, and huge numbers of studies (on which this book is based) were commissioned. The studies showed that cash transfers work: They reduce both immediate and intergenerational poverty, and they stimulate the economy and promote development. The subsequent reaction has been driven partly by attitudes about why people are in need, and partly by the desire of the North to ameliorate poverty through safety nets and welfare, without fundamental economic changes, while maintaining pressure on the South not to constrain the northern-dominated free market.

Word of the success of the three trailblazers has spread across the Global South. At least 45 countries now have cash transfers, giving money to more than 110 million families.[5] Immediate poverty is being reduced. Hundreds of thousands of children are now in school because their families can afford to buy them shoes and school clothes—and can get by without the few pennies the children could earn. And families are investing small amounts to raise their own income. Now that they have boots, they are pulling themselves up by their bootstraps. These programs are still young, and this is a global learning exercise. Experiences are being shared between continents; research and experiment are leading to rapid modifications and improvements in programs.

The influence of the US and European tendencies on the development of southern programs varies from country to country, but key patterns can be recognized. In middle-income and larger countries, domestic politicians and planners can consider the conditionality advocated by the United States and the targeting tendencies of European governments and then decide how best to deal with these from a position of relative autonomy. In lower-income countries, however, and especially in those that are smaller and dependent on aid, the degree of autonomy is restricted, and there is a real possibility that the policies selected will derive from external debates rather than arising out of a national policy discussion. The danger of donors dominating national policy formulation about cash transfers becomes real in such cases. But where there is political consensus on an action, it can be put into effect despite donor opposition.

BUILDING LOCAL SUPPORT

Building that local consensus for change is critical, but it can be complex, and the process will surely be different in each country. Political elites must champion the change, and economic elites must at least understand the need for cash transfers. Debates at the global level are also reflected nationally. The better off in poor countries frequently hold the attitudes of Victorian Britain, blaming the "undeserving poor" for their poverty. These attitudes have been reinforced by three decades of neoliberalism, which promoted the idea that it was good to get rich. A study of elites in five southern countries revealed a consensus that "trickle down"—growth in the economy as a whole working its way down to the poorest—would eventually end poverty and that education was the most important thing for the poor.[6]

In a study of elites in Malawi,[7] some admitted that elites actually benefit from poverty. The poor provide cheap labor and votes, as well as jobs in the aid industry. One commented, "Even our donors, if there was no poverty, they would be out of a job." In Malawi, there is consensus among the elite that the poor are not lazy and thus there is no division between deserving and undeserving poor. Nevertheless, elites believe that poverty will never be reduced and that the poor are responsible for their own poverty. That is, the poor do not work hard because they are resigned to poverty as a normal way of life. Thus elites are worried that cash transfers will create dependency. This may be reflected in Malawi's very narrow cash transfer program, which targets only the labor-constrained ultra-poor. The preference for the fertilizer subsidy reflected the elite view that people should be encouraged to work (and it did raise productivity and improve food security very quickly).

In Brazil, by contrast, only 1% of a sample of 311 members of the elite blamed poverty on lack of effort by the poor. Nearly half blamed lack of state effort or lack of political will, and elites believe that the state has a responsibility to provide for the poor. Brazilian elites see poverty and inequality as grave problems and are particularly concerned about criminal violence.[8] Perhaps it is not surprising that a country where the poor are not blamed for poverty, and where the state is given responsibility for alleviating it, has taken the lead in cash transfers.

Politics matters, and effective cash transfer programs can be introduced only when a critical mass of support can be created. Sam Hickey,[9] of the Institute of Development Policy and Management at the University of Manchester, makes the point that civil society does not seem to play an important role in the introduction of cash transfer programs in Africa, because the old, the poor, and the weak do not create active pressure groups. It becomes essential to mobilize support within governments, parliaments, and political parties, and to use the electoral process. It is necessary to tap the social responsibility attitudes of business and social elites, and to convince both elites and the middles classes that cash transfers are in their interest. The general shift from a narrow welfare approach targeting only the poorest to a broader developmental approach seems likely to make it easier to gain support.

Within government, cash transfers are often administered in weaker ministries. Finance and economic development ministries, which have more clout inside government, need to take on cash transfers as development programs. That, in turn, means making the case that cash transfers are not just instruments for mitigating current poverty. They are also profitable investments in longer-term development that are as effective as investments made in roads and dams.

> Why do low-income governments often prefer fertiliser subsidies to social welfare programmes (and why do donors appear to prefer welfare programmes to fertiliser subsidies)? Governments see enhanced access to agricultural inputs as an investment in production, food security and economic growth. Conversely, they regard welfarist handouts to widows and orphans as an unaffordable luxury that generates apathy and dependency among the poor. A great deal of effort has been expended on convincing skeptical governments (especially Ministries of Finance) that they are wrong about cash transfers, which can generate poverty reduction and economic growth and do not generate dependency. But this argument is not yet won,

warns Stephen Devereux.[10] "Making the case for social protection in low-income countries requires making it look politically attractive as well as fiscally affordable, to stakeholders who have to commit to it and will eventually have to pay for it. Politicians are more interested in evidence that social protection will win votes than in evidence that it reduces poverty," he adds.[11]

This point is underlined in a study of drought relief in Africa by Ngonidzashe Munemo.[12] He looked at why some governments have preferred universal food aid and others—or the same governments at different times—have opted for workfare-based relief. And he found, not surprisingly, that incumbent governments that are vulnerable to loss of power prefer measures that offer immediate benefits to a broader group of voters, whereas governments that are secure in their position can afford to opt for programs that are targeted on a smaller group, are developmental, and have a longer time horizon.

Political, and even patronage, power needs to be mobilized in support of cash transfers. This will vary radically among countries. For example, both China and Brazil have decentralized their cash transfer programs to municipalities, which enables local elected officials to take the credit.

Attitudes matter, and the media change the way people think. Repeated articles about "welfare scroungers" create a climate of thinking in terms of the "undeserving poor," but articles about rising school attendance and new businesses begun on a shoestring support approaches designed to lift people out of the household poverty trap. And there is a symbiotic relationship between political leadership and media coverage.

In Ghana, the Ministry of Manpower did not wait for media coverage but, instead, launched a strong advocacy campaign to explain to the public that giving money to poor people is not about "handouts" but rather represents support for children and the elderly and for those who cannot work.[13] In a Chronic Poverty Research Centre study of non-contributory pensions in Lesotho, Namibia, and South Africa, Larisa Pelham concluded that successful programs build a bond between citizen and state based on three factors: social solidarity linked to the value and contribution of the elderly in the household, the understanding that pensions are a permanent program that can be relied on, and acknowledgment of the role of the state in securing the welfare of its citizens.[14]

Local and global events can play an important part in creating changes and openings for introducing social protection policies. The Zapatista rebellion in Mexico, the end of apartheid in South Africa, and the fall of the military dictatorship in Brazil all created space for policy changes. Sam Hickey points to the way social protection policies come to the fore "when the social impacts of liberalised capitalist economies become too great to be borne in political terms," which was happening in Brazil and Mexico—the other half of Polanyi's double movement.

Sam Hickey's research underlines the importance of electoral politics. Parties attempting to stay in power or secure power can use cash transfers to win new constituencies or strengthen existing ones. The balance can be quite complex. Middle-class support is essential, and Hickey points to the need not to include only the very poorest. Programs that do—or could—benefit the middle class are more likely to win support. Fairness, justice, and social responsibility seem to be important intangibles.

Brazil is a good example of party political dynamics at work. Brazil had come out of the 1964–1988 military dictatorship, and the 1988 constitution stipulated that alleviation of poverty was one responsibility of the state. The idea of a child benefit as a first step toward a basic income was tabled by the Workers Party (PT, Partido dos Trabalhadores) and became a subject of public debate. Because of decentralization in Brazil, the idea was first picked up by municipalities, and by 1998, 60 municipalities and four states had child benefit programs. Fernando Henrique Cardoso was standing for reelection as national president in 1998 against the PT's Luiz Inácio Lula da Silva ("Lula"), so he adopted the child benefit (as Bolsa Escola, or School Grant) as a national program. Cardoso won a second term, and Bolsa Escola was scaled up. Lula won in 2002 and expanded the program into the Family Grant (Bolsa Família).[15] That, in turn, increased Lula's popularity, and he won reelection in 2006.

"I like Lula a lot—he gave us Bolsa Família. Many people today have a better life," Selma Aguiar, who runs a luncheonette in Vale do Mearim, in Maranhão state, told BBC Brazil. "He has improved our life, and that of many families, a lot. I receive R$122 [$67] per month. I voted for Lula and I will vote for him again," added Eliene da Silva Brito, a farmer with five children.[16]

In Lesotho, the government was reelected in 2008 partly because of the popularity of the pension introduced in 2004.

In Mexico, not only did the cash transfer survive the historic change in the government of Mexico in the 2000 elections, but the new administration of President Vincente Fox expanded its coverage from rural to poor urban areas of the country, changing the name of the program from Progresa to Oportunidades. The program was politically popular because of the overwhelming and unprecedented evidence that it was alleviating poverty and encouraging poor rural families to send their children to school.[17]

In an opinion survey conducted in South Africa, exactly two-thirds of the population agreed with the statement "The government should spend more money on social grants for the poor, even if it means higher taxes." Perhaps more important, taxpayers also agreed; the statement had the support of 59% of the poor and 63% of paid workers. Thus, in South Africa too, social grants win votes.[18]

In Bangladesh the incoming Awami League government of 2009 canceled the predecessor government's "100 days of work" cash transfer scheme, but then it immediately launched a similar scheme so as not to lose political popularity.

Globally, social pensions seem to be the most popular programs. They are inclusive, satisfy our instinctive desire to support the elderly, are successful and seem fair. For purely selfish reasons, voters are attracted to the idea of universal pensions, which provide peace of mind regarding one's own fate—or the fate of a grandparent, aunt, friend, or neighbor—in old age. Finance and social welfare ministries also see that older people spend a significant part of their pension on children and others in the household, so pensions have a broad impact. A child benefit, as exemplified in South Africa, has similar broad appeal.

It does appear that cash transfers can start small, but successful ones are not narrowly targeted at groups with whom most voters cannot identify. They are established in a way that makes expansion obvious and possible. That is, they are targeted on the poorest districts or on individual municipalities, which makes expansion to other districts a political goal, or they are targeted at younger, poorer children, which makes expansion to a full child benefit seem reasonable.

Nicaragua's Red de Protección Social (RPS, Social Protection Network) illustrates what happens to a program without broad support. Its first phase (2000–2002) was spectacularly successful, improving nutrition and health and increasing school attendance.[19] But for its second phase (2002–2005), cash payments were cut from $19 per family per month to $12. Although the second phase was also successful, the government abandoned the program in 2005, even though funding was available. It was a textbook case of how *not* to design a popular program. First, in an effort to ensure that the program was not seen as "welfare," it never mentioned poverty reduction as one of its goals; instead, the cash was presented purely as a way of buying behavior change on the part of the poor, in order to build human capital. Thus the program had no buy-in from the vast majority of people who felt they knew how to look after their children and thus would never benefit. Second, the program was almost entirely driven by the Inter-American Development Bank (IDB) and by a small group of key civil servants with experience in World Bank and IDB programs within the

Emergency Social Investment Fund (Fondo de Inversión Social de Emergencia, FISE). Program administrators were under huge IDB pressure to implement RPS quickly, so they had no time to build political support in Congress, with President Enrique Bolaños and his Constitutional Liberal Party (PLC), or with the opposition Sandanistas and their leader Daniel Ortega, who was elected president in 2006 and was openly opposed to RPS. Although there was international praise for the program, there was little domestic publicity about its success. Finally, RPS leaders failed to build support even within the civil service. In 2002 it was moved from FISE to the weaker Family Ministry, where there was grumbling about the higher donor-funded salaries of RPS staff. And it was the family minister who decided in 2005 not to continue RPS, despite the continued availability of IDB funds.

Honduras offers another example of the hazards faced by a small and politicized program. Honduras has been experimenting with its family grant (Programa de Asignación Familiar, PRAF) for more than a decade. But the program was too small to gain widespread support and was undermined by competition between IDB and government. Beneficiaries were often chosen on political grounds rather than on the basis of need. Newly elected presidents in 2002 and 2006 dismissed the entire PRAF staff and appointed new people. Not surprisingly, PRAF became identified as a political project of the governing party.[20]

But Nicaragua and Honduras are exceptions to a broader pattern. Where southern governments have been able to take the lead and build a political consensus reflecting local conditions and history, programs are proving popular, effective, and durable.

CASH TRANSFERS WORK

Cash transfers work. They provide the essential boost to lift people out of the poverty trap—they supply the boots that enable people to pull themselves up by their bootstraps. All the evidence is that people spend grant money wisely and that grants do not encourage people to be lazy or workshy. For most poor people, lack of money is the biggest problem. Small farmers in Malawi do not need agricultural extension workers to tell them to use fertilizer on their maize; rather, they need $3.50 to buy half a bag of subsidized fertilizer. Oportunidades recipients in Mexico have convinced even policymakers that they already knew how to make profitable investments and that all they needed was the money. Giving people money is proving to be the best way to stimulate local economic development in low-income countries. Cash transfers are not social programs that can wait until after development; instead, they are an essential precursor to growth and a driver of development.

Vuyiswa Magadla lives in a tiny house at the end of an alley in Khayelitsha in Cape Town, South Africa. She has diabetes and cannot walk much or see well, and she has a disability grant. But she still works selling fruits and vegetables, using money from her grant to buy fresh produce. She may not be well, but she is a good trader. To replenish her stock of vegetables, she travels to a place in Nyanga East, quite far away, rather than buying from a nearby wholesaler, where vegetables are not as fresh. Fortunately, the minibus driver does not charge her extra for the box of vegetables she brings back with her, because she can carry it on her lap.[21]

For the poorest, and for the elderly and disabled, cash transfers are essential social welfare that can lift people out of destitution and enable them to buy a bit of food for a second meal each day. But the importance of cash transfers is much broader. A key element is helping children to be better off as adults than their parents are. Breaking the intergenerational cycle of poverty starts with ensuring that children have more and better food when they are tiny, which prevents malnutrition. This is critical because stunting is mental as well as physical, and children who cannot develop when they are small never recapture that lost physical and metal growth. Next, cash enables children to go to school; they do not have to work to help support the family, and money is available for clothes and books. Children who finish secondary school are much less likely to be poor than those who do not. Thus cash transfers are a critical investment in the next generation and in the long-term elimination of poverty.

The Southern Alternative

Over the past decade, cash transfers have emerged as the response of the Global South to the need for economic development and poverty reduction. The northern-led extreme free market model of the 1980s and 1990s failed in the South, not only not bringing development but often leading to increased poverty and inequality. In the industrialized North, social protection and cash benefit schemes expanded rapidly in the second half of the 20th century, but these were largely insurance-based schemes that assumed male breadwinners employed in steady jobs. In the South, however, most people are still peasant farmers or are working in the informal sector and cannot be covered by insurance schemes. The US variant of the northern model, too, is build on a distrust of poor people and on the assumption that the poor are a relatively small group.

The South has been rethinking the problem from the bottom up. Poor people, who have struggled to survive on tiny amounts of cash, are good economists who use additional money wisely. Giving money directly to poor people solves three problems at once. First, it alleviates immediate poverty; much of the money is spent on more and better food. Second, it enables poor people to invest small amounts in their farms and in small businesses, and all the evidence suggests that ordinary people already know how to make profitable investments. Furthermore, money is spent locally, which stimulates the economy by increasing local demand and creating an upward economic spiral. Third, poor families can send their children to school, creating a healthier and better educated next generation who will play an active role in development.

The key is to trust poor people and directly give them cash—not vouchers or projects or temporary welfare, but money they can invest and use and be sure of. Cash transfers are a key part of the ladder that equips people to climb out of the poverty trap. Letting people make their own choices about how to spend money is hugely empowering and productive.

The late 20th century was a very conservative period. The North, as well as elites in many countries of the South, blamed the poor for their poverty, and some still do not believe that poor people are able to act in the best interests of their children. The first southern cash transfers began in middle-income countries that could fund them out of their own tax revenues and were under increasing political pressure to deal with worsening poverty. The huge distrust in the North meant that these programs have been extensively studied. This scrutiny only increased when "experts" simply did not believe the initial results that showed how well cash transfers were working.

The whole exercise was experimental, but these programs were big, giving money to millions of families—and not just to the poorest of the poor, but to larger groups who were still below the poverty line. Each country started differently. Programs were modified in response to initial feedback and research. And the ideas and experience spread, as more countries introduced cash transfer programs. Research continued and there was increased sharing of information, experience, and ideas.

One lesson is that cash transfers are not a magic bullet; they do not work on their own. There must be schools and health posts, and poor people must have access to them, as well as to land and jobs. But the biggest lesson has been that people must have at least enough money to take advantage of schools, health facilities, and land. And if they *do* have that money, they can take the lead in their own development.

Northern Responses and Opportunities

Middle-income countries, particularly Mexico, Brazil, and South Africa, started cash transfers, but their early success led many low-income countries to launch such programs, which brought the donors and international development banks into the picture. This increased tensions as northern institutions worried that simply giving money to the poor would waste their foreign aid and (for some) reduce their power. The Washington-based institutions, and particularly the IMF, are trying to retain power by refusing to trust the poor and advocating expenditure ceilings and hard conditions. Meanwhile, European donors are uneasy because cash transfers can be developmental and thus might replace some of their traditional development programs, so they tend to support cash transfers only as social welfare.

Northern institutions are trying to catch up, but the initiative and the action remain in the South. The southern model of cash transfers is new, and in a learning culture it is evolving rapidly. And it is not just about poverty and welfare. This is a southern-conceptualized and southern-driven rethinking of the entire development model: Give money to the poor, precisely because they *can* be trusted to make better use of it than aid industry project officers and social workers. Lessons are being learned and experience exchanged. New York is drawing on the experience of both South Africa and Mexico. Indonesia is drawing on Mexico, and Ghana on Brazil. Pensions have spread from South Africa to neighboring states. South–South cooperation is challenging the received wisdom from Washington and London as ideas diffuse from Brazil, India, Mexico, and elsewhere.

But just as cash transfers in the South have been groundbreaking, the most interesting responses in the North have come from outside the normal aid and development network. President Barack Obama of the United States specifically asked Indonesia's President Susilo Bambang Yudhoyono to speak at the G20 meeting in Pittsburg in September 2009 to promote his policy of phasing out fuel subsidies and giving the money to the poor as cash transfers instead. It was an unexpected meeting of several policy lines. From a climate change perspective, Obama is promoting an end to fossil fuel subsidies. Just two months before, Yudhoyono had been reelected president with more than 60 percent of the vote, and his landslide victory was attributed in part to increased support from the poor because of cash transfers.[22] Thus climate change, democracy, and cash transfers to help the poor are coming together in a new way.

Meanwhile, in the North there is increasingly serious advocacy of taxes on financial transactions and on the use of carbon. In both cases the intent is to increase costs—the costs of risky financial transactions and of damaging the environment. But both would raise substantial revenue. In mid-2009, both French President Nicolas Sarkozy and Lord Adair Turner, the chairman of Britain's financial watchdog, the Financial Services Authority, proposed the Tobin Tax. French Foreign Minister Bernard Kouchner argued that a tax of just 0.005% on financial transactions could bring in up to €30bn ($45bn) a year for development.[23] Other proposals that have been floated include giving individual carbon credits and providing money to help poor countries maintain rainforests.

One question that is always raised is how the money would be delivered. Cash transfers provide an obvious answer. Child poverty expert Peter Townsend promoted a worldwide child benefit, which could be funded through such a tax. But the most important point is that successful cash transfers are locally designed and transparent. Local people make the choices about targeting and about whether to impose conditions, but the distribution of funds is much easier to audit with cash transfers than with conventional northern-funded development projects. Thus with cash transfers, northern taxpayers could be assured that their money was being distributed to children, to poor families, or to the elderly.

The poorest countries, particularly in Africa, can afford only limited cash transfer programs with their own resources, so to be effective these programs will need outside finance for years to come. But the shifts in thinking, away from conventional aid projects toward budget support and block grants, and toward non-traditional revenue sources such as the Tobin Tax, all point to cash transfers as the most effective way to distribute this money. They have the potential to reduce poverty, while promoting development, slowing climate change, and reducing the likelihood of another financial crisis.

Five Principles

This book has laid out a wide range of debates about the specific goals, targets, and conditions of cash transfers. Each country is developing its own model that reflects its own needs, history, and politics. There is no single "best" cash transfer program. But we can outline five overriding principles: Cash transfers work when they are fair, assured, practical, large enough to affect household income, and popular.

FAIR: Grants must be seen to be fair in the sense that most citizens agree on the choice of who receives money and who does not. Categorical grants—those that give money to all or nearly all children or elderly—are usually seen as fair, but they may not always target the most needy. A strategy of excluding the better off, as in Brazil and South Africa, is sometimes seen as fairer than trying to distinguish among shades of poverty. Targeting the poorest or the ultra-poor requires much more care, because it can be divisive and can create conflict between neighbors when some receive a grant and others do not; proxy means tests may be relatively accurate, but they are not easily understood by beneficiaries.

ASSURED: Recipients must be convinced that the money will really arrive every month and that families can depend on it. Only then will families be able to make long-term plans and invest in schooling and income generation. The insurance function of grants is important because people know that if their crop fails or they fall ill, some money will continue to come in—and this enables people to take risks on growing new crops or going further afield to look for work.

PRACTICAL: Directly related to the requirement that grants be fair and assured is the need for a reliable system to identify legitimate recipients and to ensure that they receive their grant regularly. There must be enough trained civil servants to administer the system, and there must be a reliable and secure banking or cash distribution system to hand out the payments. Sophisticated proxy means tests and complex conditions are of no use if they cannot be applied correctly and consistently. Some countries have much more experienced civil services than others, and some countries, particularly in Africa, may be forced to adopt simpler systems because of lack of capacity. A growing number of innovative systems have proved effective in transferring cash where civil services are weak. For example, grants can be distributed through post offices, lottery agents, and even mobile phones.

NOT JUST PENNIES: Grants must be large enough to cause a real change in behavior, such as growing new crops or sending children to school. If money is only enough to enable one extra child in the family to go to school, it is not working. In communities in rural Africa where cash incomes are very low and people produce a significant amount of their own food, even a few dollars a month makes a huge difference. In more industrialized countries where the cash poverty line is higher, it requires more money to make a meaningful difference. Indications are that the grant must be not less than 20% of poor households' consumption, and where this criterion is not met, the grants are unlikely to have the desired effect.

POPULAR: Any grant program must be politically acceptable and (ideally) popular and a vote winner. Cash transfers are an important step on the path to achieving social contracts in developing countries and thus replacing conflict and corruption with solidarity and social bonds. Donor-initiated and donor-driven programs are less like to win approval than programs that have indigenous roots.

These principles need interpreting at the national level, because no "models" can be automatically transferred from country to country. High-quality technical analysis is needed, alongside the recognition that effective programs must be based on local political support. Each government will juggle with goals and competing demands for resources and, in so doing, develop its own approach. But a decade of experience shows that cash transfers work. *To reduce poverty and promote development, just give money to the poor.*

NOTES

1. Ariel Fiszbein and Norbert Schady, *Conditional Cash Transfers* (Washington, DC: World Bank, 2009).

2. Speaking at a meeting in London, May 26, 2009.

3. Elisa Reis and Mick Moore, "Elites, Perception and Poverties." In *Elite Perceptions of Poverty and Inequality,* edited by Elisa P. Reis and Mick Moore (Zed: London, 2005), p. 197.

4. Karl Polanyi, *The Great Transformation: The Political and Economic Origins of Our Time* (Boston, MA: Beacon, 1944, 1957, 2001); James Putzel, "Politics, the State and the Impulse for Social Protection: The Implications of Karl Polanyi's Ideas for Understanding Development and Crisis," Crisis States Working Paper 1 (London: London School of Economics, 2002), available at http://www.crisisstates.com/download/wp/WP18JP.pdf.

5. Armando Barrientos and David Hulme, "Social Protection for the Poor and Poorest in Developing Countries: Reflections on a Quiet Revolution," *Oxford Development Studies,* 38, no. 1 (2010).

6. Reis and Moore, "Elites," p. 19.

7. Chipiliro Kalebe-Nyamongo, "Elite Perceptions of Poverty in Malawi," Paper presented at the conference "The Roles of Elites in Economic Development," June 12–13 (Helsinki, UNU-Wider, 2009).

8. Elisa Reis, "Perceptions of Poverty and Inequality Among Brazilian Elites." In *Elite Perceptions,* p. 38; Elisa Reis, "Poverty and Inequality in the Eyes of the Elites," Paper presented at the conference "The Roles of Elites in Economic Development," June 12–13 (Helsinki, UN-Wider, 2009).

9. Sam Hickey, "The Politics of What Works in Reducing Chronic Poverty," Chronic Poverty Research Centre Working Paper 91 (Manchester, UK: CPRC, 2006).

10. Stephen Devereux, "Social Protection and the Global Crisis" (Johannesburg: Regional Hunger and Vulnerability Programme, 2009), available at http://www.wahenga.net/index.php/views/comments_view/social_protection_and_the_global_crisis/.

11. Devereux, "Social Protection."

12. Ngonidzashe Munemo, "Political Incumbency and Drought Relief in Africa." In *Social Protection for the Poor and the Poorest,* edited by Armando Barrientos and David Hulme (Basingstoke: Palgrave Macmillan, 2008).

13. Sonya Sultan and Tamar Schrofer, "Building Support to Have Targeted Social Protection Interventions for the Poorest—The Case of Ghana," Paper presented at the conference "Social Protection for the Poorest in Africa: Learning from Experience," Kampala, September 8–10, 2008.

14. Larissa Pelham, "The Politics Behind the Non-contributory Old Age Social Pensions in Lesotho, Namibia, and South Africa," Working Paper 83 (Manchester, UK: Chronic Poverty Research Centre, 2007).

15. Marcus Melo, "Political Competition Can Be Positive: Embedding Cash Transfer Programmes in Brazil." In *Development Success: Statecraft in the South,* edited by Anthony Bebbington and Willy McCourt (Basingstoke, UK: Palgrave Macmillan, 2007).

16. Alessandra Corrêa, "Desabrigados ainda Reverenciam Lula, mas Ignoram Dilma," BBC Brasil, May 29, 2009, http://www.bbc.co.uk/portuguese/noticias/2009/05/090528_maranhao_luladilma_ac_cq.shtml.

17. Emmanuel Skoufias, "PROGRESA and Its Impacts on the Welfare of Rural Households in Mexico" (Washington, DC: IFPRI, 2005), available at http://www.ifpri.org/pubs/abstract/139/rr139.pdf.

18. Michael Noble, Phakama Ntshongwana, and Rebecca Surender, "Attitudes to Work and Social Security in South Africa" (Cape Town: Human Sciences Research Council, 2008), available at www.hsrcpress.ac.za.

19. Charity Moore, "Nicaragua's Red de Protección Social: An Exemplary But Short-Lived Conditional Cash Transfer Programme," Country Study 17 (Brasilia: UNDP International Policy Centre for Inclusive Growth, 2009), available at http://www.ipc-undp.org/pub/IPCCountryStudy17.pdf.

20. Rafael Guerreiro Osório, "The Recent Impact of Government Transfers on Poverty in Honduras and Alternatives to Enhance their Effects," Working

Paper 47 (Brasilia: UNDP International Poverty Centre, 2008); Charity Moore, "Assessing Honduras' CCT Programme PRAF, Programa de Asignación Familiar: Expected and Unexpected Results," Country Study 15 (Brasilia: UNDP International Poverty Centre, 2008).

21. Andries du Toit and David Neves, "Vulnerability and Social Protection at the Margins of the Formal Economy—Case Studies from Khyelitsha and the Eastern Cape" (Cape Town: USAID and Programme for Land and Agrarian Studies, 2006).

22. Fiona Harvey and Edward Luce, "US Backs Ending of Fossil Fuel Subsidies," *Financial Times,* September 24, 2009; Nick Perry, "Indonesians Choose Reformist Yudhoyono," *UPI-Asia,* July 13, 2009.

23. Phillip Inman, "Miliband Supports Tobin Tax, Claims French Foreign Minister—Levy on Foreign Exchange Deals 'Could Raise £27bn to Help Developing Nations,'" *Guardian,* September 17, 2009.

BACKGROUND
AND RESEARCH DATA

THIS BOOK IS BASED ON JUST SOME OF THE HUGE AMOUNT OF RESEARCH data on cash transfers. There are several key reports that summarize this research, and several websites present a wide range of studies. The most important of these sources follow.

Publications

Brooks World Poverty Institute. Armando Barrientos and David Hulme, *Social Protection for the Poor and Poorest* (Basingstoke: Palgrave Macmillan, 2008).

Save the Children UK. Jennifer Yablonski with Michael O'Donnell, *Lasting Benefits: The Role of Cash Transfers in Tackling Child Mortality* (London: Save the Children, 2009), http://www.savethechildren.org.uk/en/docs/Lasting_Benefits .pdf.

World Bank. Margaret Grosh, Carlo del Ninno, Emil Tesliuc, and Azedine Ouerghi, *For Protection and Promotion: The Design and Implementation of Effective Safety Nets* (Washington, DC: World Bank, 2008).

Regional Hunger and Vulnerability Programme. Frank Ellis, Stephen Devereux, and Philip White, *Social Protection in Africa* (Cheltenham, UK: Edward Elgar, 2009).

Literature Reviews

Joint Learning Initiative on Children and HIV/AIDS. Michelle Adato and Lucy Bassett, "What Is the Potential of Cash Transfers to Strengthen Families Affected by HIV and AIDS? A Review of the Evidence on Impacts and Key

Policy Debates" (Washington, DC: International Food Policy Research Institute, 2008), available at http://www.jlica.org/.

Maxine Molyneux. *Conditional Cash Transfers and Women's Empowerment: Annotated Bibliography* (London, Institute for the Study of the Americas, University of London, 2008) http://www.americas.sas.ac.uk/about/docs/CCTAN NotatedBibDFID.pdf.

Websites

The United Nations Development Programme (UNDP) **International Policy Centre for Inclusive Growth** (IPC-IG), formerly the International Poverty Centre, in Brazil has an excellent Cash Transfers and Social Protection archive, http://www.ipc-undp.org/cct.do.

Brazil – Bolsa Família. In Portuguese: A Biblioteca Virtual do Bolsa Família, http://www.ipc-undp.org/mds.do.

Mexico – Oportunidades. External evaluations.
In English: http://evaluacion.oportunidades.gob.mx:8010/en/index.php.
In Spanish: http://evaluacion.oportunidades.gob.mx:8010/es/index.php.

Social Assistance in Developing Countries Database
http://www.chronicpoverty.org/uploads/publication_files/Social_ Assistance_Database_Version4_August2008.pdf.

Brooks World Poverty Institute. Working papers on social protection: http:// www.bwpi.manchester.ac.uk/.

Chronic Poverty Research Centre. Research on insecurity, risk, and vulnerability: http://www.chronicpoverty.org/research-themes-vulnerability.php.

ACKNOWLEDGMENTS

WE HAVE DRAWN ON THE RESEARCH OF DOZENS OF PEOPLE IN MANY COUN-tries whose meticulous study of individual cash transfer programs made this book possible. We would like to thank all the researchers who talked to us, sent us material, and shared their data and thinking. We also want to thank Nyeleti Honwana, Chris Elliott, and James Scott for helping us pull together the details. And we would like to acknowledge the financial support of the Chronic Poverty Research Centre and Brooks World Poverty Institute at the University of Manchester and the International Development Centre at the Open University.

BIBLIOGRAPHY

Adato, Michelle. *The Impact of PROGRESA on Community Social Relationships: Final Report.* Washington, DC: IFPRI, 2000, available at http://www.ifpri .org/sites/default/files/publications/adato_community.pdf.

Adato, Michelle, and Lucy Bassett. "What Is the Potential of Cash Transfers to Strengthen Families Affected by HIV and AIDS? A Review of the Evidence on Impacts and Key Policy Debates." Review for the Joint Learning Initiative on Children and HIV/AIDS. Washington, DC: IFPRI, 2008, available at http://programs.ifpri.org/renewal/pdf/JLICACashTransfers.pdf.

Adato, Michelle, Benedicte de la Briere, Dubravka Mindek, and Agnes R. Quisumbing. *The Impact of PROGRESA on Women's Status and Intrahousehold Relations.* Washington, DC: IFPRI, 2008, available at http://www.ifpri .org/themes/progresa/pdf/Adato_intrahh.pdf.

Adato, Michelle, and Terry Roopnaraine. "A Social Analysis of the Red de Protección Social (RPS) in Nicaragua." Washington: IFPRI, 2004.

Agüero, Jorge M., Michael R. Carter, and Ingrid Woolard. "The Impact of Unconditional Cash Transfers on Nutrition: The South African Child Support Grant." Working Paper 39. Brasilia: UNDP International Poverty Centre, 2007.

Altman, Miriam, and Gerard Boyce. "Policy Options to Leverage the System of Social Grants for Improved Access to Economic Opportunity. Paper 1: Overview of Grant Beneficiary Households." Pretoria: HSRC, 2008.

Angelucci, Manuela. "Aid and Migration: An Analysis of the Impact of Progessa on the Timing and Size of Labour Migration." Centre for the Evaluation of Development Policies Report EWP04.05. London: Institute for Fiscal Studies, 2004.

Ardington, Cally, Anne Case, and Victoria Hosegood. "Labor Supply Responses to Large Social Transfers: Longitudinal Evidence from South Africa," *American*

Economic Journal: Applied Economics, 1, no. 1 (2009): 22–48. An earlier version of this paper is available as NBER Working Paper No. 13442. Cambridge, MA: National Bureau of Economic Research, 2007, available at http://www.nber.org/papers/w13442.

Armendariz, Beatriz, and Jonathan Morduch. *The Economics of Microfinance.* Cambridge, MA: MIT Press, 2005.

Attanasio, Orazio, and Alice Mesnard. The Impact of a Conditional Cash Transfer Programme on Consumption in Colombia." *Fiscal Studies,* 27, no. 4 (2006): 421–42.

Attanasio, Orazio, Erich Battistin, Emla Fitzsimmons, Alice Mesnard, and Marcos Vera-Henández. "How Effective Are Conditional Cash Transfers? Evidence from Colombia." Briefing Note 54. London: Institute of Fiscal Studies, 2005.

Attanasio, Orazio, Emla Fitzsimons, and Ana Gomez. "The Impact of a Conditional Education Subsidy on School Enrolment in Colombia." London: Institute of Fiscal Studies, 2005, available at http://www.ifs.org.uk/publications/3329.

Attanasio, Orazio, Emla Fitzsimons, Ana Gomez, Martha Isabel Gutiérrez, Costas Meghir, and Alice Mesnard. "Child Education and Work Choices in the Presence of a Conditional Cash Transfer Programme in Rural Colombia." IFS Working Papers W06/13. London: Institute for Fiscal Studies, 2006.

Attanasio, Orazio, Costas Meghir, and Ana Santiago. "Education Choices in Mexico: Using a Structural Model and a Randomized Experiment to Evaluate Progresa." London: Centre for the Evaluation of Development Policies, Institute for Fiscal Studies, 2005, available at http://www.ifs.org.uk/projects/301.

Barrientos, Armando, and Jocelyn DeJong. "Reducing Child Poverty with Cash Transfers: A Sure Thing?" *Development Policy Review,* 24, no. 5 (2006): 537–52.

Barrientos, Armando, Rebecca Holmes, and James Scott. "Social Assistance in Developing Countries Database Version 4." Manchester, UK: Brooks World Poverty Institute and CPRC, 2008.

Barrientos, Armando, and David Hulme. "Social Protection for the Poor and Poorest in Developing Countries: Reflections on a Quiet Revolution." *Oxford Development Studies,* 38, no. 1 (2010).

Barrientos, Armando, David Hulme, and Miguel Nino-Zarazua. "Will the Green Shoots Blossom? A New Wave of Social Protection in Sub-Saharan Africa." Manchester, UK: Brooks World Poverty Institute, University of Manchester, 2009.

Barrientos, Armando, and Claudio Santibañez. "New Forms of Social Assistance and the Evolution of Social Protection in Latin America." *Journal of Latin American Studies,* 41, no. 1 (2009): 1–26.

———. "Social Policy for Poverty Reduction in Low Income Countries in Latin America: Lessons and Challenges." *Social Policy & Administration,* 43, no. 4 (2009): 409–24.

Barrientos, Armando. "Cash Transfers for Older People Reduce Poverty and In-
    equality." In *Institutional Pathways to Equity: Addressing Inequality Traps,* ed-
    ited by Anthony J. Bebbington, Anis A. Dani, Arjan de Haan, and Michael
    Walton, 169–92. Washington DC: World Bank, 2008.

———. "Comparing Pension Schemes in Chile, Singapore, Brazil and South
    Africa." IDPM Discussion Paper 67. Manchester: University of Manchester,
    2005, available at http://www.sed.manchester.ac.uk/idpm/research/publications/
    wp/dp/documents/dp_wp67.pdf.

———. "Introducing Basic Social Protection in Low Income Countries: Lessons
    from Existing Programmes." In *Building Decent Societies. Rethinking the Role
    of Social Security in Development,* edited by Peter Townsend, 253–73. Lon-
    don: Palgrave Macmillan and ILO, 2009.

———. "Financing Social Protection." In *Social Protection for the Poor and Poor-
    est: Concepts, Policies and Politics,* edited by Armando Barrientos and David
    Hulme, 300–12. London: Palgrave, 2008.

———. "Pensions and Development in the South." *Geneva Papers on Risk & In-
    surance,* 28, no. 4 (2003): 696–711.

———. "Pensions for Development and Poverty Reduction." In *Oxford Hand-
    book of Pensions and Retirement Income,* edited by Gordon L. Clark, Alicia H.
    Munnell, and J. Michael Orszag, 782–98. Oxford: Oxford University Press,
    2006.

———. "Social Pensions in Low Income Countries." In *Closing the Coverage
    Gap: The Role of Social Pensions and Other Retirement Transfers,* edited by
    Robert Holzman, David A. Robalino, and Noriyuki Takayama, 73–84. Wash-
    ington, DC: World Bank, 2009.

———. "Social Protection and Growth: A Review." CPRC Working Paper 112.
    Manchester, UK: Brooks World Poverty Institute and CPRC, 2008.

Bedia, Arjun S., and Jeffery H. Marshall. "Primary School Attendance in Hon-
    duras." *Journal of Development Economics,* 69, no. 1 (2002): 129–53.

Begum, Sharifa, and Binayak Sen. "Maternal Health, Child Well-being and In-
    tergenerationally Transmitted Chronic Poverty: Does Women's Agency
    Matter?" Working Paper 8. Manchester: Chronic Poverty Research Centre,
    2005.

Bellamy, Carol. "Commentary: The 6 Billionth Baby." In *The Progress of Nations
    1999.* New York: UNICEF, 1999.

de Brauw, Alan, and John Hoddinott. "Is the Conditionality Necessary in Con-
    ditional Cash Transfer Programmes? Evidence from Mexico." One Pager 64.
    Brasilia: International Poverty Centre, 2008.

———. "Must Conditional Cash Transfer Programs Be Conditional to Be Effec-
    tive?" Discussion Paper 757. Washington, DC: IFPRI, 2008.

de Britto, Tatiana Feitosa. "The Emergence and Popularity of Conditional Cash
    Transfers in Latin America." In *Social Protection for the Poor and Poorest,* ed-
    ited by Armando Barrientos and David Hulme. Basingstoke, UK: Palgrave
    Macmillan, 2008.

Budlender, Debbie, Solange Rosa, and Katharine Hall, "At All Costs? Applying the Means Test for the Child Support Grant." Cape Town: Children's Institute and Centre for Actuarial Research, University of Cape Town, 2005.

Carrera, Mauricio. *Oportunidades: Historias de Éxito.* Mexico: Secretaría de Desarrollo Social, Coordinación Nacional del Programa de Desarrollo Humano Oportunidades, 2008. Published in English as *Oportunidades: Stories of Success.*

Case, Anne, Victoria Hosegood, and Frances Lund, "The Reach and Impact of Child Support Grants: Evidence from KwaZulu-Natal." *Development Southern Africa,* 22, no. 4 (2005): 467–82.

Chaudhry, Peter. "Unconditional Direct Cash Transfers to the Very Poor in Central Vietnam." Paper presented at the "What Works for the Poorest" conference (BRAC and CPRC), December 3, 2006, Dhaka, Bangladesh.

Chen, Shaohua, Martin Ravallion, and Youjuan Wang, "Di Bao: A Guaranteed Minimum Income in China's Cities?" Policy Research Working Paper 3805. Washington, DC: World Bank, 2006.

Chinsinga, Blessings, and Aoiffe O'Brien. *Planting Ideas—How Agricultural Subsidies Are Working in Malawi.* London: Africa Research Institute, 2008.

Chronic Poverty Research Centre. *The Chronic Poverty Report 2008–09.* Manchester, UK: Chronic Poverty Research Centre, 2008.

Clark, Fiona. "Renta Dignidad." New York: Global Action on Aging, 2008, available at http://www.globalaging.org/pension/world/2008/Renta.htm.

Coady, David, Margaret Grosh, and John Hoddinott. "Targeting Outcomes Redux." Washington, DC: IFPRI, 2002, available at http://www.ifpri.org/divs/fcnd/dp/papers/fcndp144.pdf.

Collier, Paul. *The Bottom Billion.* Oxford: Oxford University Press, 2008.

Corrêa, Alessandra. "Desabrigados ainda Reverenciam Lula, mas Ignoram Dilma." BBC Brasil, May 29, 2009, http://www.bbc.co.uk/portuguese/noticias/2009/05/090528_maranhao_luladilma_ac_cq.shtml.

Cortés, Maribel Lozano. "Evaluación Cualitativa de los Impactos del Programa Oportunidades, en Alimentación, Salud y Educación en los Municipios del sur de Yucatán (2004–2005)." Quintana Roo, México: Universidad de Quintana Roo, 2006.

Davies, Simon. "Making the Most of It: A Regional Multiplier Approach to Estimating the Impact of Cash Transfers on the Market." Malawi: Concern Worldwide, 2007.

Delany, Aislinn, Zenobia Ismail, Lauren Graham, and Yuri Ramkissoon. *Review of the Child Support Grant: Uses, Implementation and Obstacles* (Johannesburg: Community Agency for Social Enquiry for UNICEF and the South African Social Security Agency, 2008.

Devereux, Stephen. "Social Protection and the Global Crisis." Johannesburg: Regional Hunger and Vulnerability Programme, 2009, available at http://www.wahenga.net/index.php/views/comments_view/social_protection_and_the_global_crisis/.

Devereux, Stephen, Rachel Sabates-Wheeler, Mulugeta Tefera, and Hailemichael Taye. "Ethiopia's Productive Safety Net Programme." Brighton, UK: Institute of Development Studies, and Addis Ababa: Indak International, 2006.

Dias, Magda Núcia Albuquerque, and Maria do Rosário de Fátima e Silva. "A Condição de Pobreza das Famílias Beneficiárias do Programa Bolsa Família no Município de Bacabal—MA: a Importância do Benefício." Brasilia: UNDP International Poverty Centre, Biblioteca Virtual do Bolsa Família, 2008, available at http://www.ipc-undp.org/publications/mds/34P.pdf.

————. "O Programa Bolsa Família no Município de Bacabal—MA: Avaliação de Implementação com o Foco nas Condicionalidades." Brasilia: UNDP International Poverty Centre, 2008, available at the Biblioteca Virtual do Bolsa Família, http://www.ipc-undp.org/publications/mds/29M.pdf.

Dirección de Comunicación Social, Programa de Desarrollo Humano Oportunidades, "Oportunidades, un Programa de Resultados." México: Sedesol—Secretaría de Desarrollo Social, 2008.

Duflo, Esther. "Child Health and Household Resources in South Africa: Evidence from the Old Age Pension Program." *American Economic Review,* 90, no. 2 (2000): 393–98.

Dugger, Celia W. "To Help Poor Be Pupils, Not Wage Earners, Brazil Pays Parents." *New York Times,* January 3, 2004.

Elliott, Larry. "Proposed Tax on Forex Trades to Raise $50bn Aid." *Observer,* London, May 24, 2009.

Ellis, Frank. "'We Are All Poor Here': Economic Difference, Social Divisiveness, and Targeting Cash Transfers in Sub-Saharan Africa." Paper presented at the conference on "Social Protection for the Poorest in Africa: Learning from Experience," Kampala, Uganda, September 8–10, 2008.

Ellis, Frank, Stephen Devereux, and Philip White. *Social Protection in Africa.* Cheltenham, UK, and Northampton, MA: Edward Elgar, 2009.

Escobar Latapí, Augustín, and Mercedes González de la Rocha. "Evaluacion Cualitativa del Programa Oportunidades. Etapa urbana 2003." Mexico City: CIESAS—Occidente, 2009.

————. "Girls, Mothers and Poverty Reduction in Mexico: Evaluating Progresa-Oportunidades." In *The Gendered Impacts of Liberalisation: Towards "Embedded Liberalism"?* edited by Shahra Razavi. New York and Abingdon: Routledge/UNRISD, 2009.

Farrington, John, and Rachel Slater. "Introduction: Cash Transfers: Panacea for Poverty Reduction or Money Down the Drain?" *Development Policy Review,* 24, no. 5 (2006): 499–510.

Ferreira, Francisco, Peter Lanjouw, and Marcelo Neri. "A Robust Poverty Profile for Brazil Using Multiple Data Sources." *Revista Brasileira de Economia,* 57, no. 1 (2003): 59–92.

Fiszbein, Ariel, and Norbert Schady. *Conditional Cash Transfers: Reducing Present and Future Poverty.* Washington, DC: World Bank, 2009.

Förster, Michael, and Marco Mira d'Ercole. "Poverty in OECD Counties: An Assessment Based on Static Income." In OECD, *Growing Unequal? Income Distribution and Poverty in OECD Countries.* Paris: OECD, 2008.

G20. "The Global Plan for Recovery and Reform, 2 April 2009." London, 2009, available at http://www.g20.org/Documents/final-communique.pdf.

Gaiha, Raghav, and Katsushi Imai. "The Maharastra Employment Guarantee Scheme." Policy Brief 6. London: Overseas Development Institute, 2006.

Gassmann, Franziska, and Christina Behrendt. "Cash Benefits in Low-income Countries: Simulating the Effects on Poverty Reduction for Senegal and Tanzania." Issues in Social Protection Discussion Paper 15. Geneva: International Labour Organization, 2006.

Gelbach, Jonath, and Lant Pritchett. "More for the Poor Is Less for the Poor—The Politics of Targeting." Policy Research Working Paper 1799. Washington, DC: World Bank, 1997, available at http://go.worldbank.org/9BTYD9ZMT0.

Gertler, Paul, Sebastian Martinez, and Marta Rubio-Codina. "Investing Cash Transfers to Raise Long-Term Living Standards." Report WPS3994-IE. Washington, DC: World Bank, 2006, available at http://go.worldbank.org/59S3O8JZP0.

Gilligan, Daniel, John Hoddinott, and Alemayehu Seyoum Taffesse. "The Impact of Ethiopia's Productive Safety Net Programme and Its Linkages." Discussion Paper 839. Washington, DC: IFPRI, 2008.

Grosh, Margaret, Carlo del Ninno, Emil Tesliuc, and Azedine Ouerghi. *For Protection and Promotion: The Design and Implementation of Effective Safety Nets.* Washington, DC: World Bank, 2008.

Gustafsson, Bjorn, and Deng Quheng. "Social Assistance Receipt and Its Importance for Combating Poverty in Urban China." Discussion Paper No. 2758. Bonn: Institute for the Study of Labor, 2007.

Haarmann, Claudia, Dirk Haarmann, Herbert Jauch, Hilma Shindondola-Mote, Nicoli Nattrass, Michael Samson, and Guy Standing. *Towards a Basic Income Grant for All.* Basic Income Grant Pilot Project First Assessment Report. Windhoek, Namibia: Basic Income Grant Coalition, 2008, available at www.bignam.org.

Haarmann, Claudia, Dirk Haarmann, Herbert Jauch, Hilma Shindondola-Mote, Nicoli Nattrass, Ingrid van Niekerk, and Michael Samson. *Making the Difference! The BIG in Namibia.* Basic Income Grant Pilot Project Assessment Report. Windhoek, Namibia: Namibian BIG Coalition, 2009, available at www.bignam.org.

Hailu, Degol, and Sergei Soares. "What Explains the Decline in Brazil's Inequality?" One Pager 89. Brasilia: International Policy Centre for Inclusive Growth, 2009.

Handa, Sudhanshu. "Raising Primary School Enrolment in Developing Countries—The Relative Importance of Supply and Demand." *Journal of Development Economics,* 69, no. 1 (2002): 103–28.

Handa, Sudhanshu, and Benjamin Davis. "The Experience of Conditional Cash Transfers in Latin America and the Caribbean." *Development Policy Review*, 24, no. 5 (2006): 513–36.

Hanlon, Joseph. "Defining 'Illegitimate Debt': When Creditors Should Be Liable for Improper Loans." In *Sovereign Debt at the Crossroads*, edited by Chris Jochnick and Fraser A. Preston, 109–31. Oxford: Oxford University Press, 2006.

Hanlon, Joseph, and Teresa Smart. *Do Bicycles Equal Development in Mozambique?* Woodbridge, Suffolk, UK: James Currey, 2008.

Harvey, Fiona, and Edward Luce. "US Backs Ending of Fossil Fuel Subsidies." *Financial Times*, September 24, 2009.

Heinrich, Carolyn. "Demand and Supply-Side Determinants of Conditional Cash Transfer Program Effectiveness." *World Development*, 35, no. 1 (2007): 121–43.

HelpAge International. "Old Age Pensions in India." *Ageing and Development* 15. London: HelpAge International, 2003.

Hickey, Sam. "Conceptualising the Politics of Social Protection in Africa." In *Social Protection for the Poor and the Poorest*, edited by Armando Barrientos and David Hulme. Basingstoke: Palgrave Macmillan, 2008.

———. "The Politics of What Works in Reducing Chronic Poverty." Chronic Poverty Research Centre Working Paper 91. Manchester, UK: CPRC, 2006.

Hoddinott, John, and Emmanuel Skoufias. "The Impact of Progresa on Food Consumption." Washington, DC: IFPRI, 2003, available at http://www .ifpri.org/divs/fcnd/dp/papers/fcndp150.pdf.

Hodges, Anthony, Anne-Claire Dufay, Khurelmaa Dashdorj, Kang Yun Jong, Tuya Mungun, and Uranchimeg Budragchaa. "Child Benefits and Poverty Reduction: Evidence from Mongolia's Child Money Programme." Working Paper MGSoc/2007/WP002. Maastricht: School of Governance, Maastricht University, 2007.

Hulme, David, and Mark Infield. "Park–People Relationships: A Study of Lake Mburo National Park, Uganda." In *African Wildlife & Livelihoods: The Promise and Performance of Community Conservation*, edited by David Hulme and Marshall Murphree. Oxford: James Currey, 2001.

Hulme, David, Karen Moore, and Faisal Bin Seraj. "Reaching the People Who Microfinance Cannot Reach: Learning from BRAC's Targeting the Ultra Poor Programme." In *The Handbook of Microfinance*, edited by Beatriz Armendariz and Marc Labie. World Scientific Publishing, forthcoming 2010.

Hulme, David, and Paul Mosley. *Finance Against Poverty (Volume 1)*. London: Routledge, 1996.

Hutagalung, Stella A., Sirojuddin Arif, and Widjajanti I. Suharyo. "Problems and Challenges for the Indonesian Conditional Cash Transfer Programme—Program Keluarga Harapan (PKH)." Social Protection in Asia Working Paper 04. Brighton, UK: IDS, 2009.

India Together. "NREGA: A Fine Balance." July 13, 2008, available at www.india together.org/2008/jul/psa-finebal.htm.

Inman, Phillip. "Miliband Supports Tobin Tax, Claims French Foreign Minister—Levy on Foreign Exchange Deals 'Could Raise £27bn to Help Developing Nations,'" *Guardian,* September 17, 2009.

Irwin, Alec, Alayne Adams, and Anne Winter. *Home Truths: Facing the Facts on Children, AIDS, and Poverty.* Final report. Boston and Geneva: Joint Learning Initiative on Children and HIV/AIDS, 2009.

de Janvry, Alain, and Elisabeth Sadoulet. "Making Conditional Cash Transfer Programs More Efficient: Designing for Maximum Effect of the Conditionality." *World Bank Economic Review,* 20, no. 1 (2006): 1–29.

Jatimulyo, Pemdes. "BLT: Bantuan Langsung Tunai (Direct Cash Assistance)." Blog Post, March 28, 2009, http://pemdesjatimulyo.blogspot.com/2009/03/blt-bantuan-langsung-tunai-direct-cash.html.

Kakwani, Nanak, Fabio Soares, and Hyun Son. "Cash Transfers for School-age Children in Africa." *Development Policy Review,* 24, no. 5 (2006): 553–70.

———. Conditional Cash Transfers in African Countries. Working Paper 9. Brasilia: International Poverty Centre, 2005.

Kalebe-Nyamongo, Chipiliro, "Elite Perceptions of Poverty in Malawi." Paper presented at the conference "The Roles of Elites in Economic Development," June 12–13. Helsinki: UNU-Wider, 2009.

Kidd, Stephen. "Equal Pensions, Equal Rights: Achieving Universal Pension Coverage for Older Women and Men in Developing Countries." London: HelpAge International. In *Gender and Development* 17, no. 3 (November 2009): 377–88.

Knox, Charles. "Response to Social Protection and the Global Crisis." Johannesburg: Regional Hunger and Vulnerability Programme, 2009, available at http://www.wahenga.net/index.php/views/comments_view/response_to_social_protection_and_the_global_crisis.

The Lancet Editorial. "Cash Transfers for Children—Investing into the Future. *Lancet,* 373, no. 9682 (2009): 2172.

———. "A New Agenda for Children Affected by HIV/AIDS." *Lancet,* 373, no. 9663 (2009): 517.

Levy, Santiago. *Progress Against Poverty: Sustaining Mexico's Progresa-Oportunidades Program.* Washington, DC: Brookings Institution, 2006.

Levy, Sarah, with Carlos Barahona and Blessings Chinsinga. "Food Security, Social Protection, Growth and Poverty Reduction Synergies: The Starter Pack Programme in Malawi." *Natural Resource Perspectives* 95. London: Overseas Development Institute, 2004.

Lin, Justin, and Joy Phumaphi. "Foreword." In *Conditional Cash Transfers,* edited by Ariel Fiszbein and Norbert Schady. Washington, DC: World Bank, 2009.

Lindert, Peter H. *Growing Public: Social Spending and Economic Growth since the Eighteenth Century.* Cambridge: Cambridge University Press, 2004.

Lund, Frances, Michael Noble, Helen Barnes, and Gemma Wright. "Is There a Rationale for Conditional Cash Transfers for Children in South Africa?" Working Paper 53. Durban: School of Development Studies, University of KwaZulu-Natal, 2008, available at http://sds.ukzn.ac.za/files/WP%2053%20web.pdf.

Maddison, Angus. "Statistics on World Population, GDP and Per Capita GDP, 1–2006 AD." Datafile, part of *Historical Statistics of the World Economy: 1–2006 AD* (2009), available from http://www.ggdc.net/maddison/.

Mahmud, Simeen. "Female Secondary School Stipend Programme in Bangladesh: A Critical Assessment." Dhaka: Bangladesh Institute of Development Studies, 2003, available at http://portal.unesco.org/.

Maluccio, John A., and Rafael Flores. "Impact Evaluation of a Conditional Cash Transfer Program—The Nicaraguan Red de Protección Social." Research Report 141. Washington, DC: IFPRI, 2005.

Martinez, Sebastian. "Invertir el Bonosol para Aliviar la Pobreza: Retornos Económicos en los Hogares Beneficiarios." In *La Inversion Prudente. Impacto del Bonosol Sobre la Familia, la Equidad Social y el Crecimiento Economico,* edited by Guillermo Aponte et al. La Paz: Fundacion Milenio, 2007.

———. "Pensions, Poverty and Household Investments in Bolivia." Paper presented at the "Perspectives on Impact Evaluation" conference, Cairo, Egypt, April 2009.

Marysse, Stefaan, and Joris Verschueren. "South Africa's BIG Debate in Comparative Perspective." Discussion Paper 2007.03. Antwerp: University of Antwerp, 2007.

Matabele, D., and F. Sidumo. "Centena e Meia mil de Idosos Recebe Assistência Social no País." *MediaFax,* Maputo, August 27, 2009.

Mather, David, Benedito Cunguara, and Duncan Boughton. "Household Income and Assets in Rural Mozambique, 2002–2005." Research Report 66. Maputo: Ministério da Agricultura, and East Lansing: Michigan State University, 2008.

Medeiros, Marcelo, Tatiana Britto, and Fabio Veras Soares. "Targeted Cash Transfer Programmes in Brazil: BPC and the Bolsa Família." Working Paper 46. Brasilia: International Poverty Centre, 2008.

Melo, Marcus. "Political Competition Can Be Positive: Embedding Cash Transfer Programmes in Brazil." In *Development Success: Statecraft in the South,* edited by Anthony Bebbington and Willy McCourt. Basingstoke, UK: Palgrave Macmillan, 2007.

Miller, Candace. "Economic Evaluation of the Mchinji Cash Transfer—Preliminary Findings." Boston: Boston University School of Public Health, 2009, available at http://childresearchpolicy.org/images/Economic_Impacts_June_15.pdf.

Miller, Candace, and Maxton Tsoka. "$13 a Month for Half a Year: Round 2 Impact of the Mchinji Cash Transfer." PowerPoint Presentation to the National Social Protection Steering Committee, Government of Malawi, Lilongwe, December 11, 2007.

Miller, Candace, Maxton Tsoka, and Kathryn Reichert. "Targeting Cash to Malawi's Ultra Poor: A Mixed Methods Evaluation." Boston, MA: Center for International Health and Development, Boston University School of Public Health, and The Centre for Social Research, University of Malawi, 2008, available at http://child researchpolicy.org/images/Cash_Targeting_Evaluation.pdf.

———. "Targeting Report—External Evaluation of the Mchinji Social Cash Transfer Pilot." Boston, MA: Center for International Health and Development, Boston University School of Public Health, and The Centre for Social Research, University of Malawi, 2008, available at http://childresearchpolicy .org/images/Targeting_Evaluation_Final_August.pdf.

Ministério da Previdência Social. "Anuário Estatístico da Previdência Social 2007," http://www1.previdencia.gov.br/aeps2007/16_01_01_03.asp.

Ministério do Desenvolvimento Social e Combate à Fome. "Desenvolvimento Social," 2009, available at http://www.mds.gov.br/institucional/secretarias/ secretaria-de-avaliacao-e-gestao-da-informacao-sagi/arquivo-sagi/pesquisas.

———. "Perfil Das Famílias Do Programa Bolsa Família No Cadastro Único," 2005, available at http://www.mds.gov.br/institucional/secretarias/secretaria-de-avaliacao-e-gestao-da-informacao-sagi/arquivo-sagi/pesquisas.

———. "Programa Bolsa Família," 2009, available at http://www.mds.gov.br/ bolsafamilia/.

Ministry of Community Development and Social Services (Zambia). "Social Cash Transfer Scheme," 2007, available at http://www.socialcashtransfers-zambia .org/social_cash_transfers_zambia.php.

Molyneux, Maxine. "Conditional Cash Transfers: A 'Pathway to Women's Empowerment'?" Pathways of Women's Empowerment Working Paper 5. Brighton, UK: Institute of Development Studies, 2009, available at http://www.pathways ofempowerment.org/PathwaysWP5-website.pdf.

———. *Conditional Cash Transfers and Women's Empowerment: Annotated Bibliography.* Waterloo, Ontario, Canada: IGLOO Network of the Centre for International Governance Innovation, 2008, available at www.igloo.org/ pathways/download-nocache/currentdoc/conditiona.

Moore, Charity. "Assessing Honduras' CCT Programme PRAF, Programa de Asignación Familiar: Expected and Unexpected Results." Country Study 15. Brasilia: UNDP International Poverty Centre, 2008.

Motta, Adylson. *TCU Evaluation of the Child Labor Eradication Program.* Official translation of *Avaliação do TCU sobre o Progama de Erradicação do Trabalho Infantil.* Brasilia: Brazilian Court of Audit (Tribunal de Contas de União), 2003, available at http://portal2.tcu.gov.br/portal/page/portal/TCU/english/ publications/institucional_publications/EXECUTIVE_SUMMARIES_3.PDF.

Moyo, Dambesa. *Dead Aid: Why Aid Is Not Working and How There Is a Better Way for Africa.* New York: Farrar, Straus and Giroux, 2009.

Mukherjee, Nilanjana, Joan Hardjono, and Elizabeth Carriere. "People, Poverty and Livelihoods: Links for Sustainable Poverty Reduction in Indonesia." World Bank Report 25289. Washington, DC: World Bank, 2002.

Munemo, Ngonidzashe. "Political Incumbency and Drought Relief in Africa." In *Social Protection for the Poor and the Poorest,* edited by Armando Barrientos and David Hulme. Basingstoke: Palgrave Macmillan, 2008.

Murgai, Rinku, and Martin Ravallion. "Is a Guaranteed Living Wage a Good Antipoverty Policy?" Policy Research Working Paper 3640. Washington, DC: World Bank, 2005.

Mwamlima, Harry, and Reagan Kaluluma. "Malawi's Director of Social Protection Responds to 'One out of Ten' Comment." Johannesburg: Regional Hunger and Vulnerability Programme, 2008, available at http://www.wahenga.net/ index.php/views/comments_view/malawis_director_of_social_protection_ responds_to_one_out_of_ten_comment/.

Neri, Marcelo Côrtes. "Poverty, Inequality and Income Policies." Rio de Janeiro: O Centro de Políticas Sociais (CPS), Fundação Getulio Vargas, 2007, available at http://www3.fgv.br/ibrecps/RET3/engl/index.htm.

Neufeld, Lynette, et al. "Impacto de Oportunidades en el Crecimiento y Estado Nutricional de Ninos en Zonas Rurales." In *Alimentacion, Volume 3: Evaluacion Externa de Impact al Programa Oportunidades 2004,* edited by Bernardo Hernandez Prado and Mauricio Hernandez Avila, 17–51. Cuernavaca: Instituto Nacional de Salud Publica y CIESAS, 2005.

Noble, Michael, Phakama Ntshongwana, and Rebecca Surender. "Attitudes to Work and Social Security in South Africa." Cape Town: Human Sciences Research Council, 2008, available at www.hsrcpress.ac.za.

OECD. *Growing Unequal? Income Distribution and Poverty in OECD Countries.* Paris: OECD, 2008.

———. *OECD Factbook 2009: Economic, Environmental and Social Statistics.* Paris, OECD, 2009.

Office of the Prime Minister of Australia. "$950 One-off Cash Bonus to Support Jobs." Media Release, February 3, 2009, available at http://www.pm.gov.au/ media/Release/2009/media_release_0778.cfm.

d'Oro, Rachel. "Alaskans to Receive $3,269 Each." *Anchorage Daily News,* September 5, 2008.

Osório, Rafael Guerreiro. "The Recent Impact of Government Transfers on Poverty in Honduras and Alternatives to Enhance Their Effects." Working Paper 47. Brasilia: UNDP International Poverty Centre, 2008.

Parker, Susan W., and Emmanuel Skoufias. "The Impact of Progresa on Work, Leisure and Time Allocation." Washington DC: IFPRI, 2000.

Paxson, Christina, and Norbert Schady. "Cognitive Development Among Young Children in Ecuador." *The Journal of Human Resources,* 42, no. 1 (2007): 49–84.

———. "Does Money Matter? The Effects of Cash Transfers on Child Development in Rural Ecuador." World Bank Policy Research Paper 4226. Washington, DC: World Bank, 2007.

Pelham, Larissa. "The Politics Behind the Non-contributory Old Age Social Pensions in Lesotho, Namibia, and South Africa." Working Paper 83. Manchester, UK: Chronic Poverty Research Centre, 2007.

Pereira, Lucélia Luiz, Leonor Maria Pacheco Santos, Micheli Dantas Soares, Flavia Conceição dos Santos Henrique, Simone Costa Guadagnin, and Sandra Maria Chaves dos Santos. *Efeitos do Programa Bolsa Família nas Condições de Vida de Beneficiários em Municípios de Muito Baixo IDH.* Brasilia: UNDP International Poverty Centre, 2008, available at http://www.ipcundp.org/publications/mds/33M.pdf.

Perry, Nick. "Indonesians Choose Reformist Yudhoyono." *UPI-Asia,* July 13, 2009.

Pogge, Thomas. "'Assisting' the Global Poor." In *The Ethics of Assistance: Morality and the Distant Needy,* edited by Deen K. Chaterjee, 260–88. Cambridge, UK: CUP, 2004.

Polanyi, Karl. *The Great Transformation: The Political and Economic Origins of Our Time.* Boston, MA: Beacon, 1944, 1957, 2001.

Posel, Dorrit, and Danila Casale. "What Has Been Happening to Internal Labour Migration in South Africa, 1993–1999." *The South African Journal of Economics,* 71, no. 3 (2003): 455–79.

Posel, Dorrit, James A. Fairburn, and Frances Lund. "Labour Migration and Households: A Reconsideration of the Effects of the Social Pension on Labour Supply in South Africa." *Economic Modelling,* 23, no. 5 (2006): 836–53.

Putzel, James. "Politics, the State and the Impulse for Social Protection: The Implications of Karl Polanyi's Ideas for Understanding Development and Crisis." Crisis States Working Paper 1. London: London School of Economics, 2002, available at http://www.crisisstates.com/download/wp/WP18JP.pdf.

Ravi, Shamika, and Monika Engler. "Workfare in Low Income Countries: An Effective Way to Fight Poverty? The Case of NREGS in India." Indian School of Business working paper. Hyderabad: Indian School of Business, 2009, available at http://www.isb.edu/WorkingPapers/Workfare_LowIncome-Countries.pdf.

Reis, Elisa. "Perceptions of Poverty and Inequality Among Brazilian Elites." In *Elite Perceptions of Poverty and Inequality,* edited by Elisa P. Reis and Mick Moore. Zed: London, 2005.

———. "Poverty and Inequality in the Eyes of the Elites." Paper presented at the conference "The Roles of Elites in Economic Development," June 13–13. Helsinki: UN-Wider, 2009.

Reis, Elisa P., and Mick Moore. "Elites, Perception and Poverties." In *Elite Perceptions of Poverty and Inequality,* edited by Elisa P. Reis and Mick Moore. Zed: London, 2005.

Riddell, Roger C. *Does Foreign Aid Really Work?* Oxford: Oxford University Press, 2007.

de la Rocha, Mercedes González. "Households and Social Policy in Mexico." Presentation made at the Bi-Regional Conference on Social Protection and Poverty Reduction, Cape Town, South Africa, June 6–9, 2007.

Rook, John. "Targeting: The Debate Goes on But What Does It Mean in Practice?" Johannesburg: Regional Hunger and Vulnerability Programme, 2009, available

at http://www.wahenga.net/index.php/views/comments_view/targeting_the
_debate_goes_on_but_what_does_it_mean_in_practice.

Rosa, Solange, Annie Leatt, and Katharine Hall. "Does the Means Justify the
End? Targeting the Child Support Grant." Cape Town: Children's Institute,
University of Cape Town, 2005.

de Sá e Silva, Michelle Morais. "Opportunity NYC: A Performance-based Conditional Cash Transfer Programme. A Qualitative Analysis." Working Paper
49. Brasilia: International Poverty Centre, 2008.

Sabates-Wheeler, Rachel, Stephen Devereux, and Bruce Guenther. "Building Synergies Between Social Protection and Small-holder Policies." Paper presented
at the conference "Social Protection for the Poorest in Africa: Learning from
Experience," Kampala, September 3–10, 2008.

Sabates-Wheeler, Rachel, Stephen Devereux, and Anthony Hodges. "Taking the
Long View: What Does a Child Focus Add to Social Protection?" *IDS Bulletin,* 40, no. 1 (2009): 109–19.

Sadoulet, Elisabeth, Alain de Janvry, and Benjamin Davis. "Cash Transfer Programs with Income Multipliers: Procampo in Mexico." Washington, DC:
IFPRI, 2001.

Samson, Michael. "The Developmental Impact of Social Pensions in Southern
Africa." Presentation at the world conference "Social Protection and Inclusion," Lisbon, October 4, 2006.

———. "The Social and Economic Impacts of South Africa's Social Grants."
Presentation at the "Growing Up Free from Poverty" seminar, November 18,
2007. London, Overseas Development Institute, 2007.

Samson, Michael, Una Lee, Asanda Ndlebe, Kenneth Mac Quene, Ingrid van
Niekerk, Viral Gandhi, Tomoko Harigaya, and Celeste Abrahams. "Final
Report: The Social and Economic Impact of South Africa's Social Security
System." Report commissioned by the South Africa Department of Social
Development, EPRI Research Paper 37. Cape Town: Economic Policy Re-
search Institute, 2004, available at http://www.epri.org.za/rp37.htm.

Samson, Michael, Kenneth Mac Quene, Ingrid van Niekerk, Sheshi Kaniki,
Karen Kallmann, and Martin Williams. "Review of Targeting Mechanisms,
Means Tests and Values for South Africa's Social Grants—Final Report."
Cape Town: Economic Policy Research Institute, 2007, available at http://
www.wahenga.net/uploads/documents/news/Main%20Report%20
Review%20of%20Targeting%20Mechanisms_Means%20Test%20and%20
Values%20of%20SA%20Grants%20final.pdf.

Sawyer, Diana Oya. *Sumário Executivo—Avaliação de Impacto do Programa Bolsa
Família.* Brasilia: Ministro do Desenvolvimento Social e Combate à Fome, 2007.

Schady, Norbert, and Maria Caridad Araujo. "Cash Transfers, Conditions and
School Enrollment in Ecuador." *Economia,* 8, no. 2 (2008): 43–70.

Schubert, Bernd. No title, posted December 3, 2008, as a response to Wahenga,
"One out of Ten," available at http://www.wahenga.net/index.php/views/user_
comment_view/1910?comm=1.

————. "The Pilot Social Cash Transfer Scheme Kalomo District—Zambia." Lusaka: GTZ, 2004.

————. "Targeting Social Cash Transfers." Wahenga Comments, 2009, http://www.wahenga.net/index.php/views/comments_view/targeting_social_cash_transfers/.

Schubert, Bernd, and Rachel Slater. "Social Cash Transfers in Low-income African Countries: Conditional or Unconditional?" *Development Policy Review,* 24, no. 5 (2006): 571–78.

Schwarzer, Helmut, and Ana Carolina Querino. "Non-contributory Pensions in Brazil: The Impact on Poverty Reduction." Extension of Social Security Working Paper 11. Geneva: International Labour Organization, 2002.

Scully, Timothy, J. Samuel Valenzuela, and Eugenio Tironi, eds. *El Eslabón Perdido: Familia, Modernización y Bienestar en Chile.* Santiago, Chile: Taurus, 2006.

Seaman, John, Celia Petty, and Patrick Kambewa. "The Impact on Household Income and Welfare of the Pilot Social Cash Transfer and Agricultural Input Subsidy Programmes in Mlomba TA, Machinga District, Malawi." Lilongwe: Malawi Vulnerability Assessment Committee, 2008, available at www.wahenga.net/uploads/documents/comments/sct/EvDev_Mlomba_Survey_2008_Report.pdf.

————. "Protecting the Ultra Poor: Lessons from Malawi's Social Cash Transfer Pilot." London: Evidence for Development, 2008, available at http://www.evidencefordevelopment.com/files/Summary_STC%20summary%202008.pdf.

Seekings, Jeremy. "Prospects for Basic Income in Developing Countries: A Comparative Analysis of Welfare Regimes in the South." Cape Town: Centre for Social Science Research, 2005, available at http://www.cssr.uct.ac.za/index.html.

Shekar, Meera, Aparnaa Somanathan, and Lidan Du, "Malnutrition in Sri Lanka: Scale, Scope, Causes and Potential Response." Report 40906-KL. Washington, DC: World Bank, 2007.

Skoufias, Emmanuel. "PROGRESA and Its Impacts on the Welfare of Rural Households in Mexico." Washington, DC: IFPRI, 2005, available at http://www.ifpri.org/pubs/abstract/139/rr139.pdf.

Skoufias, Emmanuel, and David Coady. "Are the Welfare Losses from Imperfect Targeting Important?" Washington, DC: IFPRI, 2001, available at http://www.ifpri.org/divs/fcnd/dp/papers/fcndp125.pdf.

Skoufias, Emmanuel, Benjamin Davis, and Sergio de la Vega. "Targeting the Poor in Mexico: An Evaluation of the Selection of Households for PROGRESA." Washington, DC: IFPRI, 2001, available at http://www.ifpri.org/divs/fcnd/dp/papers/fcndp103.pdf.

Soares, Fábio Veras, Rafael Perez Ribas, and Rafael Guerreiro Osório. "Evaluating the Impact of Brazil's Bolsa Família: Cash Transfer Programmes in Comparative

Perspective." *IPC Evaluation Note 1.* Brasilia: International Poverty Centre, 2007.

Soares, Fabio Veras, Sergei Suarez, Dillon Soares, Marcelo Medeiros, and Rafael Guerreiro Osório. "Cash Transfer Programmes in Brazil: Impacts on Inequality and Poverty." Working Paper 21. Brasilia: UNDP International Poverty Centre, 2006, available at http://www.ipc-undp.org/pub/IPCWorkingPaper21.pdf.

Soares, Sergei. "Distribuição de Renda no Brasil de 1976 a 2004 com Ênfase no Período entre 2001 e 2004." Brasilia: Instituto de Pesquisa Econômica Aplicada, 2006. Texto para Discussão 1166.

Soares, Sergei, Rafael Guerreiro Osório, Fábio Veras Soares, Marcelo Medeiros, and Eduardo Zepeda. "Conditional Cash Transfers in Brazil, Chile and Mexico: Impacts upon Inequality." Brasilia: UNDP International Poverty Centre, 2007.

South African National Treasury. "A People's Guide to the 2009 Budget." 2009, available at http://www.sars.gov.za/home.asp?pid=41116.

Stiglitz, Joseph. *Globalization and Its Discontents.* New York: Penguin, 2002.

Stockholm International Peace Research Institute. *SIPRI Yearbook 2009: Armaments, Disarmament and International Security.* Oxford: Oxford University Press, 2009.

Sultan, Sonya, and Tamar Schrofer. "Building Support to Have Targeted Social Protection Interventions for the Poorest—the Case of Ghana." Paper delivered at the conference "Social Protection for the Poorest in Africa: Learning from Experience." Kampala, September 8–10, 2008.

Surender, Rebecca, Michael Noble, Phakama Ntshongwana, and Gemma Wright. "Work and Welfare in South Africa: The Relationship Between Social Grants and Labour Market Activity." Oxford: Centre for the Analysis of South African Social Policy, Oxford University, 2008, available at http://www.chronicpoverty.org/socialprotectionconference/abstracts/Rebecca%20Surender.pdf.

Szreter, Simon. "A Right to Registration: Development, Identity Registration, and Social Security—A Historical Perspective." *World Development,* 35, no. 1 (2007): 67–86.

Taylor, Viviene, *Transforming the Present—Protecting the Future: Report of the Committee of Inquiry into a Comprehensive System of Social Security for South Africa.* Taylor Committee, 2002.

du Toit, Andries, and David Neves. "Trading on a Grant: Integrating Formal and Informal Social Protection in Post-Apartheid Migrant Networks." Working Paper 75. Manchester, UK: Brooks World Poverty Institute, 2009.

———. "Vulnerability and Social Protection at the Margins of the Formal Economy—Case studies from Khyelitsha and the Eastern Cape." Report prepared for USAID, 2006, available at http://www.plaas.org.za/publications/downloads/vulnerability.pdf.

Townsend, Peter. *The Abolition of Child Poverty and the Right to Social Security.* London: Lulu Enterprises, 2008, available from http://www.lulu.com/content/ 2299240.

Uganda Social Protection Task Force. *Design of a Cash Transfer Pilot for Uganda, Final Report.* Kampala: Ministry of Gender, Labour and Social Development, 2007.

United Nations. *The Millennium Development Goals Report 2008.* New York: United Nations Department of Economic and Social Affairs, 2008, available from http://mdgs.un.org/unsd/mdg/Resources/Static/Products/Progress2008/ MDG_Report_2008_En.pdf.

———. *The Millennium Development Goals Report 2009.* New York: United Nations, 2009.

UNCTAD. *The Least Developed Countries Report 2006: Developing Productive Capacities.* Geneva and New York: UNCTAD, 2006.

Valenzuela, J. Samuel. "The Missing Links: Families, Welfare Institutions and Economic Development in Latin America," Paper presented at the annual meeting of the Society for the Advancement of Socio-Economics, Copenhagen, July 2007.

Veit-Wilson, John. "Who Set the Conditions? Conditionality, Reciprocity, Human Rights and Inclusion in Society." *Global Social Policy,* 9, no. 2 (2009): 171–74.

Wahenga. "Five out of Ten." 2008, available at http://www.wahenga.net/index.php/ views/comments_view/five_out_of_ten/.

———. "One out of Ten: Social Cash Transfer Pilots in Malawi and Zambia." 2008, available at http://www.wahenga.net/index.php/views/comments_view/ one_out_of_ten_social_cash_transfer_pilots_in_malawi_and_zambia/.

Walsh, Cora, and Nicola Jones. "Alternative Approaches to Social Protection for Health in West and Central Africa." London: Overseas Development Institute, 2009, available at http://www.odi.org.uk/events/2009/06/16/1885-presentation-cora-walsh-nicola-jones.pdf.

Wang, Limin, Sarah Bales, and Zhengzhong Zhang. "China's Social Protection Schemes and Access to Health Services: A Critical Review." Washington, DC: World Bank, 2006.

Watkins, Ben. "Alternative Methods for Targeting Social Assistance to Highly Vulnerable Groups." Washington, DC: Kimetrica International, 2008, for the Technical Working Group on Social Assistance, Zambia.

Weigand, Christine, and Margaret Grosh. "Spending on Social Safety Nets: Comparative Data Compiled from World Bank Analytic Work." Spreadsheet dated June 30, 2008. Washington, DC: World Bank, 2008, available at http:// siteresources.worldbank.org/SAFETYNETSANDTRANSFERS/Resources/ SN_Expenditures_6-30-08.xls.

White, Philip, Frank Ellis, Stephen Devereux, and Katharine Vincent. "Fertiliser Subsidies and Social Cash Transfers." Frontiers of Social Protection Brief 1. Johannesburg: Regional Hunger and Vulnerability Programme, 2009, available at http://www.wahenga.net/uploads/documents/reba_studies/FOSP_ Brief_1.pdf.

Whiteford, Peter. "How Much Redistribution Do Governments Achieve? The Role of Cash Transfers and Household Taxes." In OECD, *Growing Unequal: Income Distribution and Poverty in OECD Countries.* Paris: OECD, 2008.

Wilkinson, Richard, and Kate Pickett. *The Spirit Level: Why More Equal Societies Almost Always Do Better.* London: Allan Lane, 2009.

Williams, Martin. "The Social and Economic Impacts of South Africa's Child Support Grant." Working Paper 40. Cape Town: Economic Policy Research Institute, 2007.

————. "The Social and Economic Impacts of South Africa's Child Support Grant (Extended Version)." Working Paper 39. Cape Town: Economic Policy Research Institute, 2007.

Willmore, Larry. "Universal Pensions for Developing Countries." *World Development,* 35, no. 1 (2007): 24–51.

World Bank. *World Development Report 2006: Equity and Development.* Washington, DC: World Bank and New York: Oxford University Press, 2005.

Yablonski, Jennifer, with Michael O'Donnell. *Lasting Benefits: The Role of Cash Transfers in Tackling Child Mortality.* London: Save the Children, 2009, available from http://www.savethechildren.org.uk/en/docs/Lasting_Benefits.pdf.

INDEX

ABOUT THE AUTHORS

Armando Barrientos is professor of poverty and social justice and director of research at the Brooks World Poverty Institute at the University of Manchester in the UK. He earned his BA and PhD from the University of Kent at Canterbury. His research interests focus on the links between welfare programs and labor markets in developing countries, as well as on policies addressing poverty, vulnerability, and population aging. He is a senior researcher with the Chronic Poverty Research Centre, leading research on insecurity, risk, and vulnerability. His work has been published widely, including articles in *World Development, Applied Economics,* and *Geneva Papers on Risk & Insurance.* He has acted as an adviser to the ILO, the World Bank, DFID, UNRISD, IADB, WIEGO, UN-DESA, UNICEF, and the Caribbean Development Bank. His most recent book is Armando Barrientos and David Hulme, *Social Protection for the Poor and Poorest* (Basingstoke: Palgrave Macmillan, 2008).

Joseph Hanlon is a senior lecturer in development and conflict resolution at the International Development Centre of the Open University, Milton Keynes, England, and visiting senior research fellow at the London School of Economics. He is a journalist and is the author or editor of more than a dozen books. This book continues his work on how the international context can be changed to give people in the Global South more power over their own development strategies. He is the coauthor of *Civil War, Civil Peace* (Milton Keynes: Open University; Oxford: James Currey; and

Athens, Ohio: Ohio University Press, 2006) and was policy officer for the Jubilee 2000 campaign to cancel the unpayable debt of poor countries. He has written five books on Mozambique, most recently *Do Bicycles Equal Development in Mozambique?* (Oxford: James Currey, 2008).

David Hulme is professor of development studies at the University of Manchester and executive director of the Brooks World Poverty Institute and the Chronic Poverty Research Centre. His recent publications include *Poverty Dynamics: Inter-disciplinary Perspectives,* with T. Addison and R. Kanbur (Oxford: Oxford University Press, 2009); Armando Barrientos and David Hulme, *Social Protection for the Poor and Poorest* (Basingstoke: Palgrave Macmillan, 2008); *The Challenge of Global Inequality,* with A. Greig and M. Turner, a special 2006 issue of the *Journal of Development Studies* on "Cross-disciplinary Research on Poverty and Inequality"; and many articles in other leading journals. His research interests include rural development, poverty analysis and poverty reduction strategies, finance for the poor, and the sociology of development.